# Teachers Engaged in Research

## Inquiry Into Mathematics Classrooms, Grades Pre-K–2

*a volume in*
Teachers Engaged in Research

*Series Editor*
**Denise S. Mewborn**
*University of Georgia*

# Teachers Engaged in Research

## Inquiry Into Mathematics Classrooms, Grades Pre-K–2

*edited by*

**Stephanie Z. Smith**
*Georgia State University*

*and*

**Marvin E. Smith**
*Georgia Southern University*

INFORMATION AGE
PUBLISHING

Greenwich, Connecticut • www.infoagepub.com

**Library of Congress Cataloging-in-Publication Data**

Teachers engaged in research : inquiry into mathematics classrooms, grades prek-2 / edited by Stephanie Z. Smith and Marvin E. Smith.
    p. cm. – (Teachers engaged in research)
 Includes bibliographical references.
 ISBN 1-59311-495-8 (pbk.) – ISBN 1-59311-496-6 (hardcover)
 1. Mathematics–Study and teaching (Early childhood)–United States. 2. Mathematics–Study and teaching (Elementary)–United States. 3. Elementary school teaching–Research–United States. I. Smith, Stephanie Z. II. Smith, Marvin E. III. Series.
 QA11.2.T425 2006
 372.7–dc22

                  2006007051

## LIST OF REVIEWERS

Lynn Hart
Eula Monroe
Susan Swars
Doug Clarke
Dan Siebert
Shonda Lemons-Smith
Rhina Fernandes
Rubye Sullivan
Amanda Collins
Sandra Jackson

## LIST OF CONTRIBUTORS

| | |
|---|---|
| *Mary Kay Archer* | Long Lake Elementary |
| *Marilyn Cochran-Smith* | Boston College |
| *Barbara Dougherty* | University of Mississippi |
| *Theresa J. Grant* | Western Michigan University |
| *Laurie Hands* | (currently unaffiliated) |
| *Rita Janes* | Rita Janes Educational Solutions |
| *Linda Jaslow* | Northwest Arkansas Education Service Cooperative |
| *Annie Keith* | John Muir Elementary School |
| *Kate Kline* | Western Michigan University |
| *Claire Okazaki* | University of Hawaii at Manoa |
| *Lori Renfro* | Dysart Unified School District |
| *Karen Schweitzer* | Williamsburg Elementary Schools |
| *Stephanie Z. Smith* | Georgia State University |
| *Marvin E. Smith* | Georgia Southern University |
| *Ana Vaisenstein* | Boston Public Schools |
| *Tanya Vik* | Center for Research in Mathematics and Science Education |
| *Regina Wicks* | Goulds Elementary School |
| *Fay Zenigami* | University of Hawaii at Manoa |

# CONTENTS

# SERIES FOREWORD

**Marilyn Cochran-Smith**
*Boston College*

This series, *Teachers Engaged in Research: Inquiry Into Mathematics Classrooms,* represents a remarkable accomplishment. In four books, one each devoted to teaching and learning mathematics at different grade level groupings (Pre-K–2, 3–5, 6–8, and 9–12), ninety-some authors and co-authors write about their work as professional mathematics educators. Across grade levels, topics, professional development contexts, schools, school districts, and even nations, the chapters in these four books attest to the enormous complexity of teaching mathematics well and to the power of inquiry as a way of understanding and managing that complexity.

In a certain sense, of course, the education community already knows that doing a good job of teaching mathematics is demanding—and all too infrequent—and that it requires deep and multiple layers of knowledge about subject matter, learners, pedagogy, and contexts. Nearly two decades of ground-breaking research in cognition and mathematics education has told us a great deal about this. But the books in this series are quite different from most of what has come before. These four books tell us about teaching and learning mathematics from the inside—from the perspectives of school-based teacher researchers who have carefully studied the commonplaces of mathematics teaching and learning, such as the whole

*Teachers Engaged in Research*
*Inquiry Into Mathematics Classrooms, Grades Pre-K–2,* pages ix–xx
Copyright © 2006 by Information Age Publishing

class lesson, the small group activity, the math problem, the worksheet where the student shows his or her work, the class discussion about solutions and answers, and the teacher development activity. Taking these and other commonplaces of mathematics teaching and learning as sites for inquiry, the multiple authors of the chapters in these four books offer richly textured and refreshingly insightful insider accounts of mathematics teaching and learning. Reflecting on the contrasts that sometimes exist between teachers' intentions and the realities of classroom life, the chapters depict teachers in the process of considering and reconsidering the strategies and materials they use. Drawing on students' work and classroom discourse, the chapters show us what it looks like as teachers strive to make sense of and capitalize on their students' reasoning processes, even when they don't end up with traditional right answers. Staying close to the data of practice, the chapters raise old and new questions about how students—and teachers—learn to think and work mathematically. In short, this remarkable quartet of books reveals what it really means—over time and in the context of different classrooms and schools—for mathematics teachers to engage in inquiry. The goal of all this inquiry is nothing short of a culture shift in the teaching of mathematics—the creation of classroom learning environments where the focus is deep understanding of mathematical concepts, practical application of skills, and problem solving.

These four books provide much-needed and rich detail from the inside about the particulars of mathematics teaching and learning across a remarkably broad range of contexts, grade levels, and curricular areas. In addition, the books tell us a great deal about teachers' and pupils' learning over time (and the reciprocal relationships of the two) as well as the social, intellectual and organizational contexts that support their learning. Undoubtedly teachers and teacher educators will find these books illuminating and will readily see how the authors' successes and the struggles resonate with their own. If this were the only contribution this series made, it would be an important and worthwhile effort. But this series does much more. The books in this series also make an important contribution to the broader education community. Taken together as a whole, the chapters in these four books have the potential to inform mathematics education research, practice and policy in ways that reach far beyond the walls of the classrooms where the work was originally done.

## TAKING AN INQUIRY STANCE

This series of books shows brilliantly and in rich and vivid detail what it means for teachers to take an inquiry stance on teaching and learning mathematics in K-12 classrooms over the professional lifespan. "Inquiry stance" is a concept that my colleague, Susan Lytle, and I have written about over the last decade and a half. It grew out of the dialectic of our simultaneous work as teacher educators involved in day-to-day, year-to-year participation in teacher learning communities, on the one hand, and as researchers engaged in theorizing the relationships of inquiry, knowledge, and practice, on the other. In our descriptions of inquiry as stance, we have repeatedly emphasized its distinction from "inquiry as project." By inquiry project (as opposed to stance), we refer to things like the classroom study that is the required culminating activity during the student teaching semester in a preservice program where inquiry is not integral and not infused throughout, or, the day-long workshop on teacher research or action research that is part of a catalog of professional development options for experienced teachers rather than a coherent part of teacher learning over the lifespan.

Teacher research or inquiry *projects* are discrete and bounded activities, often carried out on a one-time or occasional basis. In contrast, as we have suggested (Cochran-Smith & Lytle, 1999), when inquiry is a *stance*, it extends across the entire professional lifespan, and it represents a world view or a way of knowing about teaching and learning rather than a professional project:

> In everyday language, "stance" is used to describe body postures, particularly with regard to the position of the feet, as in sports or dance, and also to describe political positions, particularly their consistency (or the lack thereof) over time. In the discourse of qualitative research, "stance" is used to make visible and problematic the various perspectives through which researchers frame their questions, observations, and interpretations of data. In our work, we offer the term *inquiry as stance* to describe the positions teachers and others who work together in inquiry communities take toward knowledge and its relationships to practice. We use the metaphor of stance to suggest both orientational and positional ideas, to carry allusions to the physical placing of the body as well as to intellectual activities and perspectives over time. In this sense, the metaphor is intended to capture the ways we stand, the ways we see, and the lenses we see through. Teaching is a complex activity that occurs within webs of social, historical, cultural and political significance. Across the life span an inquiry stance provides a kind of grounding within the changing cultures of school reform and competing political agendas.
>
> *Inquiry as stance* is distinct from the more common notion of inquiry as time-bounded project or activity within a teacher education course or professional development workshop. Taking an inquiry stance

means teachers and student teachers working within inquiry communities to generate local knowledge, envision and theorize their practice, and interpret and interrogate the theory and research of others. Fundamental to this notion is the idea that the work of inquiry communities is both social and political—that is, it involves making problematic the current arrangements of schooling, the ways knowledge is constructed, evaluated, and used, and teachers' individual and collective roles in bringing about change. To use *inquiry as stance* as a construct for understanding teacher learning in communities, we believe that we need a richer conception of knowledge than that allowed by the traditional formal knowledge-practical knowledge distinction, a richer conception of practice than that suggested in the aphorism that practice is practical, a richer conception of learning across the professional life span than that implied by concepts of expertise that differentiate expert teachers from novices, and a rich conception of the cultures of communities as connected to larger educational purposes and contexts . (pp. 288–289)

Developing and sustaining an inquiry stance on teaching, learning and schooling is a life-long and constant pursuit for beginning teachers, experienced teachers, and teacher educators alike. A central aspect of taking an inquiry stance is recognizing that learning to teach is a process that is never completed but is instead an ongoing endeavor. The bottom-line purpose of taking an inquiry stance, however, is not teachers' development for its own sake (although this is an important and valuable goal), but teachers' learning in the service of enriched learning opportunities for Pre-K–12 students.

The chapters in these four books vividly explicate the work of Pre-K–12 teacher researchers who engage in inquiry to transform their teaching practice, expand the mathematical knowledge and skill of their students, and ultimately to enhance their students' life chances in the world. Across the 50 chapters in these books, the serious intellectual work of mathematics teaching is revealed again and again as are the passion teachers have for their work (and their students) and the complexity of the knowledge teachers must have to support students' emerging mathematical development.

## INQUIRY INTO TEACHING AND
## LEARNING IN MATHEMATICS

Over the last two decades, various forms of practitioner inquiry, such as teacher research, action research, and collaborative inquiry, have become commonplace in preservice teacher preparation programs as well as in professional development projects and school reform efforts of various kinds. Although there are many variations and often different underlying assumptions among these, the use of inquiry has generally reflected a move away from transmission models of teacher training and retraining wherein teachers are expected to implement specific practices developed by others. The move has been toward a concept of teacher learning as a life-long process of both posing and answering questions appropriate to local contexts, working within learning communities to construct and solve problems, and making all of the aspects of the work of teaching possible sites for inquiry.

As this series of books demonstrates so clearly, an inquiry stances is quite compatible with the professional standards for teaching and learning mathematics that have emerged since the mid 1980s. In fact, in a number of the chapters in these books, the explicit purpose of the researchers is to study the implementation and effectiveness of standards-driven mathematics teaching and learning. The chapters concentrate on a wide range of mathematics topics, for example: concepts of number, addition and subtraction, algebraic thinking, linear measurement, geometric patterns and shapes, classification and sorting, mathematical proofs, multiplicative reasoning, division of fractions, data analysis and probability, volume, and the concept of limit. The chapters also examine what happens in terms of students' learning and classroom culture when various strategies and teaching methods are introduced: bringing in new models and representations of mathematical concepts and operations, teaching with problems, using writing in mathematics instruction, having students share their solution strategies, supporting students' own development of the algorithms for various mathematical operations, encouraging students to work in small groups and other collaborative arrangements, including role play in one's repertoire of mathematics teaching strategies, and integrating multiple opportunities for students to participate in hands-on technology and to work with technology-rich problems. Taken as a group, the chapters in these four volumes illustrate the power of an inquiry stance to widen and deepen teachers' knowledge of the subject matter of mathematics at the same time that this stance also enhances teachers' understanding of the learning processes of their students. Both of these—deeper knowledge of mathematics and richer understandings of learners and learning—are essential ingredients in teaching mathematics consistent with today's high standards.

Some of the chapters in these four volumes are written by single authors. These chronicle the ongoing efforts of teachers to understand what is going on in their classrooms so they can build on the knowledge and experiences students bring at the same time that they expand students' knowledge and skill. It is not at all surprising, however, that many of the chapters are co-authored, and even the single-authored chapters often reflect teachers' experiences as part of larger learning communities. Inquiry and community go hand in hand. The inquiries reported in these volumes feature collaborations among teachers and a whole array of colleagues, including fellow teachers, teacher study groups, teacher educators, university-based researchers, professional development facilitators, curriculum materials developers, research and development center researchers, and directors of large-scale professional development projects.

Across the chapters, there is a fascinating range of collaborative relationships between and among the teacher researchers and the subjects/objects of their inquiries: two teachers who collaborate to expand their own knowledge of mathematical content, the teacher researcher who is the subject of another researcher's study, the school-based teacher researcher and the university-based researcher who form a research partnership, the teacher who collaborates with a former teacher currently engaged in graduate study, pairs and small groups of teachers who work together to implement school-wide change in how mathematics is taught, teachers who team up to examine whether and how standards for mathematics teaching and learning are being implemented in their classrooms, teachers who engage in inquiry as part of their participation in large-scale professional development projects, the teacher who is part of a team that developed a set of professional development materials, a pair of teachers who collaborate with a university-based research and development group, a group of teachers who develop an inquiry process as a way to induct new teachers into their school, two teachers who inquire together about pedagogy and practice in one teacher's classroom, and teachers who form research groups and partnerships to work with teacher educators and student teachers. Almost by definition, practitioner inquiry is a collegial process that both occurs within, and stems from, the collaborations of learning communities. What all of these collaborations have in common is the assumption that teacher learning is an across-the-professional-lifespan process that is never "finished" even though teachers have years of experience. The chapters make clear that learning from and about teaching through inquiry is important for beginning and experienced teachers, and the intellectual work required to teach mathematics well is ongoing.

The inquiries that are described in these four books attest loudly and clearly to the power of questions in teachers' and students' learning. These inquiries defy the norm that is common to some schools where the competent teacher is assumed to be self-sufficient and certain and where asking questions is considered inappropriate for all but the most inexperienced teachers. Similarly, the chapters in these four books challenge the myth that good teachers rarely have questions they cannot answer about their own practices or about their students' learning. To the contrary, although the teachers in these four books are without question competent and may indeed be self-sufficient and sometimes certain, they are remarkable for their questions. Teachers who are researchers continuously pose problems, identify discrepancies between theory and practice, and challenge common routines. They continuously ask critical questions about teaching and learning and they do not flinch from self-critical reflection: Are the students really understanding what the teacher is teaching? What is the right move to make at various points in time to foster students' learning? How does the teacher know this? Are new curricular materials and teaching strategies actually supporting students' learning? How do students' mathematical ideas change over time? What is the evidence of students' growth and development? How can theory guide practice? How can practice add to, even alter, theory? These teachers ask questions not because they are failing, but because they—and their students—are learning. They count on their collaborators for alternative perspectives about their work and alternative interpretations of what is going on. In researching and writing about their work, they make explicit and visible to others both the decisions that they make on an ongoing basis and the intellectual processes that are the backdrop for those decisions. Going public with questions, seeking help from colleagues, and opening up one's practice to the scrutiny of outsiders may well go against the norms of appropriate teaching behaviors in some schools and school districts. But, as the chapters in this series of books make exquisitely clear, these are the very activities that lead to enriched learning opportunities and expanded knowledge for both students and teachers.

In this current era of accountability, there is heavy emphasis on evidence-based education and great faith in the power of data and research to improve educational practice. The chapters in the four books in this series illustrate what it looks like when mathematics teaching and learning are informed by research and evidence. In some of the chapters, for example, teacher researchers explicitly examine what happens when they attempt to implement research-based theories and teaching strategies into classroom practice. In these instances, as in others, practice is driven by research and evidence in several ways. Teacher researchers study the work of other researchers, treating this work as generative and illuminating, rather than regarding it as prescriptive and limiting. They reflect continuously about how others' research can (and should) inform their curricular, instructional, and assessment decisions about teaching mathematics. They also examine what consequences these decisions have for students' learning by collecting and analyzing a wide array of classroom data—from young children's visual representations of mathematical concepts and operations to classroom discussions about students' differing solutions to math problems to pre- and post-tests of students' mathematical knowledge and skill to interviews with students about their understandings to students' scores on standardized achievement tests.

In many of the chapters, teachers explicitly ask what it is that students know, what evidence there is that students have this knowledge and that it is growing and developing, and how this evidence can be used to guide their decisions about what to do next, with whom, and under what conditions. Braided together with these lines of inquiry about students' learning are questions about teachers' own ways of thinking about mathematics knowledge and skill. It is interesting that in many of the inquiries described in these four books, it is difficult to separate process from product or to sort out instruction from assessment. In fact, many of the chapters reveal that the distinctions often made between instruction and assessment and between process and product are false dichotomies. When mathematics teaching is guided by an inquiry stance and when teachers make decisions based on the data of practice, assessment of students' knowledge and skill is ongoing and is embedded into instruction, and the products of students' learning are inseparable from their learning and reasoning processes.

Finally, in some of the chapters in this quartet of books, teacher researchers and their colleagues use the processes of inquiry to examine issues of equity and social justice in mathematics teaching and learning. For example, one teacher problematizes commonly used phrases and ideas in mathematics education such as "success," particularly for those who have been previously unsuccessful in mathematics. Another explores connections between culture and mathematics by interviewing students. A trio of teachers examines the mathematical understandings of their students with disabilities, while another teacher chronicles his efforts to construct mathematics problems and projects that focus on social justice. Each of these educators values and draws heavily on the data of students' own voices and perspectives; each works to empower students as active agents in their own learning. These examples are a very important part of the collection of inquiries in this book series. When scholars write about teaching and teacher education for social justice, mathematics is the subject matter area least often included in the discussion. When teachers share examples of teaching for social justice in their own schools and classrooms, mathematics is often the area they have the most difficulty incorporating. When student teachers plan lessons and units related to equity and diversity, mathematics is often the subject area for which they cannot imagine any connection. The chapters in these books that specifically focus on equity and social justice make it clear that these issues readily apply to mathematics teaching and learning. But even in the many chapters for which these issues are not the explicit focus, it is clear that the teachers' intention is to empower all students—even (and especially) those groups least well served by the current educational system—with greater mathematical acuity and agency.

## THE VALUE OF TEACHERS' INQUIRIES INTO MATHEMATICS TEACHING AND LEARNING

There is no question that engaging in inquiry about teaching and learning mathematics is an important (and often an extremely powerful) form of professional development that enhances teachers' knowledge, skill and understandings. This is clear in chapter after chapter in the four volumes of this series. The authors themselves describe the process of engaging in self-critical systematic inquiry as transformative and professionally life-changing. They persuasively document how their classroom practices and their ways of thinking about mathematical knowing changed over time. They combine rich and multiple data sources to demonstrate growth in their students' knowledge and skill. Undoubtedly many Pre-K–12 teachers and school- and university-based teacher educators will find the inquiries collected in these four volumes extraordinarily helpful in furthering their own work. The questions raised by the teacher researchers (often in collaboration with university-based colleagues and others) will resonate deeply with the questions and issues of other educators striving to teach mathematics well by fostering conceptual understandings of big mathematical ideas, reliable but imaginative problem solving strategies, and solid mathematical know-how about practical applications to everyday problems. The teacher researchers whose work is represented in these volumes have made their questions and uncertainties about mathematics teaching explicit and public. In doing so, they have offered their own learning as grist for the learning and development of other teachers, teacher educators, and researchers. This is a major contribution of the series.

Few readers of the volumes in this series will debate the conclusion that systematically researching one's own work as a mathematics educator is a valuable activity for teacher researchers themselves, for their students in Pre-K–12 schools and classrooms, and for other Pre-K–12 teachers and teacher educators who are interested in the same issues. But some readers will raise questions about whether or not there is value to this kind of inquiry that carries beyond the participants involved in the local context or that extends outside the Pre-K–12 teaching/teacher education community. After all, the argument of some skeptics might go, for the most part the inquiries about mathematics teaching and learning that are included in this series were prompted by the questions of individual teachers or by small local groups of practitioners working in collaboration. With a few exceptions, these inquiries were conducted in the context of a single classroom, course, school, or program. Almost by definition then, the skeptics might say, few of the inquiries in these four volumes can hold up to traditional research criteria for transferability and application of findings to other populations and contexts (especially if conceptualized as the identification of causes and effects). For this reason, the skeptics might conclude, the kind of work included in this series is nothing more than good professional development for individuals in local communities, which may be of interest to other teacher educators and professional developers.

Putting aside for the moment that good professional development is essential in mathematics education (not to mention, hard to come by), the skeptics' line of argument, as outlined in the paragraph above, is both short-sighted and uninformed. The inquiries that are part of the *Teachers Engaged in Research: Inquiry Into Mathematics Classrooms* series are valuable and valid well beyond the borders of the local communities where the work was done, and the criteria for evaluating traditional research are not so appropriate here. With many forms of practitioner inquiry, appropriate conceptions of value and validity are more akin to the idea of "trustworthiness" that has been forwarded by some scholars as a way to evaluate the results of qualitative research. From Mishler's (1990) perspective, for example, the concept of validation ought to replace the notion of validity. Validation is the extent to which a particular research community, which works from "tacit understandings of actual, situated practices of a field of inquiry" (Lyons and LaBoskey, 2002, p. 19), can rely on the concepts, methods, and inferences of an inquiry for their own theoretical and conceptual work. Following this line of reasoning, validation rests on concrete examples (or "exemplars") of actual practices presented in enough detail so that the relevant community of practitioner researchers can judge the trustworthiness and usefulness of the observations and analyses of an inquiry.

Many of the inquiries in these four books offer what may be thought of as exemplars of teaching and learning mathematics that are consistent with current professional standards in mathematics education. Part of what distinguishes the inquiries of the teacher researchers in these four books from those of outside researchers who rely on similar forms of data collection is that in addition to documenting students' learning, teacher researchers have the opportunity and the access to systematically document their own teaching and learning as well. They can document their own thinking, planning, and evaluation processes as well as their questions, interpretive frameworks, changes in views over time, issues they see as dilemmas, and themes that recur. Teacher researchers are able to analyze the links as well as the disconnects between teaching and learning that are not readily accessible to researchers based outside the contexts of practice. Systematic examination and analysis of students' learning juxtaposed and interwoven with systematic examination of the practitioners' intentions, reactions, decisions, and interpretations make for incredibly detailed and complex analyses—or exemplars—of mathematics teaching and learning.

With rich examples, the teacher researchers in these books demonstrate how they came to understand their students' reasoning processes and thus learned to intervene more adeptly with the right question, the right comment, a new problem, or silent acknowledgement and support. Braiding insightful reflections on pedagogy with perceptive analyses of their students' understandings, the authors in these four books make explicit and visible the kinds of thinking and decision making that are usually implicit and invisible in studies of mathematics teaching. Although they are usually invisible, however, these ways of thinking and making teaching decisions are essential ingredients for teaching mathematics to today's high standards. I believe that a critical contribution of this series of books—a contribution that extends well beyond the obvious benefits to the participants themselves—is the set of exemplars that cuts across grade levels and mathematics topics. What makes this series unique is that the exemplars in this book do not emerge from the work of university-based researchers who have used the classroom as a site for research and for the demonstration of theory-based pedagogy. Rather the trustworthiness—or validation—of the exemplars in these four books derives from the fact that they were conducted by school-based teacher researchers who shouldered the full responsibilities of classroom teaching while also striving to construct appropriate curriculum, develop rich teaching problems and strategies, and theorize their practice by connecting it to larger philosophical, curricular, and pedagogical ideas.

This series of books makes a remarkable contribution to what we know about mathematics teaching and learning and about the processes of learning to teach over time. Readers will be thoroughly engaged.

## REFERENCES

Cochran-Smith, M., & Lytle, S. L. (1999). Relationship of knowledge and practice: Teacher learning in communities. In A. Iran-Nejad & C. Pearson (Eds.), *Review of research in education* (Vol. 24, pp. 249–306). Washington, DC: American Educational Research Association.

Lyons, N., & LaBoskey, V. K. (Eds.). (2002). *Narrative inquiry in practice: Advancing the knowledge of teaching*. New York: Teachers College Press.

Mishler, E. (1990). Validation in inquiry-guided research: The role of exemplars in narrative studies. *Harvard Educational Review, 60*(4), 415–442.

CHAPTER 1

# INTRODUCTION TO THE PRE-K–2 VOLUME

**Stephanie Z. Smith**[1]
*Georgia State University*

**Marvin E. Smith**
*Georgia Southern University*

More than three-quarters of a century has passed since Dewey (1929) called for the active participation of teachers in investigating educational activity and creating "a constant flow of less formal reports on special school affairs and results" (p. 46). He noted, "It seems to me that the contributions that might come from classroom teachers are a comparatively neglected field; or, to change the metaphor, an almost unworked mine" (p. 46).

As elementary classrooms become more student-focused, with teachers understanding and responding to children's mathematical thinking and problem solving strategies, the work of teaching mathematics becomes more inquiry based. As teachers systematically inquire both into their students' mathematical thinking and into their own teaching practices, *teacher as researcher* becomes a natural extension of what defines a professional teacher. Carefully observing and questioning students, analyzing their needs, and adjusting learning activities and instruction to fit students'

*Teachers Engaged in Research*
*Inquiry Into Mathematics Classrooms, Grades Pre-K–2*, pages 1–14

needs are important practices of good teaching. Becoming a reflective practitioner can lead to systematically searching for insights that lead to both increased understanding of the effects of teaching and improvements in learning outcomes.

Teacher research is becoming a significant contributor to the body of research on pedagogical and curricular reforms. Much of this research is rich in classroom narrative and personal stories, dominated by qualitative methodologies involving sustained direct contact with students, and often written by the teacher-researcher in the first person voice. In teacher research, stories are critical tools for illuminating the theories and rules operating in classroom communities.

How does this view differ from the historical role of teachers in research? Certainly teachers have been the *impetus* of research studies. They also have been referred to as *consumers* of research. It has been less common, however, for teachers to be considered *producers* of research. Even when teachers have been engaged in systematic inquiry, their work has not typically been presented to colleagues for discussion and review or disseminated through publications. However, as demonstrated by the chapters in this volume, the importance of teacher research and the opportunities to share these results are increasing. Teachers are becoming engaged in research in a variety of ways, and their voices are gaining presence in the mathematics education community.

The authors who contributed to this volume were involved in research through activities that included:

- reading and reflecting on research and other literature in the field,
- interpreting findings from the research literature to influence their instructional practice,
- participating in study groups with their colleagues,
- generating research questions for themselves and others to investigate,
- participating in research studies and professional development projects led by other researchers, and
- designing and implementing their own studies and sharing their findings with others.

The authors' involvement in these research activities had a profound impact on their conceptions of teaching and learning and prompted changes in their instructional practice. Such direct impact on practice is one of the many benefits of research that emanates from the classroom and that is conducted by teachers themselves. By sharing the teacher research in this volume, we hope to broaden its impact beyond the authors' classrooms and schools to the wider mathematics education community.

## HOW THIS VOLUME CAME TO BE

### History of the Series

The idea for the *Teachers Engaged in Research* series arose from efforts by the Research Advisory Committee (RAC) of the National Council of Teachers of Mathematics (NCTM) to expand traditional conceptions of research in mathematics to include practitioner inquiry and the research questions that are of interest to practitioners. Beginning in the late 1990s, the RAC made a concerted effort to recognize teachers as producers (and not just consumers) of research. To this end, NCTM sponsored a Working Conference on Teacher Research in Mathematics Education in Albuquerque, NM in 2001. The goal of this conference was to articulate a list of issues that should be considered in developing a framework for teacher research in mathematics education. This conference led to a grant proposal that would have brought together participants from the conference for a writing workshop with the goal of producing a publication similar to this one. For a variety of reasons, that project did not come to fruition.

The RAC turned its attention to including teacher researchers as participants—both attendees and speakers—at the Research Presession that precedes the annual NCTM meeting. Also, there was ongoing dialogue in the RAC about a publication that would highlight practitioner inquiry. Simultaneously, the RAC and the Educational Materials Committee (EMC) decided that it was time to issue an update of the *Handbook of Research on Mathematics Teaching and Learning* (Grouws, 1992). Unbeknownst to many, the series titled *Research into Practice* edited by Sigrid Wagner was originally conceived by the EMC as a "companion" to the handbook. The *Research into Practice* series featured chapters co-authored by university-based researchers and classroom teachers and reflected a view of teachers as consumers of research—an accurate reflection of the field at the time. When the RAC and EMC discussed the update of the handbook and its companion, the companion was recast to reflect a view of teachers as producers of research. The *Handbook of Research on Mathematics Teaching and Learning, 2nd Edition* (Lester, in preparation) documents a portion of the knowledge base available in mathematics education; the four volumes of the *Teachers Engaged in Research* series fill a gap in that knowledge base by focusing on the research contributions of classroom teachers, allowing an additional set of voices to be heard.

The goal of this series is to use teachers' accounts of classroom inquiry to make public and explicit the processes of doing research in classrooms. Teaching is a complex, multi-faceted task, and this complexity often is not captured in research articles. Our goal is to illuminate this complexity. The ways in which this complexity can also be messy should be articulated rather than hidden.

## Identifying Authors

Using the participants of the Albuquerque conference as a starting point, the editorial board for the series generated a list of teachers, projects, and university faculty who we knew had been engaged in classroom research themselves or might know of others who had. Through personal contacts with these individuals, and those they led us to, we compiled a list of potential authors, the nature of their work, and relevant background information. For each volume, we attempted to generate a set of potential authors and topics that would span aspects of the *Principles and Standards for School Mathematics* (NCTM, 2000), such as the content standards, process standards, and principles. We also tried to find a set of pieces that would span various roles that teachers might play in research—principal researcher, co-researcher, research participant, and consumer of research. We then invited authors for specific chapters in accordance with the categories outlined above. Authors were specifically asked to highlight the following aspects of their work in their manuscripts:

- mathematical content and processes that were addressed (using the *Principles and Standards* document as a guide)
- demographic data on school/student population/community (as it pertains to the research)
- the authors' role in the research and what the experience was like for them
- data sources for the work (incorporated into the narrative as appropriate, e.g., interview transcripts, student work, teacher reflections, summary of a class session)
- explanation of data analysis process (How did the authors make sense of their data?)

- articles that influenced their work (rather than a full literature review, references to work that may have sparked their curiosity, helped them think of data collection methods, contrasted their findings, or was helpful in another way)
- implications (How did this influence the authors' subsequent teaching? What might others take away from this study?)

We particularly stressed the need for the manuscripts to reflect disciplined inquiry and for claims to be based on evidence.

## The Review Process

We took great care with the review process in an effort to both respect the varied experiences of the authors with writing for publication and to improve the quality of the chapters. Initial outlines and drafts were reviewed and commented on by the volume editors to ensure that the manuscript met the goals for the series. Revised and edited drafts were then sent to two reviewers. To the extent possible, we solicited reviewers who had experience with teacher inquiry. We asked reviewers to be sensitive to the fact that the authors were making themselves vulnerable by sharing their research with a wider audience, and we suggested they approach their task from a mentoring frame of mind, striving to both support the authors' work and strengthen the manuscript.

The timeline from first draft to final publication of this volume was a long one, and we commend the authors in this volume for their patience and willingness to engage in the challenging and arduous process of writing for publication. As editors of this volume, we have developed great respect for the ways in which our authors, as teacher researchers, have documented, analyzed, and shared their experiences integrating inquiry with teaching.

## OVERVIEW OF CHAPTERS

Table 1.1 provides an abbreviated overview of the chapters in this volume by indicating the grade level, mathematical content, context, and primary research issue for each chapter.

Table 1.1.   Overview of Teachers Engaged in Research:
Inquiry Into Mathematics Classrooms, Grades Pre-K–2

| Author | Grade | Mathematics | Context | Research Issue |
|---|---|---|---|---|
| Archer, Grant, & Kline | K | Number | Implementing *Investigations* in Mathematics (InMath) professional development project at Western Michigan University | Effects of teacher questioning on children's understandings of number combinations summing to five |
| Keith | 2 | Early Algebraic Thinking | Cognitively Guided Instruction (CGI) classroom in Wisconsin | Children's understandings of and justifications of conjectures about odd and even numbers |
| Schweitzer | 1-2 | Early Algebraic Thinking | Developing Mathematical Ideas (DMI) professional development project at EDC in Massachusetts | Effects of classroom discourse on children's generalizations about properties of addition and subtraction |
| Vaisenstein | 2 | Number, Representations | Sabbatical at the Educational Research Collaborative (ERC) at TERC in Massachusetts | How children communicate mathematical ideas through representations |
| Jaslow & Vik | 1-2 | Linear Measurement | Independent teaching/ research collaboration in California | Children's understandings of linear measurement and how to modify learning activities and classroom discourse |

Table 1.1.    Overview of Teachers Engaged in Research:
Inquiry Into Mathematics Classrooms, Grades Pre-K–2

| Author | Grade | Mathematics | Context | Research Issue |
|---|---|---|---|---|
| Okazaki, Zenigami, & Dougherty | 1 | Measurement | Measure Up (MU) curriculum development project at the University of Hawaii | Effects of beginning the elementary curriculum with measurement and comparison rather than counting and number operations |
| Renfro | K | 2-D Geometry | Arizona Urban Systemic Initiative and Cognitively Guided Instruction (CGI) | Children's definitions and understandings of shapes |
| Hands | 1 | Number Sense, Assessment | Masters degree project while teaching a unit from Investigations in Number, Data, and Space in the State of Washington | Assessing children's number sense and differentiating curriculum and instruction |
| Wicks & Janes | 1 | Pattern | Canadian school district's Teacher as Researcher professional development project | Uncovering children's thinking and reasoning about patterns to improve instruction and learning |

Archer, Grant, and Kline describe their experiences working together in the context of the Implementing *Investigations* in Mathematics (InMath) Project co-directed by Grant and Kline. As a multi-year professional development project funded by a grant from the National Science Foundation,

InMath involved more than 350 elementary teachers from six school districts in systematic inquiry into their teaching practices. As a kindergarten teacher-researcher who participated in the project, Archer's multi-year inquiry focuses on (a) how her questioning affected students' understanding during a particular lesson from a number unit and (b) how she revised the lesson and her teaching in response to her systematic inquiry relating to the lesson.

Keith describes an action research study she conducted in her second grade Cognitively Guided Instruction (CGI) classroom to better understand her students' early algebraic thinking—specifically their understanding and justification of conjectures about odd and even numbers. Over the course of the school year, she documented and analyzed the generalized ideas her second graders held about odd and even numbers and the ways they were able to justify that these generalizations are always true. This particular study was conducted in a school district which has, for many years, encouraged, supported, and published action research conducted by its teachers.

Schweitzer describes some of her experiences learning to find what she calls *the research in teaching* in the context of children beginning to make generalizations about properties of addition and subtraction. As a teacher of students in first and second grades, she participated in a collaboration among researchers and teachers that produced the set of *Developing Mathematical Ideas* (DMI) professional development materials. Over the course of two years, Schweitzer systematically studied her classroom discourse about properties of addition and subtraction and learned that use of models is an important element in her students' approach to proving that their generalizations about operations always work.

Vaisenstein describes her efforts to systematically examine and analyze the work of second-grade students across time. As part of this inquiry, she deliberately chose to focus on how her students communicated mathematical ideas through their representations. She discovered how introducing a new representation (the 100 chart) required students to make connections to representations they already understood (vertical stacks of ten cubes) before the new representation could be used with understanding and success.

Jaslow and Vik describe their experiences researching children's understandings of linear measurement and using what they learned to inform their instructional decisions in Vik's California classroom. Applying Jaslow's previous experiences with a university-based research project on measurement, the authors examined how to modify their learning activities and classroom discourse to better help first- and second-grade students make sense of measurement concepts, learn to successfully measure length with non-standard and standard units, and understand how to make and use a ruler.

Okazaki, Zenigami, and Dougherty describe their work as researcher-teachers at the Education Laboratory School, a charter school associated with the Curriculum Research & Development Group at the University of Hawaii. They share experiences teaching in first grade with new materials they were developing that begin the elementary curriculum with measurement and comparison rather than counting and number operations.

Renfro shares her experiences collaborating with a kindergarten teacher in documenting young children's definitions and understandings of geometric shapes. Their inquiry was supported by an urban systemic initiative with the goal of engaging teachers in systematic inquiry to improve children's mathematical experiences, especially in the areas of geometry and measurement. This chapter provides a clear example of the iterative nature of classroom research and the evolution of research questions and research designs intended to answer those questions.

Hands describes her inquiry into her first-grade students' number sense in the context of teaching a unit from the *Investigations in Number, Data, and Space* curriculum. To document her students' growth in understanding she developed both a pre-assessment that included individual interviews and an end-of-unit summative assessment. She also describes how she differentiated learning activities and instruction based on the pre-assessment results. This chapter provides an example of how thorough assessment of students' understandings can support instructional decisions as well as systematic inquiry into the effects of classroom events.

Wicks and Janes describe their experiences as a first-grade teacher and professional development facilitator, respectively, involved in a collaborative teacher-as-researcher project in one school district in Newfoundland, Canada. They focus on systematically examining children's thinking and reasoning about mathematical patterns in an effort to improve instruction and learning in the classroom.

## REFLECTIONS ON COMMON THEMES

Although there are many common themes in these chapters, we will highlight three in this introduction that we consider to be most important to understanding the processes involved in teacher inquiry. These include the value of focusing on children's thinking and understanding, the benefits of collaborating with others, and the iterative nature of inquiry in teaching.

## Focusing on Children's Thinking

The Learning Principle in NCTM's *Principles and Standards for School Mathematics* (2000) emphasizes learning mathematics with understanding and constructing new knowledge from experience and prior knowledge. Similarly, the Teaching Principle speaks of knowing students as learners and how to assess students' understanding. These ideas point to the central theme of this volume: Teachers are engaging in the pursuit of greater insight into students' thinking, their understanding of important mathematical ideas and processes, and how various classroom experiences affect learning. All of the methodological choices about what evidence to gather and how to analyze what students say, do, and produce play out in the authors' efforts to document and make sense of the effects of classroom activities on children's thinking and understanding.

Generally, the research reported by these authors focuses on answering questions that address relationships between very specific classroom activities and equally specific elements of students' mathematical understanding. As Hubbard and Power explain, "Understanding learning from the students' perspectives is central to teacher research. Strategies for research emerge and evolve from these close, intense, shifting relationships between students and teachers" (1999, p. 4). Many of the authors who are able to "hear the mathematics in students' talk" (Bass & Ball, 2003, p. vii) have used students' explanations as evidence of their thinking and understanding and have found the answers to their research questions among the words of students.

## Collaborating with Others

Collaborating with others and apprenticing with more experienced researchers is an important element of the process of becoming a teacher-researcher. Whether as part of formal collaborations such as those designed primarily as professional development or as part of informal collaborations among colleagues supported by readings, the process of doing research includes opportunities to learn from others about systematic gathering and analysis of evidence to understand and explain the effects of classroom events. The authors of this volume reflect varying levels of experience doing research, and they have collaborated with others in a variety of ways.

Often collaboration includes participation in some type of research community. Hubbard and Power argue that "there are examples of teacher-researchers doing fine studies without support, but usually sustained inquiry in schools or districts over time involves the development of a research community" (1999, p. 6). Participation in a research community can be accomplished in various ways, such as through forming a new research community among participants in a professional development project or connecting to others through district-sponsored publication of action research projects (see Caro-Bruce & McCreadie, 1995, for elaboration of the district support of the Keith chapter in this volume). Some of these connections can be facilitated by technology (e.g., e-mail or list servers). Connections can also be made with existing research communities, such as through participating in NCTM Research Presessions or through publishing articles in NCTM periodicals and other publications, including this series. The chapters in this volume describe the creation of or connection to a variety of research communities.

## Iterative Nature of Inquiry in Teaching

The methods of inquiry used by the authors of these chapters demonstrate the iterative nature of inquiry in teaching, which refines both its process and its outcomes each time the cycle is repeated. These methods progressed through periods of planning classroom events and evidence to be collected, collecting evidence, and analyzing evidence before beginning anew with more planning, collecting, and analyzing. There are some similarities between this inquiry cycle and the familiar teaching cycle of planning, teaching, and assessing. Adding the element of reflection to this teaching cycle results in a basic inquiry methodology built upon practices that are familiar to teachers (Dadds & Hart, 2001). Increasing the degree to which this process is systematically planned and conducted transforms reflection into analysis and reflective teaching into systematic inquiry. As Thomas (2005) summarizes:

> Observant teachers, from their daily experiences in the classroom, compile a wealth of educational problems to solve, topics to investigate and issues to ponder. From those experiences, they also gain valuable insights into potential solutions to those problems, various methods of investigating topics, and ways to settle issues. Some teachers are not satisfied to contemplate such matters in a casual, cursory fashion. Instead, they yearn to investigate issues in a systematic manner.... (p. v)

Action research methods provide a good fit with this interest in examining issues of teaching and learning more systematically by moving beyond the informal reflection that is a central element of good teaching. As Ball (2000) describes it:

> Action research, although tied closely to one's own ongoing work as a teacher, is typically more planful. With a focal question in mind, the teacher investigates an issue, designs and tries a new method or new materials, and seeks to examine it or them systematically. Some forms of inquiry make communication with others central—teacher narratives, for example. Teachers writing about their teaching concentrate on representing the experience—problems, puzzles, excitements—of practice to themselves, to close colleagues, and sometimes to a wider audience. Within this arena, practitioners examine their practice thoughtfully with the goal of learning about teaching and learning and ultimately, improving it.... The agendas may vary, from representing teachers' experiences to asserting the primacy of teachers' perspectives to contributing to scholarship and theory. (p. 367)

The process of preparing these chapters has also reflected this iterative nature of inquiry. For some, the formality of presentation in their chapter is more an artifact of the process of writing the chapter, with the benefit of hindsight, than a reflection of the initial design of the experiment. This is consistent with the process of teacher research described by Brown: "Teacher research is a method of gaining insight from hindsight. It is a way of formalizing the questioning and reflecting we, as teachers, engage in every day in an attempt to improve student learning" (as cited in Dana & Yendol-Silva, 2003, p. 5).

## HOW THIS VOLUME MIGHT BE USED

This volume was written primarily for teachers who have developed (or who are being encouraged to develop) an awareness of and commitment to teaching mathematics for understanding. The research findings presented in these chapters suggest instructional implications worthy of these teachers' consideration. Often, the authors in this volume describe instructional practices or raise issues that have the potential to broaden views of teaching and learning mathematics. These chapters provide interesting problems and tasks used in the authors' work that readers can use in their own classrooms.

The volume can also be used with courses for preservice and inservice teachers, collaborative teacher study groups, and other professional development activities. A hallmark of good research is its connection to the relevant literature in the field, and the authors of this volume have themselves drawn from the research literature to inform their work. The reference lists accompanying these chapters can be useful resources and should not be overlooked. Most importantly for teacher education, this volume showcases the variety of ways teachers can become engaged in research, and we hope that readers will recognize that teacher research can be both accessible and beneficial in the preparation and professional development of teachers.

This is not to suggest, however, that this volume is intended only for teachers and teacher educators. It is also intended to be an interesting, informative resource for other researchers, school administrators, and policy makers. The research presented in this volume is intended to provide an opportunity for those outside the classroom to gain insight into the kind of issues that matter to teachers, the ways in which those issues might be researched, and the contributions that classroom research makes to mathematics education.

## An Invitation to Reflect as You Read

These teachers' accounts make public various aspects of their beliefs about teaching and learning. You are invited to critically examine their instructional approaches and the rigor of their research methods. It is generally expected that published research stand up to such scrutiny. We encourage you, however, to also reflect upon your own classroom experiences and to acknowledge the accomplishments of these teachers in systematically studying and learning from classroom events. They deserve our respect for the work they have done and the risks they have taken in opening their teaching and research to public inspection. Whether you are a teacher, teacher educator, researcher, administrator, or policy maker, we hope that these stories will inspire you to pursue your own interesting questions of teaching practice and student learning.

## NOTE

1.  This chapter was written, in part, as a result of collaborative conversations with the editors of the other volumes of this series and the series editor. We wish to acknowledge the contributions of Cynthia Langrall, Joanna Masingila, Laura Van Zoest, and Denise Mewborn.

## REFERENCES

Ball, D. L. (2000). Working on the inside: Using one's own practice as a site for studying teaching and learning. In A. E. Kelly & R. A. Lesh (Eds.), *Handbook of research design in mathematics and science education* (pp. 365-402). Mahwah, NJ: Erlbaum

Bass, H., & Ball, D. L. (2003). Foreword. In T. P. Carpenter, M. L. Franke, & L. Levi, *Thinking mathematically: Integrating arithmetic & algebra in elementary school* (pp. v–vii). Portsmouth, NH: Heinemann.

Caro-Bruce, C., & McCreadie, J. (1995). What happens when a school district supports action research? In S. E. Noffke & R. B. Stevenson (Eds.), *Educational action research: Becoming practically critical.* New York: Teachers College Press.

Dadds, M., & Hart, S. (2001). *Action research in education.* New York: Routledge/ Falmer.

Dana, N. F., & Yendol-Silva, D. (2003). *The reflective educator's guide to classroom research: Learning to teach and teaching to learn through practitioner inquiry.* Thousand Oaks, CA: Corwin Press.

Grouws, D. A. (Ed.). (1991). *Handbook of research on mathematics teaching and learning.* New York: Macmillan.

Hubbard, R. S., & Power, B. M. (1999). *Living the questions: A guide for teacher-researchers.* York, ME: Stenhouse.

Lester, F. K. (Ed.) (in preparation). *Handbook of research on mathematics teaching and learning* (2nd edition). Greenwich, CT: InfoAge/NCTM.

National Council of Teachers of Mathematics. (2000). *Principles and standards for school mathematics.* Reston, VA: Author.

CHAPTER 2

# USING YOUR OWN TEACHING AS A SITE FOR RESEARCH INTO PRACTICE

**Mary Kay Archer**
*Long Lake Elementary, Traverse City, MI*

**Theresa J. Grant and Kate Kline**
*Western Michigan University*

The purpose of this chapter is to convey the authors' journey as they participated in a long-term process of systematically analyzing classroom teaching in order to uncover what it takes to support children to learn mathematics with understanding. This occurred in the context of a five-year professional development project involving the implementation of the *Investigations in Number, Data, and Space*[1] (*Investigations*) curriculum across several different districts. We begin by briefly describing the professional development project that provided the context and impetus for our drive to pursue more deliberate inquiry into teaching, and then describe the specific journey of one teacher—Mary Kay Archer. Although most of the chapter is written in Mary Kay's voice, the words, thoughts, and insights into teaching represent our collective attempt to convey the depth to which this experience has affected us all.

*Teachers Engaged in Research*
*Inquiry Into Mathematics Classrooms, Grades Pre-K–2*, pages 15–34
Copyright © 2006 by Information Age Publishing
All rights of reproduction in any form reserved. reserved.

## THE INMATH PROJECT

The project, Implementing *Investigations* in Mathematics (InMath)[2], was created in response to the needs expressed by six local districts for assistance in their efforts to implement a standards-based elementary mathematics curriculum, *Investigations*. This project involved more than 350 teachers who used their own teaching as a site for systematic inquiry. This process of inquiring into one's own teaching practice formed one of the project's main approaches to enhance teacher learning. In order to obtain funding from the National Science Foundation for this project, all teachers at every school had to commit to 100 hours of professional development over the 5 years of the project. Unlike many small-scale, experimental professional development projects, the InMath project included teachers who were not necessarily convinced of the merits of this new curriculum. With this in mind, a multi-year professional development plan was created to support these teachers to rethink what it means to teach children mathematics, and simultaneously rethink what professional development could offer them. Another critical component of the project was the cultivation of teacher leadership in order to help plan and facilitate professional development based on the needs of the participants.

From the outset, we recognized that it was important to design professional development opportunities that were closely tied to teachers' practice in a variety of ways. For example, many sessions involved teachers experiencing curriculum activities while facilitators modeled instructional approaches, often with a focus on how a mathematics idea is developed, either in a single unit at a particular grade, or over several units and grades. Other sessions utilized examples of student work, for the purposes of exploring student understanding of a particular mathematical idea and/or assessing that understanding. (See Grant & Kline, 2004 for a more detailed description of the entire InMath professional development project.)

Although the professional development formats offered were effective in enhancing participants' understanding of mathematics content and the curriculum itself, there was evidence that teachers were not making the kind of fundamental changes in their teaching that was necessary to implement *Investigations* well. They continued to struggle with the shift from dispensing knowledge to facilitating their students' sense-making of the mathematics they were learning. In addition, project teachers began to express a need for more grade-level specific professional development that dealt with the day-to-day decisions of implementing *Investigations*. This afforded the opportunity to design a new format, the Reflecting on Teaching (RT) session that would center on teaching, as the project teachers had requested, yet revolve around the complex decisions inherent to teaching for understanding and the diverse opinions and beliefs that underlie those decisions.

## The Reflecting on Teaching Professional Development Session

The Reflecting on Teaching (RT) format used videotaped practice as the focal point for reflection in order to bring different, and often competing, notions of teaching and learning to the surface. In order to foster an environment of collaborative reflection, videotapes of *Investigations* lessons taught by InMath project teachers were used. One lesson was used for each RT session, and was edited to include: the launch or introduction to the lesson, several teacher-student exchanges while the students are at work, and the closure. These segments were then used as a site for reflection during an all-day session for teachers of a particular grade level. Thus the session can be thought of as progressing through the following sequence of activities for each segment of videotape: first the participants anticipate what they might do during a particular portion of the lesson (launch, students at work, or closure) and discuss their rationale for doing so; next, the participants watch the segment of video corresponding to that portion of the lesson; finally they discuss their reactions to what they viewed. The overall format of the RT session and the specific questions utilized during the session are shown in Figure 2.1. The intent was to pose questions that were broad enough to allow a multitude of issues to surface and a variety of perspectives to be shared. (See Grant, Kline & Van Zoest, (2001) for a more detailed description of RT sessions.)

1. Introducing the Reflecting Session:
   - ➢ Introduce the activity and the difference between discussing recollections about teaching versus reflecting on an actual lesson, read the article, "The Role of Reflection in Teaching," and describe the context for where this lessons falls within the unit and what students have done previously.

2. Thinking about the Launch of the Lesson:
   - ➢ Give participants a few minutes to read through the investigation/lesson you will be watching and then discuss:
     - • What are the mathematical ideas in this lesson?
     - • What would you need to think about to launch the lesson?

3. Watching the Launch:
   - ➢ Watch the videotape of the launch and discuss in small groups:
     - • What appeared to be the goals of this introduction?
     - • Were they achieved? If so, how?

- What could be done differently?

4. Thinking about Supporting Students as They Work:
   ➤ Before watching the teacher talk to students as they are working, give participants a few minutes to review specific problems that will be discussed on the video. Then discuss in small groups:
     - What mathematics do you anticipate students struggling with while working on the problem(s) in this lesson?
     - What questions would you have prepared to ask students who are struggling?
     - What questions would you have prepared to ask students who are "getting it?"

5. Watching Students at Work:
   ➤ Watch the videotape of the exchanges with the students as they are working and debrief as a whole group:
     - What was effective about this exchange?
     - What might you do differently?

6. Thinking about the Closure of the Lesson:
   ➤ Discuss whole group what you would do as a closure to this lesson and watch videotape if available.
     - What do you need to think about to close this lesson?
     - Was there a particular mathematical idea that the students seemed confused about or divided on?
     - Were there particular strategies or ways of thinking that warrant highlighting?

7. Watching the Closure of the Lesson:
   ➤ Watch the videotape of the closure and discuss whole group:
     - What appeared to be the goals of this closure?
     - What could be done differently?

8. Concluding the Reflecting Session:
   ➤ Step back and debrief reactions to the reflecting session to think about how it will impact participants' teaching.

Figure 2.1.   Reflecting on Teaching Session Format

All project teachers, including teacher-leaders, were invited to attend RT sessions appropriate for their grade levels. Sessions for each grade level (K–5) were offered during each of the years of the project starting in year 2. The sessions were highly attended with between 25–30 participants at each. The teacher-leaders attended the RT sessions as participants in year 2, and then those who agreed worked as co-facilitators and co-planners with the project-directors for the remaining years of the project.

## The Inquiry Into Teaching Process

As the teacher-leaders first became involved in the process of planning and facilitating RT sessions, it was clear that they were embarking on an experience that would make them more introspective and impact the way we all thought about teaching and learning. The teacher-leaders went through the Inquiry into Teaching Process (ITP), which consists of the following six elements:

- Each teacher was videotaped teaching a single lesson and then watched and analyzed the videotape independently.
- With co-facilitators and project directors, the teacher watched and analyzed an edited version of the videotape that included the launch, 2-3 clips of exchanges with students while they were working, and the closure.
- With co-facilitators and project directors, the teacher anticipated issues that would arise from the edited videotape when facilitating an RT session with colleagues and possible ways to encourage discussion around these issues.
- The teacher co-facilitated an RT session with colleagues using the videotape. The teacher then discussed reactions to the RT session with project directors.
- The teacher was videotaped while teaching the lesson again after the RT session. The teacher then watched and analyzed this second videotape independently.

This ITP experience allowed some of the teacher-leaders to conduct a systematic inquiry into their practice. The focus of the remainder of this chapter is on one such teacher's experience.

## MARY KAY'S STORY[3]

I have been an elementary teacher for over 20 years, during which I have taught primarily in kindergarten and first grade. I have also worked for many years with the staff at a day care center and preschool through a government agency, and I am very committed to young children and the enthusiasm they bring to their learning. I have always been a reflective teacher, in the sense that I thought deeply about what did or did not go well during my lessons, and I often made adjustments accordingly. But it was not until I joined the InMath professional development project that I began to understand the power of scrutinizing my teaching more formally and more deliberately. As we discussed the approach *Investigations* has towards learning, we noticed the ways activities were designed to provide students the opportunity to reflect on what they were learning. We recognized the importance of reflection as a process through which students solidified their learning and I began making connections between this and seminal work by those who have advocated the critical nature of the reflective process in learning with understanding (e.g., Dewey, 1933; Piaget, 1971). As we began to work on teaching and thinking about our practice, it made sense to consider the role of reflection in our own efforts to learn about teaching as well. Interestingly, many recommendations have also been made about the importance of reflecting on teaching as a necessary part of how teachers learn to teach (e.g., Artzt & Armour-Thomas, 2002; Hart, Schultz, Najee-ullah, & Nash, 1992).

Toward that end, I welcomed the opportunity to participate in the intensive process of inquiry into my teaching that was a part of the InMath project. When I first began analyzing my videotapes independently, I was encouraged to consider one or two aspects of my teaching that I would like to study more in depth as a way to focus my inquiry. I was immediately drawn to investigating the ways in which I questioned students and the degree to which this impacted student understanding. More specifically, my inquiry revolved around the degree to which my questioning supported students in understanding the mathematics they were learning and how the alterations I made in my teaching from year to year impacted student learning.

To describe my experience during the intensive Inquiry into Teaching Process (ITP) developed for InMath teacher-leaders, I will use one complete cycle through the ITP, emphasizing how the more deliberate kinds of reflection I did helped me answer the questions that drove my inquiry and impacted my thoughts about teaching, learning, and understanding.

**The Lesson**

The *Investigations* curriculum at the kindergarten level is comprised of six units dealing with number sense, patterns, data, measurement, and geometry. Each unit contains a series of investigations that include an introductory focus lesson followed by several days of choice-time lessons, where children choose from among several different activities on a particular mathematical topic. The lesson that is the focus of this chapter is called "Five Crayons in All," which is the beginning lesson from the last investigation in the book "How Many in All?" (Kliman, Mainhart, Murray, & Econo-mopolous, 1998). In this beginning lesson, students solve a problem in which they have five crayons altogether, some blue and some red. Students find one or more combinations of blue and red crayons they could have to make up five in all and then share their solutions. The Teacher's Guide lists the main goals as:

- Finding combinations of five;
- Using pictures, numbers, and words to record solutions to a prob-lem; and
- Beginning to recognize that some problems have more than one solution.

The Teacher's Guide is explicit about recommendations for implement-ing the lesson. It suggests that the activity be introduced by holding up sev-eral blue and red crayons and an empty crayon box that holds at least five crayons. It then suggests saying, "I want to put five crayons in my box. I need some blue ones and some red ones. What could I have? How many blues? How many reds? Remember, I need five crayons in all." The Teacher's Guide recommends that two different student solutions be accepted and modeled with crayons. To help students develop their *own* ways of representing their work for this activity, this unit recommends that students' suggested solutions *not* be represented on paper. Although mod-eling how to record a child's solution is often helpful—and is often encouraged in the *Investigations* units—doing so may inhibit children from developing their own representations. The development of methods for representing ones work is a critical part of learning how to communicate mathematically. Also, because this is intended to be the last unit of the year, not modeling representations of solutions encourages students to think on their own. This can provide valuable information to the teacher about students' independent thinking.

Students are then given a choice to work alone, in pairs, or in small groups to find solutions different from those suggested. They are encour-aged to share their ideas with one another and use crayons or counters as they work on the problem. The teacher's responsibilities at this time are to notice if students are collaborating on the problem, notice which solutions students are tending to find, notice whether students stop after one solu-tion, and question students on their solutions to see if they can justify them. When everyone has found at least one additional solution, the stu-dents are then called back together with their papers to share some of their solutions. As students share, the teacher records the solutions on chart paper, only adding to the list those that are not yet recorded. As the list grows, students are encouraged to look carefully at the display list and then at their own work to find new combinations. If at some point the teacher (or students) notice that all the possible solutions have been recorded, the teacher asks once more for other ways to add to the list to encourage students to carefully consider if all possibilities have been accounted for.

## FIRST-ROUND ALTERATION OF LESSON

In planning for this lesson, I decided to make one major alteration in the way the unit authors suggested the lesson be taught. Instead of having all students work in small groups on the same problem at the same time, I planned to have a few students work independently at a table with me while other students were actively engaged in other related activities. Once the students at my table were finished, they would return to choice-time activities and a new group would join me at my table. As the students worked, I would question them about their solutions and how they knew they were correct. In some instances, I would also challenge students with larger numbers if they easily found all the solutions for 5 crayons.

I made this alteration from small groups to individual work at my table for several reasons. First, I hoped that I would have a better chance to interact with individual students and pose questions to probe and push their thinking. Second, I thought that through the exchanges with the small groups, I might be better able to prepare students for the whole group discussion at the end of the lesson. I wanted to ensure that all students were feeling successful and viewed themselves as mathematical thinkers.

### Independent Reflection on the Lesson

One of the main issues I considered when deliberately reflecting on a lesson was whether the alterations I made were effective. On the one hand, having a small number of students work on the problem while I interacted with them provided the opportunity to collect more information on how individual students were thinking as well as the opportunity to probe their thinking. On the other hand, by requiring them to work individually, I perhaps undermined the potential support and collective thinking they could have done through communicating with other students. As this was the first time students were working on this type of problem, it may have been more appropriate to give them the opportunity to work with others and assess the ways in which they use other students as resources to help them think through problems. I could have then utilized the remainder of the week, where problems of this type would be available as part of choice time, to assess individual students' approaches to the problem as well as their understanding.

As I watched the videotape of the lesson, I focused mainly on my exchanges with students while they were working on the problem. In one exchange, I interacted with a student, Brittany,[4] who had two different solutions for the problem. Her first solution was 5 blue crayons. Her second solution was 5 blue crayons and 1 red. I began my conversation with her by pointing to the second (incorrect) solution and asked, "Is that 5 crayons?" Right away, Brittany seemed to understand from my question that the solution must be incorrect and she used a black crayon to cross out the drawing of the red crayon.

As I thought about this exchange, several issues came to mind. First of all, I think it would have been more useful to begin with a general request for Brittany to explain her thinking. I could have asked something like "Tell me about your drawing," "Explain how you thought to draw what you drew" or "Prove to me that what you drew answers the problem." This would accomplish several things. First, it would have given Brittany a chance to verbalize what she was thinking, and perhaps, through the process, given her opportunities to discover the solution that did not make sense in relation to the problem. This would place the responsibility onto Brittany to determine whether her solutions were correct or not, and provide her the chance to think about her representations. Second, it would also have provided me with stronger evidence about how Brittany thinks about these problems, how she approaches them, how she monitors her own work, and what kinds of arguments she is developing to support her work. With the way I initiated the conversation, I indicated what was incorrect (albeit not purposefully) and did not ever really collect information on where that incorrect solution came from.

As I continued to think about this in greater depth, I realized that this is probably a very common misstep that I make when interacting with children as they work. Often, I want to quickly help them identify mistakes so they can reach correct solutions without further confusion. I seem to make those on-the-spot decisions about what types of support I need to offer students to help them find the correct solution. The problem with this is that my decisions about what types of support would be most beneficial for students are not as effective when I don't take time to figure out how a student is thinking in the first place. Too often these decisions are based on "assumptions" about what a student understands and suggestions are made for moving forward that may actually turn out to be disconnected from the way a student was thinking. I cannot emphasize enough how it was only through the purposeful analysis and scrutiny of my own videotape that I was able to productively wrestle with these ideas and consider strategies in which I could interact more effectively with my students.

I also analyzed an exchange with Aaron, a student who seemed to be solving the problem quite easily. Interestingly, I began our exchange in the way I had hoped to begin with Brittany by asking Aaron to first explain his work. I started by saying, "Alright, tell me about it." Aaron described what he did with the physical crayons and the drawing by saying, "I had 3 reds in the box and I drawed 3 reds. And I had 2 blues in the box, and I had to draw 2 blues." I tried to come up with questions that would probe his understanding of combinations for 5, so I asked Aaron if he could show me another way to solve the problem. Aaron described additional combinations, such as 3 blues and 2 reds and 4 blues and 1 red, but I continued to wonder about his understanding. It seemed as though he was just telling me what he did and not how he was thinking. Was the number 5 so comfortable to work with that he was having difficulty describing his process, or were my questions worded in such a way as to elicit descriptions rather than explanations of thinking? I decided that 5 was probably a comfortable number for Aaron, so I suggested he now think about the number 7. I hoped changing the number would bring to the surface Aaron's understanding of how combinations of numbers are related. It would also allow me to ascertain whether this larger number would entice an explanation from Aaron rather than just a reporting of the results. The following conversation took place between us.

Mary Kay: Now you had 7. Now tell me about this.

Aaron: I had 3 reds and 4 blues.

Mary Kay: All right. Now what would happen if I said, 'Do it another way but stay with 7?' Okay. What are you going to do?

Aaron: 6 blues and 1 red.

Mary Kay: Uh huh. What would happen if I took the box away from you and you couldn't play with the crayons? Could you still figure it out? How would you figure it out?

Aaron: Get some crayons out of there.

Mary Kay: You could get some crayons out of here. Okay. Let's pretend I take all the crayons away, and now all you have would be one crayon to draw with.

Aaron: Well, I did 3 up here, and 4 down here, so I decided to take 2, 1 crayon away, 1 red crayon away and put 1 blue crayon there, so there's 5 blues and 2 greens, I mean, reds.

Mary Kay: If you had room to do it again, like if this paper were longer, and I would say you had to do it again (which I'm not going to tell you to do), what would you draw down here?

Aaron:      I couldn't do all blues, because I don't have enough crayons.

Mary Kay:   Well, you can draw them, right? You're right, you don't have enough crayons in here to show that, do you? You could borrow them.

Aaron:      4 reds and 3 blues.

Mary Kay:   And that's what would come next? That's very interesting. Do you think you should put any numbers on your paper besides 7?

Aaron:      Okay.

Mary Kay:   What would you put on it?

Aaron:      2 down here, and 3 right here, 4 right here, and 5 down here.

As I look back at this conversation, I wonder if the questions I posed for Aaron really encouraged him to think flexibly or pushed him to investigate how to explain and justify his solutions. I was attempting to identify whether Aaron was going about finding different solutions for 7 crayons in all using a systematic method. I think I garnered some information on that when Aaron suggested how he could use his 3 red/4 blue combination to find a new one by explaining how he could take 1 red crayon away and put 1 blue crayon there, so that there would be 5 blues and 2 reds." However, when I pressed him further, he then suggested all blues as his next solution and then 4 reds/3 blues as his next. These were interesting suggestions that were somewhat surprising, because I had expected Aaron to continue the pattern of taking away one/adding one to find other combinations. My surprise at his responses perhaps resulted in a missed opportunity in that I did not probe him further to see how he was generating those new solutions. It is reasonable that he had some other "system" in his mind, but because it did not seem to match what I had anticipated, I missed the chance to uncover his understanding. I suppose I was not prepared to think flexibly about this problem myself and was surprised by his process. This exchange made me wonder whether sometimes my curiosity about students' thinking gets undermined when they do or say things I do not anticipate. In other words, do I tend not to probe when I'm surprised? This almost seems counter-intuitive, because shouldn't it be when you're surprised that you do the most probing? Maybe in the heat of a teaching moment some of our other intuitions take precedence.

## Collective Reflection on the Lesson With Colleagues

Reflecting independently on the videotape allowed me to identify and rethink particular issues that struck me personally. However, a key part of moving further out of my box, so to speak, was to reflect on teaching with other colleagues. I've had the opportunity to do this several times during RT sessions offered as part of the InMath project, as an attendee and co-facilitator, and often as the teacher on tape.

You may wonder how it is that a teacher can conjure up the courage to open up her teaching for others to scrutinize. Perhaps it was the way the tone was set in these sessions that made it not only possible, but essential for me to take that leap. The notion of critical friends (Costa, 1993; Dunne, 1998) was utilized to establish and build community among the teachers who attended these sessions. The purpose was explicitly discussed as involving sincere inquiry into *teaching* rather than judgments about *teachers*. To begin sessions with first-time participants we read "The Role of Reflection in Teaching" (Hart, Schultz, Najee-ullah, & Nash, 1992). This article is about the importance of deliberate reflection in changing one's practice and provides a variety of suggestions for undertaking such reflection, including analysis of videotaped instruction. It helps set the tone that formal reflection must be part of the work of teaching and that collaborative analysis of videotaped instruction can be powerful if approached with collegiality and shared curiosity about teaching and learning.

The deliberately chosen questions focused on both what was effective about the exchange and what could have been done to make the interaction more effective. These were extremely helpful and resulted in professional discourse that included both positive commentary as well as an acceptance that in any given teaching episode there are ways to make the episode more effective. As a result of this tone setting, the Reflecting sessions where I was the teacher on the tape were quite rewarding. The participating teachers seemed to truly appreciate my willingness to be videotaped and to allow them a look into my classroom. It felt as though we were collaborating on the common challenge of considering ways to make all of our teaching more effective as we honestly and openly grappled with some of the decisions that were made and constructively scrutinized my lesson.

In the sections that follow I will utilize the second and third phases of the RT session (Figure 2.1, items 5 and 7) to convey some of the ways that my thinking was enhanced and extended by this experience of collective reflection.

*Collective Reflection on Students at Work Exchanges.* What kinds of things were discussed by the teachers in the RT session on the Five Crayons in All lesson? As you might expect, we spent a good deal of time on the exchanges with students while they worked. A very interesting discussion ensued among the teachers that pinpointed a key struggle we all face when we interact with students while they work. As teachers were considering ways in which they interact with students while they work in general, they realized the importance of having a clear goal in mind when questioning students. One teacher used the word "nudging" to refer to the kind of questioning we do when we try to push students' thinking. She then referred to the questioning that probes students' thinking as "assessing." As a group, the teachers then generated several examples of questions they would use to probe students' thinking and those they would use to push students' thinking. Some questions that were generated to assess students' thinking included "How did you get started?" and "How did this (the representation on paper) help you think about the problem?" Questions generated for nudging students' thinking included "Are there other ways to do this problem?" and "What would you do if I told you there were (some number larger than 5) crayons all together?"

After generating these questions, the teachers considered ways in which they are challenged to operate in both domains and voiced frustration about how to make the decision at any given time as to whether to nudge or assess. They also considered the implications of rushing to "nudge" before assessing how students are thinking. This discussion was similar to the reaction I had to my videotape when I reflected independently, particularly on the exchange with Aaron, and the tension between getting sufficient information about how he was thinking and working to push him further in ways that were appropriate. However, the conversations with colleagues about the juxtaposition of nudging versus assessing, and the interplay between the two, helped me think more deeply about my role when interacting with students at work and provided me with a new "consciousness" about this issue when I returned to my classroom.

*Collective Reflection on the Closure.* One of the main goals of this lesson was to think about all the different combinations of blue and red crayons that could be used to make five crayons in all. Although I thought I had a clear understanding of this goal, it was only through our collective reflection on the closure of this lesson that I came to recognize the complexities of this idea. Many questions were raised by the teachers as we discussed my closure, and as we reflected on the purpose of the lesson: Is 5 reds and no blues an acceptable answer? Should 2 reds and 3 blues be considered to be the same as or different from 3 reds and 2 blues? Is the solution 1 red, 3 blue and 1 red the same as 2 reds and 3 blues? While many of you may think the answers to these questions are clear, you should know that my students and my colleagues disagreed on several of these points. Our reflections on these questions helped me think more clearly about the mathematical issues underlying this seemingly simple problem. Since my students focused mainly on the second of these questions, I will use it as the context for sharing how our collective analysis and reflection on the closure extended my thinking in ways beyond what I had considered when reflecting on my own.

During the closure of my lesson, we created a list of the different solutions the students had come up with for this problem. As each solution was offered, I asked whether or not that solution was already represented on our list before adding it to the list. At one point the solution 3 reds and 2 blues was offered and the following discussion ensued about whether or not it was the same as, or the opposite of, another solution (2 reds and 3 blues) already on our list.

| | |
|---|---|
| Daniel: | I had 3 blues and 2 reds. |
| Mary Kay: | Do we have yours up here? |
| Daniel: | No. |
| Mary Kay: | No? Aaron, do we have his up here? |
| Aaron: | No. |
| Mary Kay: | What do we do then? |
| Aaron: | Oh, yes, you do, but they're in different colors. |
| Caleb: | Uh, there's not 3 blues, and there's not 2 reds. |
| Mary Kay: | Do you have a question to make—All right. Aaron and Caleb, what do you think? |
| Aaron: | It's still 3 and 2. |
| Caleb: | Yeah, but Daniel gots the opposite of Nathan's. That needs to be a blue instead of a red. |
| Mary Kay: | What do you think, Aaron? Hmm. What do you think? I'm going to write Caleb's up here, when he said he had the opposite. |
| Jessica: | Why don't you write the word "opposite?" |
| Mary Kay: | Oh—write the word "opposite." Between those two? |
| Jessica: | Uh huh. |
| Brittany: | Or you could write "the same." |
| Mary Kay: | Or I could write "the same." Well, what do I write? Do I write the opposite or the same? Are they the same or opposite? |
| Jessica: | Opposite. |
| Mary Kay: | Pretend these were shells. All the same color shells, all the same shape, all the same texture. |
| Mary Kay: | Let's say 2 and 3 more is— |
| Nick: | 5. |
| Mary Kay: | Or, 3 and 2 more is— |
| Nick: | 5. |
| Mary Kay: | So, Carrie, is it the same, or is it opposite? |

Carrie:    Opposite.

Mary Kay:    Now look at their work. Now you have to turn around. Look at their work. Is it the opposite or is it the same now, Daniel?

Daniel:    What?

Mary Kay:    Is your work opposite or is it the same as Nathan's?

Daniel:    Um—the opposite.

Mary Kay:    Opposite—you still say opposite. We're going to … Robin, why do you think the same?

Robin:    Because it's 3 and 2.

Mary Kay:    Because it's 3 and 2. We'll come back to this on Tuesday.

As we considered this segment of the discussion, we recognized that my students were picking up on some very important mathematical ideas in considering how these solutions were similar, and how they were different. On the one hand, the two solutions involved the same two numbers, 3 and 2, and the sum of those two numbers would be 5 regardless of whether you use 3 and 2 or 2 and 3. The underlying mathematical concept here is that addition is commutative, a concept that is very important, particularly when learning basic facts. However, notice how this issue changes when considering the context in which this question is embedded. In the 5 crayons in all context, a solution of 3 reds and 2 blues is clearly different from a solution of 3 blues and 2 reds.

Keeping this duality in mind, we then considered the ways in which I chose to participate and guide this particular discussion. I introduced a new context, changing the crayons to shells, and making all the shells the same—the same color, the same shape and the same texture. In doing so I totally changed the nature of the problem from one in which the two subgroups were distinct, to one in which the two subgroups were indistinguishable. As the teachers pondered this move, they questioned several things. First, by changing the context of the problem in this way, it seemed to make more sense for students to view the solution 3 and 2 as being the same as 2 and 3. And while this might be useful in helping them begin to develop an intuitive notion of commutativity, it most likely confused the issue further, causing them to question whether this implied that 3 reds and 2 blues was indeed the same as 2 reds and 3 blues and could be considered as "opposite" of 3 blues and 2 reds.

Having said that, there was an even bigger pedagogical issue that was discussed in terms of the choice I made to introduce a new situation rather than attempting to pursue the lines of thinking that were already beginning to emerge. The teachers wondered if the issue about the phrases being the same or opposite may have surfaced if I had simply recognized what the students were saying at the time. Consider Aaron's early response to the question of whether the solution was already on our list: "Yes, you do, but they're in different colors," and then Caleb's comment that "Daniel gots the opposite of Nathan's. That needs to be a blue instead of a red." Teachers wondered if it would have been more effective to simply pursue these two comments in greater depth by encouraging both Aaron and Caleb to support what they were saying and go from there. The seeds of the ideas seemed to be there. But rather than pushing students to justify their statements with reasoning, the conversation was directed towards a new context that in the end may not have been helpful. I realized again the importance of not overlooking opportunities to utilize the ideas that students find confusing as places where powerful learning can occur.

This discussion with my colleagues, as well as others that followed, had a major impact on my thinking about teaching. It seemed that for a while I had been moving towards encouraging students to speak more in class and "explain" their thinking as part of doing mathematics. But I then recognized that I was still developing my ideas about what was involved in "explaining." It seemed too often "explaining" became little more than getting students to either state their opinion, sometimes with a hint of rationale (as in the case of Aaron's and Caleb's statements), or having students only describe their thinking by often describing each step of a process. What I realized was that I hadn't been pushing beyond statements and descriptions to elicit the reasoning underlying students' thinking. Why do they believe some things are true? How can they prove to their classmates that their solution is correct? It is only through exposing and scrutinizing reasoning through questions like these that students can develop understanding. And, as a teacher, making this a key goal dramatically alters the moves I make when facilitating discussions about mathematical ideas.

Although many of us emerged from this discussion of the closure with a sense of awe at the sophisticated mathematics that kindergartners can grapple with, some teachers reacted to this by concluding that my students were somehow different from theirs. I listened to a few teachers commenting that their students were not capable of participating in this kind of closure, implying that I was only able to have the discussion because my students were more advanced. I wanted to tell them that my students were just typical kindergartners, and that if they were to have seen a videotape of my students at the beginning of the year, they would not have seen this difference between their students and mine. My students did not come to me with this ability to communicate their thinking. I worked deliberately all year long to create a community where ideas were valued, regardless of their mathematical validity, where there was trust that these ideas wouldn't be ridiculed and where risk-taking was rewarded. This does not mean that we weren't searching for correct answers. Rather, as a class, we recognized the usefulness of listening and thinking hard about the ideas voiced by a member of our collective group. It is only through this process that we confront misconceptions about particular mathematical concepts, and move to a deeper understanding of the topic at hand.

I understand the tendency to dismiss the work of one group of students by arguing that "those kids are special, regular kids can't do that." I'm sure that I have been guilty of expressing this same sentiment on occasion. The process of videotaping and reflecting on my work as a teacher has pushed me to move beyond this understandable reaction to a new realization: To determine what students are capable of I need to delve deeper into the mathematics underlying the tasks I use with students into what students are telling me about the mathematics and into what I am doing as a teacher to support their efforts to publicly grapple with sophisticated mathematics.

## Lesson Revisited

As I thought about teaching the Five Crayons in All lesson again the next year and having the opportunity to be videotaped again, I recalled many of the discussions that had occurred during the Reflecting sessions and the impact those discussions had on my teaching. Could I make important changes when teaching the same lesson the second time? Which changes should I focus on so that I don't lose the focus? How would I know I actually followed through with changes? Would viewing the same lesson on videotape the second time lead into another area or level of awareness for my own professional growth?

As I considered these questions, I recognized that my experiences in RT sessions not only made me reconsider how to teach the Blue and Red crayons lesson, but they affected my teaching in a much broader sense. Questioning techniques were constantly on my mind as I worked with my students the next year, not only in mathematics but in all areas. Thinking harder about my questioning also required that I listen more carefully to my students' responses. And as I listened to their responses, I found myself working harder to find a balance between assuming understanding and collecting more evidence of understanding. Since kindergarten children are very verbal, I wanted to focus on listening to their conversations to try to determine any differences or similarities between types of reasoning. I wanted to make a point of using their representations more carefully as they explained, justified, or clarified their reasoning. I also wanted to identify opportunities where students might be able to use an individual solution to discover and investigate other solutions. As I articulate these ways in which I sought to change my teaching, I recognize these changes all stem from a focus on how and why I question students.

During that second year I was conscious of the differences in my teaching and I felt that I was successful in elevating the mathematical understanding of my students through in-depth discussions of mathematics. However, only by watching and reflecting on the videotape of teaching the "Five Crayons in All" lesson again could I analyze the degree to which I was successful in making the changes in teaching I was attempting and see the results of these changes on my students' learning. While I was pleased with aspects of this second videotaped lesson, I discovered that I still had many issues to clarify for my own understanding of how young children reason mathematically. This time I launched the lesson as the curriculum materials intended, and was pleased to see that I encouraged students not only to look at one child's solution but also compare that solution with other solutions. I was also pleased with my facilitation of the closure, in which I kept a better focus on having students discuss multiple solutions. However, as I analyzed the interactions between myself and my students as they worked on this problem, I began to identify additional issues that I needed to reflect on as a teacher.

While the students worked on this task, they seemed to stay focused, with guidance, through a fairly long period of time and I seemed to allow sufficient time for students to think about their ideas. However, even with this time allowance, I still was missing opportunities to investigate mathematical understanding! How did this happen? I was allowing more time for students, yet I still positioned myself as center stage amongst the students. I needed to let go of this authority and trust the knowledge of my students. I hoped I would have more readily utilized teaching strategies that were discussed in the RT session; e.g., having one student explain his thinking to another student (rather than to me), or having a student explain the work of another by talking to each other.

So, analyzing my teaching the second time around on the same lesson allowed me to reflect on the changes I made, what resulted from those changes, and what I needed to continue to work on. It also allowed a new issue to surface about the stance I was taking during group discussions and how this might affect the ways in which students do or do not explain their thinking. Researching my own teaching in this way will necessarily involve a cyclical process that helps me work on certain aspects of teaching, but also identify new aspects that will add to my ability to make more grounded decisions while I am teaching.

## CONCLUDING REMARKS

Researching my own teaching has changed the way I look at my profession and my own pedagogy. It has allowed me to grow in ways that I have not been able to previously, and I recognize that there are numerous complex issues around teaching for understanding that must be revisited over and over again. It is the old adage of taking two steps forward and one step back that I needed to embrace in order to realize any kind of meaningful change in my practice. The most significant lesson I learned revolves around the many implications of what it means to focus my teaching on student thinking and determining what constitutes evidence of understanding.

Before I began this intensive inquiry into my teaching, I would have said that I did focus my teaching on student thinking. Perhaps in many ways I did. But what I came to realize, through individual and collective analysis of my teaching on videotape, were the multitude of ways that I could sharpen this focus. While I had a strong curiosity about how children were thinking, which is a crucial characteristic for teachers to possess, I tended to let other factors get in the way of letting that natural curiosity guide how I would interact with my students. By developing a clearer vision myself of the mathematics I teach, I am better prepared to stay focused on the intent of the lessons, and thus keep student thinking center stage.

I have attended many professional development sessions in which we analyzed lessons in the curriculum, discussed the mathematics being developed, discussed potential struggles that students might have, and considered possible teaching moves. I learned a tremendous amount from these sessions that I know helped prepare me to teach for understanding. However, I cannot reiterate strongly enough how much further the purposeful and systematic analysis of videotape, both individually and collectively, pushed me beyond the conversations we had in other types of professional development sessions. My recollections of how a lesson went did not provide me with the specific details necessary to productively reflect on my teaching. It was not until I was faced with a vivid image of what my interactions with students looked and sounded like, and the ways in which I utilized student responses during whole group discussions, that I was able to alter my practice in significant ways. I still have room for growth in my own understanding of teaching, but that is one of the benefits and pleasures of being in the profession I chose over 20 years ago, teaching young children. I trust that future intensive inquiry into my teaching will take me down roads of professional growth I have yet to imagine.

## NOTES

1.  The *Investigations* curriculum was developed by TERC in collaboration with Kent State University and the State University of New York at Buffalo. The work was supported in part by the National Science Foundation.

2.   This chapter is based on work supported by National Science Foundation grant ESI-9819364. The opinions expressed are those of the authors and do not necessarily reflect the views of the National Science Foundation.

3.   Although the remainder of this chapter is written in the first person singular, the entire chapter is the collaborative effort of all three authors.

4.   All student names are pseudonyms.

## REFERENCES

Artzt, A., & Armour-Thomas, E. (2002). *Becoming a reflective mathematics teacher.* Mahwah, NJ: Erlbaum.

Costa, A. L. (1993). Through the lens of a critical friend. *Educational Leadership 51* (2), 49-51.

Dewey, J. (1933). *How we think: A restatement of the relation of reflective thinking to the educative process.* Boston: Heath.

Dunne, F. (1998). *That group really makes me think! Critical friends groups and the development of reflective practitioners.* ERIC document ED423228.

Grant, T. J. & Kline, K. (2004). Embracing the complexity of practice as a site for inquiry. In R. Rubenstein (Ed.), *Perspectives on teaching mathematics* (pp. 195-206). Reston, VA: National Council of Teachers of Mathematics.

Grant, T. J., Kline, K., & Van Zoest, L. (2001). Supporting teacher change: Professional development that promotes thoughtful and deliberate reflection on teaching. *The NCSM Journal of Mathematics Education Leadership 5,* 29-37. Available online at http://www.ncsmonline.org/NCSMPublications/journal.html.

Hart, L., Schultz, K., Najee-ullah, D., & Nash, L. (1992). The role of reflection in teaching. *Arithmetic Teacher 40* (1), 40-42.

Kliman, M., Mainhart, C., Murray, M., & Economopolous, K. (1998.) *How many in all?* Kindergarten unit from the *Investigations in number, data, and space curriculum.* White Plains, NY: Dale Seymour.

Piaget, J. (1971). *Science of education and the psychology of the child.* New York: Viking.

CHAPTER 3

# MATHEMATICAL ARGUMENT IN A SECOND GRADE CLASS

## Generating and Justifying Generalized Statements About Odd and Even Numbers

**Annie Keith**

*John Muir Elementary School, Madison, WI*

The notion that mathematics is for the select few is on the decline. The current push for mathematics to be accessible to all people requires the examination of, and a change in, how we teach our mathematics courses. "Algebra for All," a catch phrase similar to "Success for All," needs to be examined by teachers, researchers, policy makers, and the general public.

The National Council of Teachers of Mathematics' (NCTM) *Principles and Standards for School Mathematics* (2000) calls for "... a common foundation of mathematics to be learned by all students" (p. 5). One piece of that common foundation is algebra. Historically, algebra has been a filter that discourages or stops further study of mathematics for some people. In short, algebra has been and often continues to be the gatekeeper to higher mathematics courses and opportunities (Chambers, 1994;

*Teachers Engaged in Research*
*Inquiry Into Mathematics Classrooms, Grades Pre-K–2*, pages 35–68
Copyright © 2006 by Information Age Publishing

Chappell, 1997; Chazan, 1994; Kaput, 2000; Strong & Cobb, 2000). Chappell (1997) contends "Preparing students to enter the gate to algebraic thinking contributes to minimizing the differences in mathematics-course participation and achievement that have long existed between males and females and different racial and ethnic groups. To close these gaps in achievement, we need to open the gate to algebraic thinking in elementary schools" (p. 267).

In order to make algebra accessible to more students, our focus should be on building student's understanding instead of on learning a series of skills to be memorized and applied (Chazan, 1994; Carpenter & Levi, 1999; NCTM, 2000). Unfortunately, few descriptions are available that illustrate this vision in action.

Researchers advocate for algebraic reasoning to begin in the elementary years (Carpenter, Franke & Levi, 2003; Carraher, Schliemann & Brizuela, 2001; Flores, 2002: NCTM, 2000; Sowder & Harel, 1998; Szombathelyi & Szarvas, 1998; Whitenack & Yackel, 2002). This early algebraic thinking is not the formal algebra of the high school setting. Rather it focuses on recognizing and understanding equality, relationships, and generalized ideas. The algebraic thinking in elementary school lays the groundwork for the later understanding of formal algebra and making formal mathematical arguments.

## A Mathematical Argument in Second Grade

Historically, mathematical argument has been reserved for high school. This is changing as elementary and middle-school teachers engage students in discussions about mathematical argument and proof. The following conversation took place in my second-grade classroom in the spring. The students describe what it means to make a mathematical argument.

| | |
|---|---|
| Ms. Keith: | What does it mean to convince? |
| Kevin: | It means making someone think what you're thinking. |
| Melia: | It's kinda, to prove to people that it's the truth. |
| Mario: | I was thinking the same as Melia. |
| Taylor: | It's trying to get people to think how you are thinking. |
| Ms. Keith: | What is a mathematical argument? |
| Melia: | In a mathematical argument you can't say, "You just know it is true." |
| Jolie: | One group needs to convince the other that their idea is correct. |

Ms. Keith:  What is the difference between an argument and a mathematical argument?

Theo:  Well, a mathematical argument is like when we try to like, try to figure out things. We're not mad at each other, like in an argument.

Mario:  A mathematical argument is when you try to convince about math.

Ms. Keith:  How do you know when you have convinced another person?

Kevin:  Depends on the person. Some people will tell you, "Oh, that's enough" or "I'm not convinced. Can you tell me more?"

Ms. Keith:  What does a person mean if they say, "I'm not convinced"?

Taylor:  They want more evidence. You have to convince!

Diana:  Maybe they don't understand.

Tad:  Tell them if they don't get it. Then they might say, "Hmm, this makes me think."

Lewis:  You need to explain, really well. They might say, "Oh, so there are number sentences, so what?" You have to explain that there is more. You need to show why. You might have to explain it better.

Ms. Keith:  For whom do you think number sentences would be a convincing argument?

Kevin:  Kids with young minds.

Tad:  Yeah, kids younger than us, maybe kindergarten or first grade.

Ms. Keith:  What could you use to make a more convincing argument?

Jennifer:  Well, writing number sentences is just giving you more of the same evidence. I don't think number sentences are enough.

Tad:  You could write more.

Eun Joo:  Number and explain with words.

Theo:  You could use fingers, math cubes, counting frame, you know, math tools.

Diana:  Base ten blocks.

Eun Joo:  Facts.

Taylor:  Read a book.

Allen:  You could use a pencil to draw a picture.

Diana:   More number sentences.

Throughout the school year, these students were engaged in many mathematical experiences, including solving a variety of word problems, working with a variety of number sentences, writing conjectures for the general mathematical principles embedded in their work, and wrestling with how to justify to others that the conjectures would be always be true. By the end of the school year, these students were truly engaged in mathematical argument.

## Research on Algebraic Thinking and Justification in the Elementary Grades

The *Principles and Standards for School Mathematics* (NCTM, 2000) Algebra Standard promotes making generalized ideas explicit, encouraging teachers to work with a variety of mathematical activities that help their students to see patterns and relationships. The role of teachers-as-questioners, helping to make students' mathematical ideas explicit and generalized is highlighted. "By encouraging students to explore and model relationships using language and notation that is meaningful to them, teachers can help students see different relationships and make conjectures and generalizations from their experiences with numbers." (p. 92)

The Reasoning and Proof Standard (NCTM, 2000) focuses on the importance of encouraging students to use mathematical arguments to support their thinking and to develop more sophisticated reasoning. This Standard supports the idea of working with students on justification of mathematical ideas, and promoting justification that is based on mathematical properties and relationships. Such justifications will help students rely on their own knowledge and understanding, not on justification by authority. "The ability to reason systematically and carefully develops when students are encouraged to make conjectures, are given time to search for evidence to prove or disprove them, and are expected to explain and justify their ideas" (p. 122).

Greenes and Findell (1999) promote algebraic reasoning problems as a means by which elementary students can experience the big ideas of algebra. They define the big ideas to include: inductive and deductive reasoning, representation, equality, variable, function and proportion. The problems outlined all have multiple solution paths and can be represented symbolically. Greenes and Findell reason that in classrooms where students are expected to document, share, and discuss their thinking, gains will be made in the area of communication as well as making connections between arithmetic and algebra.

Carpenter, Franke, & Levi (2003) propose, "That the teaching and learning of arithmetic be conceived as the foundation for algebra" (p. 6). Their work shows that while children implicitly use basic mathematical properties to solve problems, the properties are not made explicit, and often are not generalized to being true for all numbers. They argue that it is important for children to have opportunities for making implicit generalizations explicit. They state:

> Our goal is to make these properties the explicit focus of attention so that
> - All students have access to basic mathematical properties;
> - Students understand why the computation procedures they use work the way they do;
> - Students apply their procedures flexibly in a variety of contexts;
> - Students recognize the connections between arithmetic and algebra and can use their understanding of arithmetic as a foundation for learning algebra with understanding. (pg. 5)

Researchers are taking a closer look at algebra in the elementary school (Ball & Bass, 2000; Bastable & Schifter, 1998; Carpenter, Franke & Levi, 2003; Carpenter & Levi, 1999; Carraher, Schliemann, & Brizuela, 2001; Kaput & Blanton, 1999; Schifter, 1999). Common to all of these research projects is the importance of generalized statements, often referred to as conjectures, and the justification of those ideas in the form of argument or proof.

Carpenter, Franke, and Levi (2003) promote the engagement of elementary students in generating and justifying conjectures. They write, "We want students to learn the importance of expressing [the fundamental properties of arithmetic] precisely and accurately using words and symbols" (p. 5). They have found that generating conjectures leads students to think about mathematical ideas and is a basis for mathematical argument. They emphasize the importance of students engaging in the justification of the conjectures.

Knuth, (2002) promotes proof as a tool for learning mathematics with meaning. He advocates for classrooms where students understand that proof is more than explaining that statements are true: that proof also includes *why* the statements are true. The sharing and discussing of different student arguments can provide a vehicle for student conversation about what constitutes proof. Knuth encourages the recognition and use of counterexamples that are more general in nature, as a part of proof. "In short, mathematicians recognize that a primary role of proof in mathematics is to establish the truth of a result, yet perhaps more important, particularly from an educational perspective, is their recognition of its role in fostering understanding of the underlying mathematics" (p. 487).

## Levels of Proof

Proof is an important element of algebraic reasoning. What constitutes proof has been established by the rigorous standards set by mathematicians. Carpenter, Franke, and Levi (2003) utilize the term *justification.* They state, "We have chosen to use the term *justification* to encompass a broader range of arguments that children use to show that a conjecture is true" (p. 85). They found as the students discussed conjectures, the need for a more complete general justification was sought after and used by the students. Carpenter, Franke, and Levi identified three levels of justification used by elementary students:

- Appeal to authority
- Justification by example
- Generalizable arguments

### *Appeal to Authority*
Appeal to authority refers to students relating their reasoning or argument to a rule or procedure that was taught or told to them by someone with authority. Their argument does not contain any mathematical justification.

### *Justification by Example*
Student justifications that are embedded in specific numbers are justifications by example. When using examples to justify conjectures, students often compute number sentence after number sentence. When asked, "How do you know the conjecture is true," these students will say, "because I wrote all these number sentences and it was always true, so I think it is true." Carpenter, Franke, and Levi found justification by example to be the most common justification by elementary school students. Many students who use examples to justify may have an idea that this type of justification is not enough to prove a conjecture being true for all numbers, but are not sure what other argument to draw upon.

### *Generalizable Arguments*
Generalizable arguments grow out of the students' understanding that examples are not enough to convince another person that a conjecture is true for all numbers. In a generalizable argument a student presents a logical argument that applies to all cases included in the conjecture. These

arguments may be verbal, symbolic, or even concrete. However, unlike justification by example, students do not compute to find answers. At this level students need to explicitly understand that the process they use can be generalized to all numbers. For example: when justifying that the sum of an even number and an odd number is odd, a student may use pairs of blocks to construct an even number and pairs of blocks plus one block to make an odd number. The exact amounts may be known, but the argument generalizes to any even or odd number. To find the sum the student may take one from each of the original pairs, create a new pair, and see that the collection is made up of pairs and one left over, so the sum is odd. On their own or with additional questioning students will note that this will work for joining any odd and even number. Although the student is using a concrete material that represents a specific number, the justification is not embedded in a specific set of numbers and the student can generalizes to any set of numbers. This use of concrete materials is similar to Fujii and Stephens' (2001) notion of quasi-variables, in that the students use specific numbers to make a general argument.

Sowder and Harel (1998), working with high school and college students, also identified three levels of justification. The levels are: external based proof, empirical proof, and analytical proof. External proof is when students rely on outside sources such as teachers, parents, or books. Empirical proof is when students base their reasoning on an example or series of examples. Analytic proof is described as arguments that incorporate mathematical reasoning and are of a more general nature.

## Studies at the Elementary Level

Flores (2002) found that elementary students had difficulties when asked to provide proof. He reported that students frequently said they just knew it or gave evidence that did not provide any proof. He contends that teachers can help their students develop convincing arguments through experiences that promote mathematical reasoning and by questioning both correct and incorrect results.

Valentine (1999) worked with sixth grade students on justification and proof of classroom conjectures for the commutative property of multiplication. She found the majority of her students progressed in their notion of what constitutes proof. The students moved away from relying on external proof to providing analytic proof for their ideas. She, like Knuth, noted the importance of her students engaging in mathematical conversations. Valentine attributed her students' growth to the discussions where reasoning and mathematical argument were a focus and to arguments where students were expected to justify their ideas.

Bastable and Schifter (1998) describe several cases in which teachers and students engaged in classroom conversations where students expressed ideas and reasoned as to the validity of their ideas. Several of the teachers working with Bastable and Schifter focused on the exploration of odd and even numbers as a means to bring about discussion of conjectures and proof. In their commentary, Bastable and Schifter raised questions about students' mathematical argument. They asked: "Do the children see any differences between these types of arguments? Do they recognize that some are more powerful than others? How do students develop a sense of mathematical argument? What constitutes proof to students and how does that view change over time?" (p. 13).

In summary, algebraic reasoning is important in the elementary school. Recognizing and stating general principles is an important part of algebra, and such fundamental ideas eventually need to be justified.

## Significance of this Study

This case study provides a preliminary understanding of the development of elementary students' thinking about generating and justifying conjectures through odd and even numbers. It also provides an inside look at second grade students working, as a community, to articulate and justify ideas about odd and even numbers. Additionally, it begins to fill the gap in literature on primary students' thinking about conjectures and justification of conjectures, specifically for odd and even numbers.

## Statement of the Research Question

To better understand elementary students' understanding of conjectures and justification of conjectures, this study looks at how second graders think about odd and even numbers. Specifically, it asks,

1. What kinds of generalized ideas do second graders have about odd and even numbers?
2. At what level are second-grade students able to justify that these ideas are always true?

## METHODOLOGY

### Teacher Background

I have been an elementary teacher in the Madison Metropolitan School District in Madison, Wisconsin for 17 years. For 6 years, I worked with Tom Carpenter and Linda Levi, at the University of Wisconsin-Madison, on their work in Early Algebraic Thinking. (Carpenter & Levi, 1999) The focus of the Early Algebra Project is on children's understanding of equality, relational thinking, and the generating and justifying of generalized mathematical ideas. Teachers involved in this project work on helping their students to use these ideas in their work with arithmetic. The teachers help their students make explicit their implicit ideas about mathematics.

Linda Levi and I also worked for 4 years with teachers in the Phoenix, Arizona area on Cognitively Guided Instruction (CGI; see Carpenter, Fennema, Franke, Levi, & Empson, 1999) and Early Algebraic Thinking. In the fall of 2000, 15 teachers from Phoenix and 7 teachers from Madison formed a joint classroom action research project (CARP). Each group held a monthly meeting at their site throughout the school year. The Madison group visited Phoenix in October and February, and the Phoenix group came to Madison in April. Classroom visitations and the sharing of participants' action research occurred during the three joint meetings. The CARP participants wrote about their students' algebraic thinking in their elementary classrooms (Bostrom, Keith, Nordness, Smith, Wiesner, & Wiesner, 2001). Fourteen members of the Phoenix-Madison CARP group decided to continue the action research project for a second year. We followed the same format of monthly meetings and again had the opportunity to visit each other's sites. Five of the Madison teachers visited Phoenix in September, two went again in February, and in April nine of the Phoenix teachers came to Madison. Teachers from the two sites also communicated about their action research and their students' thinking via emails. We supported each other in the learning and teaching of algebraic thinking in our elementary classrooms. This paper describes the question I investigated during the second year of the Phoenix-Madison CARP.

### Nature of the Case Study Site

The subjects for my study were the students in my second-grade class. The class was comprised of six boys and nine girls. Four of the students were African American, four were Asian and seven were Caucasian. One of the students received ESL services. Fourteen of the 15 families gave permission for student work, ideas, and interviews to be used in this paper. The school, located on Madison's west side, serves 460 students. Of those 460 students, 19% are African American, 14% are Asian, 9% are Latino and 58% are Caucasian; 29% of the students at the school qualify for free or reduced lunch.

## Classroom Expectations and Norms

Children and adults made up the community of learners within our classroom. I am a learner, a teacher, a questioner, and an investigator. I also want the students to be learners, teachers, questioners, and investigators. Student and teacher actions and interactions are based on respect, and all are expected to have a voice in classroom discussions and decisions. As we worked to become a community, we had discussions about the expectations in our classroom. We often talked about:

1. Why we take the time to discuss our ideas or problem solutions.
2. Why it is important to listen.
3. What is active listening?
4. What do you know now that you didn't know before?
5. How did the discussion help you?
6. What is a mathematical argument?
7. How do we prove a conjecture, and what is enough evidence to prove that a conjecture is true to other people?

Students worked on solving and recording solutions to their math problems in at least two different ways. Our math conversations frequently revolved around the students' explanations and justifications for how a math problem was solved. As students worked through problems, basic mathematical properties emerged and our conversations would shift to focus on the different properties. As a class, the students wrote conjectures for those basic mathematical properties.

## Data Sources

The data sources and artifacts for this paper were:

1. My notes from ten sessions where the whole class focused on odd and even numbers.
2. Photocopies of student journal work and student worksheets related to those ten sessions.

3. Audiotapes of several class discussions.
4. Classroom Action Research teacher reflection notes.
5. Student work for a word problem given in April.

The data was analyzed after each session. I looked for evidence of mathematical argument. I sorted student work into levels of justification, as represented by the students' recordings on their papers. I used the levels of justification identified by Carpenter, Franke, and Levi (2003) for classifying my students' justifications of odd and even conjectures. I looked for a change over time in the levels of justification used by the students. As I sorted the students' work there were several student strategies that I accepted and placed into the generalized argument level. In the context of my second-grade class, the arguments, although incomplete, were more general in nature, and the students recognized that justification by example was not enough. I realize that in other communities rigorous standards would apply and these arguments would not constitute proof.

I read my notes and listened to the tapes to confirm that my field notes were accurate and detailed.

I shared the data with my classroom action research group. As I talked about my students' thinking and my study, another teacher wrote notes. A synopsis of my sharing, with questions asked by other participants, was later given to me. The conversations I had with the other teachers engaged in classroom action research pushed my thinking and promoted further reflection about my students' understanding of justification.

In April I also gave a word problem similar to the problem discussed in a case study by Bastable and Schifter (1998). The problem I gave read:

Kenji counted 31 pieces of candy. He has jawbreakers, lollipops, gumballs, and Hershey Kisses. Kenji doesn't have an even number of any of the candies. What are the possibilities? Did he count right?

In giving this problem I was not asking for proof of a conjecture; rather I was interested in whether or not the students would use generalized knowledge to solve the problem. I sorted their work accordingly.

Together these items provided a picture of growth, not only in students' thinking about odd and even numbers, but also in what constitutes justification and proof of generalized mathematical ideas. I chose to write about the tasks and conversations the class and I had, in the order they happened, over six months.

# RESULTS

## November

I wanted my students to work with generating and justifying conjectures. I knew that conjectures about odd and even numbers would provide a good site to begin our discussions on justification. I thought that many if not most of my students would have had prior experiences with odd and even numbers and having that knowledge would help in our discussions. I gave the students a worksheet and asked them to indicate whether the following numbers were odd or even: 254, 1,230, and 3,745.

As the students started to work I heard, "What is an odd number? What is an even number?" Some of the students were able to define these terms, but most seemed unsure. At the class discussion later that day, I was surprised to find that only five of the students remembered talking about odd and even numbers in kindergarten and/or first grade. As a class we talked about the three numbers on the worksheet. Many students built the amount of each number with base ten blocks and then worked through each group of blocks (thousand cubes, hundreds flats, tens rods and ones cubes). They split the blocks into two equal groups starting with the thousands, then hundreds, tens and ones. The number was described as being even if the groups each had the same amount of cubes. If one of the groups held "an extra" cube, then the number was described as odd.

Several of the students followed the same procedure but did not use the cubes. They expanded the number in written form and then split each number into two groups. An example of this is Jennifer who said, "I think 3,745 is odd because 3,745 is 3,000 + 700 + 40 + 5 and the three thousand can be split into 1,000 and 1,000. And then you could split the other 1,000 into 500 and 500. The seven hundred would be 300 and 300 and 100 but the one hundred would be split into 50 and 50. The forty would be twenty and twenty. Five is two plus three. Two and three are not the same, so there would be different amounts in the groups."

Eun Joo followed up what Jennifer said by saying, "I think the same as Jennifer except for the five [pointing to the five in the ones place]. Two could go with [this] group, and two could go with [this] group, and one is left over, so the number is odd." The class discussed the other two numbers in a similar fashion. A few students began to verbalize that the oddness or evenness of the number was determined by the ones. The students were asked to think about their ideas of odd and even for homework that night.

## December

Several weeks later, I asked the students to write about odd and even numbers in their math journals. We then shared the ideas as a whole class. Of the fourteen students in this study, seven wrote definitions, three described interesting qualities or characteristics, three did not write anything, and one was absent. As the students talked, it became clear that as a class we needed to write a definition for odd and even numbers.

The class's definition for even numbers had two parts. Initially it read: *Even numbers won't have any left over when divided by two.* After more discussion by the students, it was agreed upon that our definition should also include: *Even is when you have an amount that two people can share and each person will have the same amount. It will be fair.*

The definition for odd numbers read: *Odd numbers cannot be divided into two groups that are equal without splitting or having one left over.* Again there was much discussion and the following was added: *With an odd number you will have one left over after dividing by two.* Several students then said, "But we can cut that left over in half and then the number is even." So, *when numbers are kept whole* was added to the definition. The final definitions were written on construction paper and posted on the wall under the word "Definitions." They read:

*Even Numbers*

- Even Numbers won't have any left over when divided by two.
- Even is when you have an amount that two people can share and each person will have the same amount. It will be fair.

*Odd Numbers*

- Odd numbers cannot be divided into two groups that are equal without splitting or having one left over.
- With an odd number you will have one left over after dividing by two when all numbers are kept whole.

Justine then said, "I have a question. If you have an even number and an odd number and you plus them, how do you know if that is even or odd?" This brought responses from her classmates. They wanted her to say her question again, talk a bit about it, and explore this idea. I wrote her question on chart paper. The question read: *If you add an even number and an odd number, will the sum be even or odd?* The students started exploring her question individually and recorded their ideas in their math journal.

Two days later they came together to discuss their results. It was unanimous; all the students thought that when you added an even number and an odd number the sum would be odd. All fourteen students came to this conclusion by writing number sentences, as examples. One of the fourteen, after writing 37 number sentences, also wrote an incomplete generalized argument for even plus odd equals odd. This is what she wrote:

> I think that whenever you add an even and an odd number it will equal an odd number because there's 1 extra after you divide an odd number and you don't have any left over when you divide an even number in 2.

> Example: $2 \div 2 = 1$, $5 \div 2 = 2\frac{1}{2}$

> If you minus 1 from an odd number, it will be even. So, if you, say, had $11 + 10 = 21$ (odd), the answer... If you add an even and an odd, I think it will always be odd because the even number is even and the odd number is odd, so you will always have one left over. So *that's* why I think an even number plus an odd number will always equal an odd number.

The students decided that since they all thought it true, it should be written as a conjecture in words, with a few examples, and posted in our classroom. The conjecture read:

*Classroom Conjecture 2*

> When adding an odd number and an even number the sum will be odd.

> Example: $5 + 38 = 43$

I made the teacher decision to wait on a deeper discussion of justifying whether or not this conjecture was true for all numbers. One of the recommendations from my classroom action research last year was to wait for the justification piece until the students had more experiences working with the conjecture idea and there was a larger group of students thinking more generally about the idea. I decided that as a class we needed more time. We were not ready to talk about levels of justification and what constituted a good mathematical argument.

After working with Justine's question, other students raised questions about odd and even numbers. These questions were written on chart paper with the heading Questions We Have about Odd and Even Numbers and posted in the classroom. The questions were:

1. If you add even numbers together, will the sum be odd or even?
2. If you add two odd numbers, what will the sum be, even or odd?
3. If you add three odd numbers, what will the sum be, odd or even?
4. What will the sum be when adding an odd number of odds?
5. When you double an even number will it be even every time?
6. What even numbers can be divided evenly into two groups *and* three groups?
7. Is zero odd or even?
8. If I have an odd number like five and I cut it in half will it be even?
9. When counting from 1-101, how many odd numbers would you say?

Note that the first six questions are at a higher level. These questions could lead to the generation of conjectures and into discussions on justification. The last three questions are more specific. They can be answered on a simpler level.

The following day the class worked to find whether the sum of two even numbers was odd or even. Two students also explored what the sum would be for more that two odd numbers, and several other students started to explore what happens when two odd numbers are added together. In each case all of the students wrote number sentences as examples in their math journals. Again the exception was Jennifer who, on this occasion, first wrote an incomplete generalized statement and then wrote 31 number sentences. Her generalized statement read:

What will the sum be when adding even + even? I think that when you add 2 even numbers together it will always be even because you don't have any leftovers in an even number when it is divided in 2 groups.

Examples:

1) 68 + 50 =118 even
2) 88 + 26 = 114 even
3) 70 + 46 = 116 even
...
31) 0 + 0 = 0 even

She then wrote, "What will be the sum when adding odd + odd? I think that it will always be even because odd numbers have one extra after being divided in two." Her statement was again followed by many examples.

The class met as a whole group. After each person shared examples they discovered that they all agreed the sum of even numbers is an even number. The students decided that we had another conjecture. Classroom Conjecture 3 stated:

*Classroom Conjecture 3*

When adding even numbers the sum will always be even.

Examples: 20 + 4 + 8 = 32 32 = 16 + 16

Later several students started talking about odd and even numbers. Soon the whole class was involved. By the end, of what was supposed to be a short class meeting, we had a sheet of chart paper with the heading: *Interesting Ideas We Have about Odd and Even Numbers.* Under the heading were eight ideas that the class wanted posted in the classroom. The interesting ideas were:

1. Even and odd are opposite.
2. We think zero is an even number.
3. You can share an odd number but… you would have to split the left-over or just have one left over.
4. Odd and even numbers take turns being the higher number.
5. With even numbers the numbers stay whole when divided into two groups.
6. Some even numbers can be divided equally into two or three groups with the numbers staying whole. Some even numbers you can't divide into three groups.
7. If you count by twos starting with an even number you will never say an odd number.
8. If you count by twos starting with an odd number you will never say an even number.

As students stated each idea, the class would opt to talk about the idea and/or ask the person questions for clarification. For instance, the student with the idea of opposites, when questioned said, "Well, by opposite I mean a number is one or the other and that if it is not even then it is odd. If it is odd then it is not even. They are just opposites."

There was little disagreement on the idea of zero being an even number. The students convinced the few who were not sure with two arguments. The first argument was that numbers go in a pattern …odd, even, odd, even, odd, even… and since two is even and one is odd then the number before one, that is not a fraction, would be zero. So zero would need to be even. The second argument was that if a person has zero things and they put them into two equal groups then there would be zero in each group. The two groups would have the same amount, zero.

The idea that odd and even numbers take turns being the higher number was greeted with agreement after several students commented, "Well, that's true when you are counting up."

Idea 6 is reminiscent of a conversation in "Sean's Numbers," reported by Ball and Bass (2000). Ball's student, Sean, shared with his class his thinking that some even numbers could be both odd and even. He asserted that some even numbers could be divided both into an odd number of groups of two and into two equal groups with an odd amount in each group. Although my student's initial claim sounded like Sean's; it was different. Like Ball's student she agreed that an even number can be divided equally into two groups, but she asserted within the set of even numbers some even numbers could also be divided equally into three groups. When pushed to explain what she meant, she wrote: $6 \div 2 = 3$ and $6 \div 3 = 2$, and said " if we divided six into two groups there would be three in each group and if we divided six into three groups there would be two in each group." She then wrote and talked through another example: $12 \div 2 = 6$ and $12 \div 3 = 4$. Finally, she gave an example of an even number that could be divided by two but not three: $10 \div 2 = 5$ and $10 \div 3 = 3\frac{1}{3}$. When another student noted that she did divide 10 into three equal groups. She answered, "I mean dividing into three equal groups without splitting anything. You know where the numbers stay whole and there isn't a leftover."

The following week the students looked at our *"Questions We Have about Odd and Even Numbers"* poster once again and decided to think about the sum of odd plus odd and the sum of an odd number of odds. Just trying to figure out what was meant by "an odd number of odds" was a puzzle in itself.

After spending several days working on this idea the students shared their findings; all of the students thought that the sum of two odd numbers was an even number and all of the students used examples to justify their thinking. It is interesting to note that the idea (the sum of two odd numbers is even) did not get written into a conjecture until April. At that time, the students thought they had a new idea for a conjecture.

Several of the students also worked on what the sum of an odd number of odds would be and shared their thinking with the class. Jennifer wrote examples and then wrote in words a more generalized statement: "I think that odd + odd + odd will always equal odd because odd + odd equals even, and even + odd = odd." Another student, Justine, tried many examples and then wrote: "If you add odd + odd + odd (or maybe more) will the sum be even or odd? I think the answer is: if they'er [sic] is [an] even amont [sic] of odd it will be even and if they'er [sic] is an odd number of odds it will be odd." Both students were showing movement to more generalized thinking, although their statements were incomplete.

I was intrigued to hear, on and off throughout the next few months, students spontaneously bringing up odd and even numbers in their conversations.

## February

In mid-February, nine students once again wrote in their math journals about the sum when adding an odd amount of odds. This time three students wrote more generalized statements, one wrote a page full of examples and then a description, and five students wrote examples only. Most of the number sentences had combinations of single and multi-digit numbers. Students also used higher numbers than in the past.

## March

Our work on justification for our odd and even number conjectures began with the following question: *True or false? When you add an even number to another even number the sum will be even.* The students were asked to decide if the statement was true or false and then write about why. They were also asked to think about how they would convince another person. When asked what convince meant, Mario said, "That's like, prove it to somebody." The students wrote for 25 minutes. All but one went right to work, writing explanations or number sentences the entire time. Only one student said, "I don't get this. What are we supposed to do? Am I supposed to write number sentences? I don't get what we are doing?" Then she decided to write number sentences as examples. During the writing time several students remarked, "This is hard Ms. Keith" but they kept on working.

The following conversation took place after the writing time. It was our first discussion about mathematical argument.

|  |  |
|---|---|
| Ms. Keith: | I heard several people say this was hard. What made it hard? |
| Jolie: | We haven't done this before. |
| Eun Joo: | We have to think about if it was true and how to explain it. |
| Taylor: | We really had to think about what would make sense. What is even and um, and we are not talking about odds. |
| Jennifer: | Sometimes it is hard to explain what you are thinking. Other people don't always understand what you're thinking. |

| | |
|---|---|
| Ms. Keith: | What do you think I mean when I say mathematical argument? |
| Kevin: | That's when somebody is trying to prove to another person why they think it's true and why they think it's false. |
| Jolie: | You need more ideas. You can't say, "Someone told me," That's not actually explaining… |
| Taylor: | …why you think it is true. That's someone else's thinking. |
| Melia: | That's not enough evidence! |
| Ms. Keith: | How would you convince another person that our Classroom Conjecture 3 was true? [even plus even equals an even] |
| Tad: | You could explain by giving some math problems that add even numbers. |

Our conversation continued after the students elicited examples, which I wrote on a piece of construction paper.

| | |
|---|---|
| Ms. Keith: | Will these number sentences convince others that our Conjecture 3 will always be true? Do you think you have convinced me? |
| Jennifer: | Maybe [pointing to the construction paper]. These turned out true but maybe you want more. There are more number sentences. |
| Ms. Keith: | How many number sentences would it take to prove that this is true? |
| Jennifer: | About a million. That would be cool, if we could each write 1,000. |
| Theo: | We wouldn't have time to do one million [glancing at the clock]. |
| Ms. Keith: | Would that be enough number sentences? |
| Several voices: | Yes, |
| | Wait; there are numbers we don't know the name of. |
| | Maybe. |
| Jolie: | Numbers go on forever! |
| Eun Joo: | You can write more than one million. |
| Melia: | Because then we would have to be at school all our life to get them all. |
| Tad: | Numbers never stop. |
| Justine: | It would take us five more notebooks for everyone. |

Ms. Keith: What would be convincing? What would be a convincing argument?

Mario: Put it in words. Explain why the number sentences explain why it's an even number.

Jennifer: Kind of, like Mario, only [explain] why you think that whatever you are trying to prove is true or false.

Justine: Like that is just showing [pointing to the examples] it's true for those number sentences but maybe in words it would be different, more details.

Jolie: It depends on how much the person you are telling wants. Maybe number sentences are enough. Maybe another person would want more.

Taylor: Maybe if a person wants more evidence they could just write more number sentences.

The children grappled with the idea of what constitutes a convincing argument. Most of the students seemed to understand that examples did not provide a complete convincing argument but they were unsure of what else they could use to justify this classroom conjecture. Only two of the students had started to think in more general terms.

Several weeks later we returned to Classroom Conjecture 3. I wanted to know if they still thought it was true and how would they justify to others that it would always be true. It was during this discussion that the ideas about partners and patterns emerged and our definition of even numbers (dividing by 2) was used in a mathematical argument.

Eun Joo: I think it is true because even numbers has a partner. [She wrote:]

00 + 00,

partner + partner

Tad: She just gave me an idea.

Eun Joo: If everything makes a partner, then it's an even number. Even numbers is partners. Even plus even is like partner plus partner.

Theo: Every even number has a partner. Yeah!

Tad: Like, if I tried to add some odds, there would be one thing less.

Theo: Eun Joo just made me think about odds—odds don't have a partner.

Eun Joo: Yeah, one left.

At this point Theo went to the board. He talked as he worked, saying, "Okay, now I need to add an even and an odd, right? So, I'll do 2 and 3." He drew two circles and three circles, and then drew lines to connect the partners.

0-0 0-0 0

Theo:    Okay, there's one left over. Now I need [to] try even numbers. I'll do 4 and 2. [Theo drew lines to connect the partners]

0 0 0-0

| |

0 0

It is interesting to note that in Theo's first picture (2 + 3), he kept the partners within each set. For his second example (4 + 2), he made partners between and within the sets.

Theo:    Yep, there's all the partners. I think partners will only work for evens. Odds don't have all partners.

Ms. Keith:    Do even numbers all have partners?

Theo:    Yes.

Ms. Keith:    Did you think about this before today?

Theo:    No, Eun Joo just made me think about it.

Taylor:    Theo just made me think about partners. I mean that each set of even numbers has a partner.

Justine:    I don't get what they mean. "Even numbers have partners?"

Kenisha:    When you put even numbers on both sides.

Jolie:    Can I go show it on the board?

Jolie drew four circles and put a ring around two and a ring around two. Jolie then said, "Four is an even number and it has partners, these two and these two; and there's nothing left over like an odd number would have."

Theo:    So, if you made 5 then you put two together and two together and one is left over.

Jolie:    That's right. That's odd. Odds have one left over.

Ms. Keith:    What could you do to make the picture show an even number?

Taylor:    You could take one away.

Jennifer:    You could add one.

Tad:    It goes in a pattern. Even, odd, even, odd…

Ms. Keith:    Does the pattern ever stop?

Class:    NO!

Lewis:    No, because numbers never end. Even and odd numbers go in a pattern. Even, odd, even, odd... So that means that if you count by twos starting at an even number you will only say even numbers and when you count by twos starting at an odd number you will only say odd numbers. An even plus one is an odd number and an even plus two is an even number. AND an odd plus one is an even number and an odd plus two is an odd number.

Toward the end of our discussion, a new idea related to our odd and even number definitions was introduced.

Jennifer:    I'm thinking that Conjecture 3 is true because even numbers can be divided by two. So, if you added two even numbers there wouldn't be any extras.

She went to the board and wrote:

XX + XX = ___  No extras when ÷ by two
XX

Even numbers have even groups, no extras

Jennifer:    There wouldn't be any extras so there would be an even sum.

Taylor:    Yeah, cause when there is an odd number there is one left over.

Theo:    What's going on in my head is: If you take an even and an odd will it still have a partner?

Allen:    I have a question for Jennifer. Why did you do that, that dividing by two?

Jennifer:    Because I think that an even number does not have any extras when dividing by two. So, if you add two even numbers there are not any extras to make the number odd.

[She pointed to each set of X's on the board and then wrote:]

No extras when divided by 2

(2 + 2) (1+1)

Jennifer:    So there are no extras when divided by two. That is the same for all even numbers. That means that there aren't any left over to make it be odd.

The following day we returned to the question, "Would writing a lot of number sentences be a convincing argument to prove Classroom Conjecture 3?" I was interested to see if the discussion from the preceding day had an impact on the students' thinking.

Eun Joo: Using number sentences can only convince a little bit. Numbers go on forever.

Justine: We didn't do all the numbers.

Mario: Even plus even equals an even because even numbers have partners.

Melia: Numbers go on forever so you can't do all the number sentences. It would take your whole life, forever.

Tad: And you couldn't convince...

Melia: And you couldn't convince the person you are trying to convince.

Ms. Keith: What else could you do?

Diana: You could use a picture. [Diana draws circles on the board, and revisits the partner idea.] Partners means they are with each other.

Theo: Evens have partners.

Eun Joo: If partner is even number you can divide.

Allen: Like for 42. Each gets 20 and then you split the 2 and each gets one more. So each person gets 21.

Kevin: You only need to look at the ones. All the tens, 10, 20, 30 40 can be split.

Justine: All the tens are even. Then if it's nine you know it's odd.

Tad: You can split seven. It's 3½ and 3½.

Jennifer: But seven is odd because evens go into two groups without fractions.

Justine: Just whole numbers.

Ms. Keith: So, if I give you a group of cubes, can you figure out if it is an even or odd amount without counting? [She hands towers of cubes to Diana and Theo.]

Diana immediately broke her tower into groups of two, partners. Theo broke his tower into two towers and adjusted the towers until both sets had equal amounts. Both students determined that the initial set was an even amount.

| Ms. Keith: | How do we know Diana and Theo each have an even amount? |
|---|---|
| Various: | They have partners and no leftovers. |
| | They have the same amount. |
| | No extras. |
| Ms. Keith: | But Diana and Theo's piles don't look the same? |
| Jennifer: | Diana checked it Eun Joo's way, with partners. She made all partners and there weren't any leftovers. |
| Justine: | And Theo did it Jennifer's way by dividing it into two groups. The groups have the same amount and no extras. |
| Ms. Keith: | So we agree that Theo and Diana each have an even amount. What could we do to show that the sum of those two sets is even? |
| Tad: | I think I know. I can show you. |

Tad took all the cubes, connected them, made one long train, and then broke the cubes all off into partners.

| Tad: | See, it's even. |
|---|---|
| Justine: | Why did you put them all together if you were going to take them apart? |
| Jolie: | Because he first had to add them together. 'Cause we're adding 2 even numbers together. |
| Ms. Keith: | Do we have to count to make sure we have an even number for the sum? |
| Aliyah: | No, we don't because they are all in partners. It's even. |
| Ms. Keith: | Do you all agree with Tad? Is the sum even? |
| Class: | Yes. It's even. |
| Ms. Keith: | So Tad showed us a way that uses the partner idea. Is there another way to think about it? |

The cubes were back in two separate towers, with different even amounts in each tower, lying on the carpet.

| Tad: | Yeah, you could break them into even groups like this. |
|---|---|

Tad took the towers and broke each tower into two even groups. Now the class and I were looking at two sets with two towers in each set. Although the towers were different lengths, within each set the towers were the same length.

| Lewis: | Same length, same number. So we can just add each tower to the other. |
|---|---|

He put one tower from one group on a tower from the second group. He then repeated this.

> Jolie:  The sum is the same because the two parts are equal.
>
> Tad:  How do you know the sum is even?
>
> Jolie:  Well, you could split them into partners again.
>
> Justine:  That would be going into Eun Joo's way.
>
> Lewis and Justine:  Hey! It's a cycle!
>
> Jolie:  Divide by two and partners. Jennifer's way and Eun Joo's way. They both work.

I asked the students to write in their math journals about what they knew about even numbers and how they could prove Classroom Conjecture 3 to someone else. Three of the students wrote generalized arguments. Six of the students wrote arguments that were more general in nature although not complete. These students showed movement away from proof by example. Four of the students wrote about the characteristics of even numbers but did not write a justification for Classroom Conjecture 3. One student only wrote the date on her paper; other than that her paper was blank.

Lewis was very excited to share his journal entry with the class. He said, "Conjecture 3 is true because, uh, here let me read it. *When you count by two you alwys* [sic] *say even numbers so even numbers are made out of two and sens* [sic] *their* [sic] *made out of two even plus even is even."* Several students said, "But you can count by two's starting at an odd and you say odd numbers." Lewis responded, "Yeah, but I mean when you count by two's starting with an even you always get an even number." Lewis's argument, though incomplete, showed evidence of generalized thinking.

## April

Eun Joo brought the class back to justifying Classroom Conjecture 2, our conjecture about adding an odd plus an even number. She had been thinking and working on this conjecture at home. She brought to school her written generalized arguments for why there is an odd sum when adding an odd and an even. She was eager to share her ideas. Before our class discussion started, all the students had time to write their thoughts on Classroom Conjecture 2. The students brought their math journals to the carpet for our discussion.

> Diana:  I think Conjecture 2 is true because I did some problems.
>
> Kenisha:  What do you mean?

Diana:   I'll show you.

Diana wrote:   4 + 5 = 9.

When pushed as to how she knew if the numbers were odd or even, Diana drew 4 circles and then 5 circles. She drew a ring around each set of two circles.

Diana:   See, I can make the four circles into partners, and there aren't any left over. Then I can do that with the five, but I have a leftover. Odd numbers have one left over. So the answer is odd."

Justine:   Actually, you could split that last one into half and half.

Jolie:   Half is not a whole number. We're keeping the numbers whole, remember.

Lewis:   I think it [Conjecture 2] is true because odd plus one is even, so odd plus two is odd.

Tad:   Lewis, what do you mean?

Allen:   I don't get it.

Lewis:   When you split an odd number into two even groups you have one left over. So, if you add one you will get an even. And evens are made out of evens. Evens are made out of twos, so even plus two will always be evens.

Allen:   Oh, I get it. He's right.

Ms. Keith:   Do you understand what Lewis is thinking about?

Eun Joo:   He's talking about pattern. Odd plus odd is even and odd plus even is….uhhh

Lewis:   Odd.

Eun Joo:   I think it's true. Take odd number and take one away. Now it is even number. We know that even plus even is even. Now add the one more. It's odd number because numbers are like order: even, odd, even, odd. Like Lewis said, even plus one makes odd.

Kevin:   I think if you take an even plus odd you will get an odd. You count by two when you say even numbers and if you add an odd you will not say an even number.

Jennifer:   I think Conjecture 2 is always true 'cause an even number can be divided equally into two groups, but if you do that to an odd number there will be one left over. The left over makes the sum odd

Lewis: Oh I get it. Even plus even is even, plus one is odd.

Ms. Keith: Allen do you have anything more you want to add to this argument?

Allen: No, not yet.

Ms. Keith: Justine, what are you thinking?

Justine: Well, since the even number can be split into two equal groups, you put them [the groups] together and you make an even number. You can make the odd number even by splitting it into two equal groups and keeping the one leftover. And as we know that after an even comes an odd number. So after you add the even numbers, you add one more, making an odd.

Taylor: Hey, it's even plus even plus one!

Various: Yeah. She's right.

Lewis: That's what I was saying.

Ms. Keith: Kenisha, why do you think Conjecture 2 is true?

Kenisha: 'Cause I did lots of problems. I did some for even plus even and I always got even. I tried some for even plus odd and I always got odd, and I tried some for odd plus odd and I got even.

Ms. Keith: You tried all those different even and odd combinations in number sentences?

Kenisha: Yes. See. [Holding her paper up]

Aliyah: Ms. Keith, I think she said a new conjecture.

Ms. Keith: What new conjecture did you hear Kenisha say?

Aliyah: I think it was an odd number plus an odd number made an even number.

Ms. Keith: Hmm, do we have that idea yet?

Various: [Looking at conjectures hanging from the ceiling] No. We have the other ones Kenisha said but not the one Aliyah said.

Theo: And Ms. Keith, I know how it looks. It would be like this.

Theo drew seven squares on the board. Under the squares he drew nine circles. He then proceeded to draw a ring around each set of two.

Theo:  See, this here is an odd number. I can make partners. Evens have partners. Odds have one left over. This here got one left over [pointing to the squares], so it's an odd number. Same with here. [Pointing to the circles] But then I can take this one left over, and this one left over, and make another partner. Now they're all partners. So it's even.

Jennifer:  I agree with Theo. Let's add it to our conjectures.

Various:  Yes.

Lewis:  That would be Conjecture 7.

Classroom Conjecture 7 read:

*Classroom Conjecture 7*

When you add two odd numbers the sum will be an even number.

Later that week, twelve of the students wrote in their math journals why they thought Classroom Conjecture 7 was true. Two of the students chose to continue writing about Classroom Conjecture 2. All of the students began their explanations with pictures or words. They did not write lists of examples, as had been done with past conjectures. Three of the students later added number sentences to their papers, perhaps as a means for providing more specific evidence or because they had time and they wanted to keep writing more ideas.

Kenisha who in the past said, "I don't get it. What do you want us to do? What should I write?" or would not write anything at all went right to work. She based her explanation on the examples she had worked on earlier in the week. Although her written justification was example based, she did not feel the need to add any more examples to her paper. Kenisha wrote: "I think that odd + odd always equals an even number because an odd always has one left and I did a lot of odd + odds and I only got a even number."

During this time two students used justification by example; four students used weak or incomplete generalized arguments; and eight students were able to independently write a generalized argument.

## Student Use of Generalized Knowledge to Solve a Word Problem

I was intrigued by a story problem I had seen in earlier readings. (Bastable & Schifter, 1998). A teacher gave her third and fourth grade students the following problem:

*Lilah counted 71 pieces of candy. She has Milky Way Bars, Rollos, Lifesaver Packs, Kit Kat Bars, Hershey Kisses, Mars Bars, Blow Pops, and Hershey Bars. Lilah doesn't have an even number of anything. What are the possibilities? Did she count right?*

The teacher reported that this problem led her students into the exploration of odd and even numbers and their properties. The teacher stated that her students worked for a long time to find combinations of eight odd numbers that would total 71. When they came together as a group they did not have consensus as to whether or not the girl in the problem had counted correctly. During their whole class discussion a variety of justifications emerged. Justifications included the use of examples and properties of odd and even numbers. Specific to the arguments using the properties were the use of an odd, even, odd, even, odd pattern when adding odd numbers and a generalized argument about adding an odd number to an odd number and getting an even number.

Toward the end of April I gave my students a similar problem, with lower numbers. I was interested in whether or not my students would translate their thinking about generalized argument to a word problem situation. The problem read:

*Kenji counted 31 pieces of candy. He has jawbreakers, lollipops, gumballs, and Hershey Kisses. Kenji doesn't have an even number of any of the candies. What are the possibilities? Did he count right?*

Unlike the third- and fourth-grade students, when we came together as a group to discuss the problem we had consensus. All of the students agreed that Kenji had not counted correctly. Also in contrast, only one of the second graders used computation to try to find a combination of numbers to make 31. Thirteen of the 14 students started by thinking of the total first. Two of those students divided the 31 cubes into specific sets of odd numbers. The other 11 students moved away from specific sets of numbers and used concrete materials to build a generalized argument. All 11 showed evidence of solving the problem using generalized thinking, although many of their arguments were incomplete.

## SUMMARY OF RESULTS

The second grade students in this study had many ideas and questions about odd and even numbers. The students wrote conjectures about the sums of odd and even numbers. Specifically, ideas about the sums of (a) an even number and an even number; (b) an even number and an odd number; and (c) an odd number and an odd number. Although, the students'

Table 3.1.   Types of Justification Used by Scond Grade Students

|  | Examples | Emerging/ Incomplete Generalized Argument | Generalized Argument |
|---|---|---|---|
| November | 14 | 0 | 0 |
| December | 12 | 2 | 0 |
| March | 4 | 6 | 3 |
| April | 2 | 4 | 8 |

conjectures revolved around the operation of addition, the conjectures provided a basis for deep discussions on justification.

During the six months of this study, growth in the kinds of justifications used by students to prove conjectures was observed and recorded (Table 3.1). At the start of this project all 14 students used examples to prove why they believed a conjecture was true. They were satisfied that examples provided enough proof. As the class engaged in conversations and discussions about what constitutes enough proof, the students' mathematical arguments became more general and more convincing.

By March, most of the children had a sense that proof by example was not enough—that more was needed to make a convincing argument.

By April, 8 out of the 14 students were able to give a generalized argument to justify why one or more of the odd/even conjectures would be true for all numbers. Four more students used emerging or incomplete generalized arguments and 2 students continued to use examples. Eleven of the 14 students were also able to transfer their generalized thinking to a problem situation.

## DISCUSSION

Knuth (2002) highlights the importance of giving students opportunities to present differing mathematical arguments to their classmates. He advocates these discussions as a means by which students may build a deeper understanding of proof as well as fundamental mathematics.

I also found this idea to be advantageous when working with my second graders. Repeated discussions about what constitutes convincing arguments for why a conjecture is true were often the results of students sharing justifications. In March when many in the class realized they needed more than examples for proof, continued discussions about justifications helped in building their understanding of a generalized argument.

Similar to the teachers in the Bastable and Schifter (1998) case studies, I found my students to be very interested and excited by odd and even numbers. Students' notions about the properties of these numbers were eagerly written as conjectures. The odd and even conjectures turned out to be an important vehicle for engaging students in discussions about justification.

Like Carpenter, Franke, and Levi (2003), I saw students using different levels of justification. Reminiscent of their findings, my students went through a limbo stage during which they knew examples were not enough, but didn't have other alternatives for proof. Carpenter, Franke, and Levi described three broad levels of justification, including one about making generalizable arguments. Based on my students' justifications, I felt the need to make further distinctions within this level. I found it helpful to classify my students' generalizable arguments into two sub-categories: concrete generalized argument and abstract generalized argument. This distinction was helpful as I worked with the students to articulate their generalizable arguments. Seeing a distinction enabled me to help my students build relationships between different arguments. The students worked to see how the arguments were similar and how they were different. In addition, the distinction provided a way for me to both learn about and better understand proof.

When I began this study I was not sure at what level second grade students would be able to justify their ideas. Prior to this year I had both second and third grade students working together on algebraic thinking. I saw evidence of generalized thinking with that class, although we only touched upon the notion of what constitutes a convincing argument. At the time, I wondered if the third graders in the group were the impetus for pushing the bigger ideas in our class conversations. With this study I have learned that second graders are quite capable of engaging in mathematical arguments, pushing thinking in more generalized ways and seeing differences between mathematical arguments. I continue to wonder how their experiences with justification will affect their work with mathematics in the future.

Students' use of generalized argument is not a trivial issue, as illustrated in the candy word problem. Additionally, I asked a friend who was teaching an undergraduate math method course to give the original problem (71 candies and 8 groups of odd amounts) to her students. She agreed, and when we looked over the finished work we found 15 of the 18 college students wrote examples (looking for combinations of odd numbers that would equal 71) while 3 of the college students began with examples and moved to more generalized, although incomplete, arguments. This small sample suggests that some teachers leave college without understanding proof. It also causes me to reflect on changes in my own thinking. Before I started working with my students on algebraic thinking, I too would have used examples for my justification and thought that it constituted enough proof.

The experience of working on algebraic reasoning with my students has increased my own knowledge. My understanding of what constitutes a convincing argument has grown deeper. I have a heightened awareness of proof as a tool for learning why something is true, not just for justifying that it is true. I find myself working to think in a more generalized way.

In my classroom students have always been expected to justify to each other their answers; to prove how they know they have the correct answer. We are now working to lift the mathematics out of the arithmetic and use justification to prove why properties are true for all designated numbers. I consciously think about the mathematics my students engage in and make deliberate decisions about the tools I use to highlight the fundamental properties embedded in their work. I am much more aware of students' implicit ideas and work to make these ideas explicit to the classroom community.

Working with teachers and university researchers on early algebraic thinking has also contributed to my deeper understanding of mathematics. Being a part of a classroom action research project helped to focus and deepen my thinking about my students' work. The teachers and facilitators were a consistent source of support—acting as listeners, encouragers, questioners and mind stretchers. Working on classroom action research with a focus on algebraic thinking for two years was also a wonderful opportunity. I was able to use what I learned from the first project in my second project. I also enjoyed the deeper sense of community and friendship that comes from working with the same people for a longer period of time. Working with researchers gave me the opportunity to expand my knowledge about algebraic thinking and was also another community in which discussions about children's' thinking was discussed.

For teachers to meet the goals outlined in the *Principles and Standards for School Mathematics* (NCTM, 2000), I believe it is increasingly important for teachers to engage in mathematics and to become a part of the mathematics' communities inside and outside of their classrooms.

## ACKNOWLEDGMENT

The Madison Action Research Group was funded by a grant at the University of Wisconsin-Madison directed by Dr. Thomas P. Carpenter and by the Madison Metropolitan School District. I would like to thank Nancy Beck and Sue Berthouex for their work as group facilitators. A version of this chapter was published previously by the Madison Metropolitan School District which has granted permission for this work to be published here.

## REFERENCES

Ball, D. L., & Bass, H. (2000). Making believe: The collective construction of public mathematical knowledge in the elementary classroom. In D. Philips (Ed.), *Constructivism in education* [Yearbook of the National Society for the Study of Education] (pp. 193-224). Chicago: University of Chicago Press.

Bastable, V., & Schifter, D. (Unpublished Manuscript). Classroom stories: Examples of elementary students engaged in early algebra.

Bostrom, M., Keith, A., Nordness, C., Smith, R., Wiesner, B., & Wiesner, R. (2001). *Classroom action research: Early algebraic thinking.* Madison, WI: Madison Metropolitan School District.

Carpenter, T. P., Fennema, E., Franke, M. L., Levi, L., & Empson, S. B. (1999). *Children's mathematics: Cognitively guided instruction.* Portsmouth, NH: Heinemann.

Carpenter, T. P., Franke, M. L., & Levi, L. (2003) *Thinking mathematically: Integrating arithmetic and algebra in elementary school.* Portsmouth, NH: Heinemann.

Carpenter, T. P., & Levi, L. (1999, April). *Developing conceptions of algebraic reasoning in the primary grades.* Paper presented at the annual meeting of the American Educational Research Association, Montreal, Canada.

Carraher, D., Schliemann, A. D., & Brizuela, B. M. (2001). Algebra in the early grades? *Hands On! 24*(1), 8-11.

Chambers, D. L. (1994). The right algebra for all. *Educational Leadership,* March, pp. 85–86.

Chappell, M. F. (1997). Preparing students to enter the gate. *Teaching Children Mathematics, 2,* 266–267.

Chazan, D. (1994). *Algebra for all students?* National Council for Research on Teacher Learning, East Lansing, MI and Office of Educational Research and Improvement, Washington, DC.

Flores, A. (2002). How do children know that what they learn in mathematics is true? *Teaching Children Mathematics, 8,* 269-274.

Fujii, T., & Stephens, M. (2001). The future of the teaching and learning of algebra. In H. Chick, K. Stacey, J. Vincent, & J. Vincent (Eds.), *Proceedings of the 12th ICMI study conference* (Vol. 1, pp. 258-264). Victoria, Australia: University of Melbourne.

Greenes, C., & Findell. C. (1999). Developing students' algebraic reasoning abilities. In Stiff, L. V. (Ed.), *Developing mathematical reasoning in grades K–12* [NCTM Yearbook] (pp. 127–137). Reston, VA: National Council of Teachers of Mathematics.

Kaput, J. (2000). *Transforming algebra from an engine of inequity to an engine of mathematical power by "algebrafying" the K–12 curriculum.* Dartmouth, MA: National Center for Improving Student Learning and Achievement in Mathematics and Science.

Kaput, J. & Blanton, M. (1999). *Enabling elementary teachers to achieve generalization and progressively systematic expression of generality in their math classrooms: The role of authentic mathematical experience* (Working paper). Madison, WI: National Center for Improving Student Learning and Achievement in Mathematics and Science.

Knuth, E. (2002). Proof as a tool for learning mathematics. *Mathematics Teacher, 95,* 486–490.

National Council of Teachers of Mathematics. (2000). *Principles and standards for school mathematics.* Reston, VA: Author.

Schifter, D. (1999). Reasoning about operations, early algebraic thinking in grades K-6. In Stiff, L. V. (Ed.), *Developing mathematical reasoning in grades K–12* [NCTM Yearbook] (pp. 62–81). Reston, VA: National Council of Teachers of Mathematics.

Sowder, L., & Harel, G. (1998). Types of students' justifications. *Mathematics Teacher, 91,* 670–675.

Strong, D. S., & Cobb, N. B. (2000). Algebra for all: It's a matter of equity, expectations, and effectiveness. *Mathematics Education Dialogues, 3*(2), 3.

Szombathelyi, A., & Szarvas, T. (1998). Ideas for developing student's reasoning: A Hungarian perspective. *Mathematics Teacher, 91*(8), 677–681.

Valentine, C. (1999). Conversations about proof and justification in a sixth grade classroom. Unpublished master's thesis, University of Wisconsin, Madison.

Whitenack, J., & Yackel, E. (2002). Making mathematical arguments in the primary grades: The importance of explaining and justifying ideas. *Teaching Children Mathematics, 8,* 524–527.

CHAPTER 4

# TEACHER AS RESEARCHER

## Research as a Partnership

**Karen Schweitzer**
*Williamsburg Elementary Schools, Williamsburg, MA*

For most of the day, as I nurture children, mediate problems, zip snow suits, and teach my class to reason, think, and question, I am a teacher. Teaching is what I do each day as I work with my class of first and second graders, and it is what I have done for more than 20 years.

So what does it mean when I also take on the role of teacher-researcher? What does it mean for me to engage in research as I am also doing the work of educating my students? What does it mean for me and for others to consider the work that I am doing research?

In this chapter, I will first discuss the professional development experiences that contributed to me seeing myself as a researcher and beginning to value the research I do in my own classroom. Then I will share the story of my most recent exploration into the early algebraic thinking of first- and second-graders, specifically in the area of making generalizations about operations.

*Teachers Engaged in Research*
*Inquiry Into Mathematics Classrooms, Grades Pre-K–2*, pages 69–94
Copyright © 2006 by Information Age Publishing

I have always thought of my teaching as being both guided and supported by research. Research has given me a way to make sense of the hundreds of little things that happen in my classroom throughout the day. It gives me a framework into which I can fit my student's ideas and behaviors. When I find research that connects to things that are happening in my class, I think, "Oh! That's why my students do that." It had never occurred to me that my teaching could have any other connection to research.

Then I became involved in a series of professional development projects that caused me to change my perspective on research. These projects have spanned the past 13 years (with a few scattered breaks) and have had some important common features that I feel are responsible for my change in perspective. I would like to share my experiences and my observations of the process of change that I have experienced as a participant in these projects.

## LEARNING TO FIND THE RESEARCH IN TEACHING: PROFESSIONAL DEVELOPMENT PROGRAMS THAT CHANGED MY PERSPECTIVE

All of the projects I will be talking about have been connected with SummerMath for Teachers, a program at Mount Holyoke College that is engaged in mathematics education for teachers of grades K-8. All but the first project have been collaborations among SummerMath for Teachers, the Education Research Collaborative at TERC, and the Center for the Development of Teaching at the Education Development Center (EDC).

I work in a small rural school in the western part of Massachusetts. The town is economically diverse, though not racially diverse. Our school has a commitment to small classes, and my class size varied between 15-18 children during the time described in this chapter.

In 1992, I participated in the Mathematics Process Writing Project (Schifter, 1996a, 1996b). In this program, a group of teachers engaged in weekly seminars facilitated by Deborah Schifter, then the director of SummerMath for Teachers. Each week, the teachers wrote about some piece of mathematics that was happening in their classrooms. Two things happened with these pieces of writing. First we met with other teachers to share our writing. We also received written feedback on our writing from the facilitator. Eventually, each of us compiled our writing into a longer paper that explored a piece of mathematics or pedagogy in more depth.

This project was one of the most meaningful and transforming experiences I had had as a teacher. I learned how powerful writing could be as a tool for reflecting on my own teaching, and how reflecting on my teaching could cause me to change my practice. In order to write about the mathematics in my classroom, I had to think very deeply about what my students were saying and what that told me about their understanding of the mathematics. I had never before had the experience as a teacher of taking the time to sit back and reflect deeply on one part of my day. I learned that the processes of reflecting and writing could help me to identify my students' understandings and guide my teaching decisions. This project was the beginning of the process of learning to carefully observe my students and listen to what they say.

It was also my first experience with having another pair of eyes that, through my writing, could look into my classroom and see my teaching and my students' thinking. The feedback I received and the questions I was asked by Dr. Schifter pushed me to reflect on both the mathematics and on my teaching at an even deeper level.

As I look back now, I can see that this project was also the beginning of a kind of collaboration that, for me, is a crucial piece of being a teacher researcher. Working with researchers who see our work as a partnership provides not only essential support but also a larger context for my work. I think that this will become clearer as I describe the next project in which I participated: Teaching to the Big Ideas.

The Teaching to the Big Ideas (TBI) project was a collaboration among researchers from SummerMath for Teachers, TERC, EDC, and 36 K-8 teachers (Schifter, Russell, & Bastable, 1999). From the perspective of the teachers, the project was designed to explore the big ideas that children encounter in their elementary mathematics education. The TBI project lasted four years and produced a set of professional development materials based on the work we did together.

Although there were similarities between TBI and the Mathematics Process Writing Project—particularly reflective writing—there were some components that made this experience different. This project had a particular focus on learning more about the mathematics of the elementary curriculum. This focus meant that we, as participants, engaged in exploring the mathematics for ourselves. For many of us, actually doing the mathematics activities and not just talking about what the children might do was a huge change. For some of us, it meant working through our anxieties about mathematics—the baggage we brought with us from our own school experiences. For others, it meant realizing that there was a lot more to understand even if we had been successful mathematics students. I was startled by the notion that I needed to know more about the mathematics in order to understand what my students were doing and what I needed to teach them.

There was another difference between these two projects that had a large impact on me. During the time that we were writing cases for TBI, a staff person visited our classrooms every 2 weeks to observe a mathematics lesson. After my students and I completed the lesson, the observer and I spent time talking about it. Together, we analyzed the activity and looked for the interesting parts and the confusing parts. Working in this way with a researcher helped me to learn to look at my teaching even more carefully and to identify the mathematics in my students' work.

These experiences helped me to develop a habit of reflection that is the basis for what I now consider to be my research. The experiences I had in TBI taught me to look into classrooms—my own and those of my peers—and look to the mathematical thinking of students in order to identify big ideas to think about. Sometimes I wrote cases about the activities that had been observed. At other times I wrote about the process of being observed and how reflecting with the observer helped me to think more deeply about the mathematics and to see something else that I might write about—thereby continuing the process of systematically reflecting on my classroom experiences and the big ideas of the mathematics. As in the previous project, the TBI staff responded to our cases and asked questions that pushed us to think more deeply about the mathematics embedded in them.

Another aspect of the project was that we were bringing these cases to our seminar, talking about them with our peers and doing related mathematics as adults. I remember the excitement of discovering that similar things were happening in different classrooms across the grades and connecting what students were doing in classrooms to our discoveries as mathematics learners. It was exciting to exchange cases with other teachers who were also working on these ideas and to begin to make connections between what a second grader was doing mathematically and what a fifth grader was doing. In our cases, we saw older children continuing to grapple with some of the same ideas on which the younger ones were working, sometimes refining them, sometimes expanding them. Through this process, we were able to begin to see a progression of the mathematical ideas through the elementary curriculum.

As the staff read these cases, they began to organize them based on the mathematics explored in them. This organization of the cases contributed to the process I described above of developing a bigger picture of what was happening across grades and within each grade. Eventually, these cases were put into a larger context as the staff also organized them into chapters and casebooks and put them together with mathematics activities and research findings to create a professional development seminar (Schifter, Bastable, & Russell, 1999a, 1999b). These materials supported what we were seeing in our classrooms.

This was the beginning of a move toward seeing *my* classroom as a place where I could begin to build my own framework for my students' ideas—a framework that I used to rely on other research to provide. We, as teachers, had made observations about the thinking and understanding of our students. The staff had helped us to understand that when we looked at all of our observations, common themes and patterns began to emerge. In addition, the work of researchers outside of our project was consistent with what we were seeing and writing about. I remember thinking for the first time about what research meant and how what we were doing as teachers was comparable to what researchers do.

The other formative experience I had during this time was reading the work of the researchers with whom we were collaborating—the staff of the project (Hammer & Schifter, 2001; Russell, 1999; Schifter, 1998; Schifter, 1999a; Schifter & Szymaszek, 2003). I read journal articles and book chapters and attended presentations about the work we had done. I learned the ways in which the work of the teachers was integrated into the work of these researchers. These experiences enabled me to see our work in an even larger context—how it contributed to the body of research that was changing the teaching of mathematics.

I have taken from the work that began with TBI the idea that my classroom and my students can be a site for developing research questions and for embarking on research. In addition, when paired with a collaborator, I can be an integral part of the research team and actually consider myself a teacher researcher.

## A RESEARCH QUESTION BEGINS TO TAKE FORM

Since that first TBI project, which focused on number and operations, the work has continued over subsequent years, focusing on geometry, measurement, data, and most recently on algebraic thinking. I would like to share my experiences working as a teacher researcher in more detail by describing the work that I have done in this most recent project on algebraic thinking.

In this project, classroom teachers were again working with researchers. One of our tasks was to explore algebra and its role in the elementary curriculum. My personal question at the onset of the project was: What does algebra look like for first and second graders?

As I stated earlier in the chapter, my previous work had taught me that in order to make sense of what my children were grappling with, I had to have a grasp on the mathematics myself. When we began our work with algebra, my only experience had been that of my ninth- and twelfth-grade mathematics classes in high school, and I did not see what connection those experiences would have to the work of my first and second graders. I saw the work in the early grades as preparing children to do algebra later in their lives, but there was nothing that they were doing that I could identify as algebra or algebraic thinking.

However, the staff of the project, the guiding force in our research team, had a larger and more informed perspective. To get us ready for the work ahead, they asked us to read some current research on algebraic thinking in the elementary grades. The readings focused on algebraic thinking involved in making generalizations about operations (Ball & Bass, 2003; Bastable & Schifter, in press; Carpenter & Levi, 1999; Schifter, 1999b). As we read this research, we became aware that these were new ideas.

These readings pointed out that young children notice and describe generalizations about numbers and operations. For example, students often recognize that when you switch the order of addends in an addition problem you get the same answer. Later in their schooling they might express these generalizations in algebraic language, but as young children, they use the everyday language that they have available to them to express their understanding of this idea. We began to look for examples of those generalizations and to push our students' thinking about those ideas.

As the fall went on, the teachers attended a monthly seminar facilitated by the project staff. As many of us had done before, we engaged in mathematics activities as adults and shared our writing about the work our students were doing. Our focus was on algebraic thinking, but many of us were having a hard time figuring out just what that was. Sometimes, the staff would ask us to have our children think about a specific idea. At other times, we would try what a colleague had done with our own classes so we could see how it worked in another class with other children.

In trying to figure out what to do with my own students, I began looking at the work they were already doing. In the years since the first project described above, I had learned to look for patterns or commonalties in what my students were doing. I tried to identify the things that were puzzling for them and the things that were coming up over and over in their work. In this very early stage, I felt like I was fumbling in the dark, trying to figure out what was interesting, where the children were getting stuck, and what their misunderstandings were. Since there was little prior research in this area, we understood we were exploring new territory.

I was teaching a multiage class made up of first and second grade students. During our math class, I taught a single grade by trading students with the other teacher of a multiage class. At other times during the day, we did mathematics as a mixed-grade class.

In order to listen to the thinking of my students more carefully, I taped some of our conversations, listened to them, and transcribed them. I then reflected on what they said and wrote up my reflections with parts of our dialogue to create episodes that could be discussed with other teachers and researchers.

To try to find more clarity, I returned to the mathematics we were exploring as adults. I looked at what I was learning to help me think about what my students might learn. Under the guidance of our facilitators, our teacher group began talking about what it means to make a generalization. When does an observation become a generalization? How do you know something will always work? What does it mean to prove something? As we explored these ideas ourselves, we turned our attention to how our children could deal with these ideas. How is this idea of generalizing part of what it means for young children to engage in algebraic thinking?

I had been noticing that in one of our daily mathematics routines, called "Today's Number," I was seeing what I was starting to look for—children using the same set of strategies over and over, even when the numbers involved were different. In this routine, the children are given the number of the day and are asked to write different expressions that equal the number. For example, if Today's Number were 12, a child might write $10 + 2 = 12$, $14 - 2 = 12$, and $12 + 3 - 2 - 1 = 12$. As I looked at my students' daily work with this new lens—trying to find the algebra in their work—I began to notice that the children had strategies that they used day after day for coming up with their equations. The children understood that something was the same in this class of problems. There was something predictable about what was happening in the mathematics, and they could apply that to different numbers. This caught my attention as a place where I might begin to explore my students' algebraic thinking.

## LEARNING TO MAKE GENERALIZATIONS: THE BEGINNING OF ALGEBRAIC THINKING IN FIRST AND SECOND GRADE

The question I was dealing with at this point was: Did I see evidence of generalizing in the work of my own first and second grade students, and if so, where was it and what did it look like? I looked to their work with Today's Number to explore this question.

One of the patterns I noticed the children using early in that first year was the way they often made an ordered sequence of equations that equaled Today's Number (e.g., $5 - 0 = 5$; $6 - 1 = 5$; $7 - 2 = 5$; $8 - 3 = 5$). They knew the answer had to be five, and they seemed to know that this method of writing equations where both numbers of the subtraction were increased by one got them correct equations. I saw this pattern in the work of several children, so this is where I chose to begin my exploration of my students' thinking.

The children were excited to share their accomplishments; even proud that they had come up with this strategy they thought of as a trick. They had found a way to easily manage creating several equations for Today's Number no matter what the number was. However, they were unable to articulate what was happening mathematically that made this method work or how they knew it would always work. In these early discussions with my students, I was hoping that we could move from noticing that something was occurring to thinking about why it was happening. This beginning work was slow and difficult. The children had not been asked to think about these things before, and I was still learning what questions to ask to help them.

I continued to ask my students the same set of questions: "Why does that work?" "Does it always work?" "How do you know?" and "Could you explain that to someone else?" Perhaps I persisted in asking these questions because of the researchers with whom I was collaborating. They had said that they were very interested in how these ideas developed in young children. Or perhaps I persisted with these questions because each time I asked them the answers seemed to change just a little.

Here is an excerpt from an episode I wrote in December of that first year that shows my first steps toward getting children to think about how they knew something was always true. The discussion focused on knowing how to start one of those sequences of equations for Today's Number.

Paul… was one of the children who had used that string of related number sentences that we had talked about, almost every day. Paul started us off by telling us that for ten, it would be $11 - 1$. When asked how he knew it was 11 and not $12 - 1$, he replied, "because 10 is before 11, and 11 is after 10, so if you take away one that equals 10." My sense was that much of the class was in that same place of understanding, so I jumped in with, "Does that always work?" I heard yeses and nos. So I asked, "If I asked you any number, could you tell me what you had to start out at to take away one and end up at that number." Molly offered this:

Molly:   If you had any number… pretend I had 31, and then I took away
         one… then it would equal 30. (Episode, December 10, 2001)

Molly was taking the first step in learning to generalize. She picked "any number," which happened to be 31. For a first grader, 31 can seem like "any number," or a number that could represent a generalization. It was bigger than she probably could create a mental image for, but not so big that it seemed too big to work with.

Though we moved on to exploring some others pieces of algebra in our seminar, I was very interested in continuing to focus the work with my students on finding the algebraic thinking in what we were already doing. I had made a shift from thinking that there was nothing algebraic in my first- and second-grade class to being quite certain there was. However, I was still uncertain about how deeply my students were capable of understanding those ideas.

I decided to stick with the work we were doing on making generalizations. For myself I had answered the first part of my research question—that algebraic thinking was present in the mathematical work of my students. That answer led me to my next question. I needed to figure out what kinds of mathematical ideas my students would make generalizations about. I did not know what those ideas were, but my experience had taught me where to look. I looked to the work that my students were doing for guidance.

## HOW DOES GENERALIZING ABOUT OPERATIONS SUPPORT COMPUTATION?

At this same time, I was beginning to think that part of making the mathematics we were doing accessible to all students meant making the strategies and the thinking of my proficient students more explicit. For many years, my students had shared computation strategies with their classmates during class discussions, but sharing strategies alone was not helping my less proficient students develop more fluency in their computation. It seemed to me that there was a step missing in the work I was doing with my students. My explorations were being motivated by this curiosity as well as the charge to investigate algebraic thinking. Consequently, I began forming a new research question that connected these two areas of interest.

I knew that one strategy children could use to make computation more efficient was to use an easier, related number sentence to help solve the computation (e.g., using 25 + 100 to help solve 26 + 99). Since I had seen evidence of children thinking about these related number sentences in their Today's Number work, I decided to try to put what I saw the children doing into a set of story problems so that we would have a context in which we could explore what was happening with the quantities.

In the following episode, you will see children exploring a set of related problems designed to help them explore how knowing an answer to one problem might help them solve another related problem. I wanted the arithmetic to be easy enough so that the children would not get stuck on it and could look past it to what was happening mathematically. I structured the problems to work on the following idea: If an addend increases by 1, the sum increases by 1. This idea can also be represented algebraically: If $a + b = c$, then $a + (b + 1) = c + 1$.

The two problems the children worked on during this episode were as follows:

*Maura found 13 beautiful rocks. Then she found 8 more. How many rocks did she find all together?*

*Trevor found 13 rocks and then he found 9 more. How many rocks did he find together? Is there a way you can use the previous problem to help you with this problem?*

The children worked on these problems, and then we came together to share their work. After a quick sharing of strategies for the first problem, we moved on to the second problem. Here are the observations I wrote from that conversation:

Someone read the second problem, and I asked that since they knew 13 + 8 = 21, could they figure out the answer to the second problem without counting on their fingers or counting cubes. Paul said that it was one more, so it was 22. Marissa clarified that you took the one more from the nine and added that to the 21, that makes the answer one more. Several children restated some variation of the idea that nine is one more than eight. Scott said that it was the eight that helps you.

I gave the children another problem to think about right on the spot to see what they were getting out of the conversation. I asked, "How about 13 + 10?" Many children answered that it was 23, without counting. When I asked how they knew that, Molly said that the answers were always one more than each other. (Episode, March 11, 2002)

Though we can see that the computation strategies of some of the children were beginning to change in the context of this work, I was not yet sure that the connection was clear enough to be useful over time. I did not think they had generalized enough to know they could use it in all situations. The episode went on:

I decided that I wanted to create another set of problems to see if this time, they would use the strategies we had just discussed to actually solve the problems.

The next set of problems was:

*Andrew was fishing. He caught 17 fish before lunch. Then he caught 5 fish after lunch. How many fish did he catch that day?*

*Corey went fishing also. He also caught 17 fish before lunch. He caught 6 fish after lunch. How many fish did Corey catch that day? Is there a way you can use the previous problem to help you with this problem?*

This time, as I watched the children solve the problems, I noticed that many of them used the first problem to help them solve the second problem. (In fact, when I look at their work, the children who didn't were children whose number sense was not as developed.)

When I was planning the discussion of this piece of work, I wondered if it would go further than the previous discussion, since we had that previous discussion as a common starting place.

As we began to discuss Corey's fish, I realized that we were in familiar territory. Brandon showed us that he took one more cube to make the 22 into 23, and Eleanor explained that the 6 was one more than the 5 and they both had 17. Were we going to get past this, this time? As Eleanor was explaining, I decided to put the information she was giving us into a chart, in hopes that showing the information in a different way would trigger other understanding.

|        | Morning | Afternoon |
|--------|---------|-----------|
| Andrew | 17      | 5         |
| Corey  | 17      | 6         |

I asked her how knowing six was one more than five helped her to know the answer. She couldn't articulate it so I turned the question to the group. "Is there anyone who has words to describe that? How does knowing this ($17 + 5 = 22$) help you know that ($17 + 6 = 23$)?" Kathleen volunteered.

Kathleen: First you have five and then you have six. There's one more… less… there's one less than six then… um

Teacher: So how does that tell us about how many fish all together? Let's say this is all the fish. (I drew/circled something on the board.) How does knowing that this is one more than that help us figure out all the fish together?

Kathleen: Like if you count… um… you would have five first and then six.

Teacher: Let's go back to what we already knew. We already knew that Andrew had 22 all together, right?

Many: Um hmm.

Teacher: And Eleanor and Kathleen have both been pretty clear that six is one more than five. What does that tell us about how many Corey has?

Corey: It means that I have one more than Andrew.

> Teacher:    Why does it mean that you have one more? Corey says that it means that he has one more than Andrew. Why does it mean that? (Episode, March 11, 2002)

One can see Kathleen struggling to describe the relationship between five and six and how that relationship affects the answer. Corey, however, seems to be clearer about the effect, though he is also not articulating it. In the next section, as they are talking about the counting sequence, the boys are trying to explain that you are adding one each time—that is the constant thing that is happening.

> Corey:    The first number is the same. But if you were counting the right way, five and then six, six would come after, so six is a bigger number.
>
> Teacher:    The first number is the same...
>
> Scott:    So you go 1, 2, 3, 4, 5. If you were counting up you would go 1, 2, 3, 4, 5, 6. It wouldn't go 1, 2, 3, 4, 6.

At this point, I made a decision: to move forward, I needed to offer a paraphrase. "I heard Corey say that the first number is the same, and the second number is one more." Cory agreed that this is what he had said. Now I wanted to move toward creating a rule.

> Teacher:    So Corey has come up with an idea kind of like a rule that says if the first number is the same and the second number is one more, then the answer is going to be one more. Does everyone agree with that rule?
>
> Class:    Yea...
>
> Teacher:    Can you prove to me that it's going to be true?
>
> Class:    Yea. No. Yes
>
> Scott:    No, because it could be a times, then it wouldn't be true.
>
> Teacher:    Ah, so...
>
> Scott:    It's only true for plusses and minuses.

We worked to amend Corey's rule. As we amended it, the children became very concerned about whether the wording continued to match what they understood to be true.

> Teacher:    So we have to add something to Corey's rule. When you add two numbers, if the first number is the same and the second number is one more, then the answer is one more. So let's try two numbers and see if this works.

We moved on to trying this statement out with another problem. I decided that the consistent context helped to make the connection between the problems, so we stuck with fishing. We tried Heather catching 17 fish in the a.m. and 7 in the p.m. We also tried Carol catching 17 fish in the a.m. and 8 in the p.m. We decided that the rule worked.

Molly said that they are catching the same number in the morning and everyone is catching one more fish than each other in the afternoon. I didn't quite understand this, and Irene made sure to tell me that what I was writing didn't match what was being said. It seemed that, all of a sudden, there was an understanding that they needed to pay attention to the words to make sure that what I wrote was really what they meant to say. (Episode, March 11, 2002)

By the end of this set of activities, I think that my students and I were all in a different place in our thinking than we had been when we started. The work had helped my students to move from noticing what was happening in one particular set of problems to identifying a relationship and then realizing the relationship will always be true in this situation. The group was then able to realize they could put into words what it was that would always be true. I think that their investment in the wording showed a shift in their level of generalization.

Things had also become clearer to me about what this work was about. I realized that the children needed to understand the mathematics in the problem before they could begin to make a generalization about it. I also realized that working with related sets of story problems was going to be an important part of our work.

## A CONSOLIDATION OF IDEAS AS THE FIRST YEAR ENDS

My research question was once again becoming narrower in focus. I was beginning to see the connection between the strategies that my children were using and the algebraic thinking I was looking for. I was now focusing on generalizations about the number system and operations and how these were related to computational fluency.

As that first year of the project ended, we were asked to write about what we now understood about our students and algebra. I looked back at my writing from that year to help guide my reflections. In the same way that looking at the same piece of work from many students helps me get a bigger picture of the mathematics the children are doing, looking at my writing over time helped give me a better picture of what had happened over the year.

For the first time that year, I could see significant progress in our work. In fact, the ways in which the children were able to answer the questions "Does it always work?" and "How do you know?" had changed. They were not articulating clear and concise generalizations, but they no longer met these questions with silence. The children had grappled with making the words they were telling me match what they understood to be happening. While they were not talking completely abstractly when explaining why a rule always worked, they had begun to think about trying a rule out with "any number."

I also had a clearer picture of where I wanted to go in the next year. I had found what seemed to make sense for me both in that it fit with the work that was an important piece of my mathematics curriculum and that it was helping me and my students think about making generalizations. I knew that next year we would continue the work with word problems while I emphasized the question, "How can you use what you know to help with what you don't know?"

By the end of the year, the children had created the following rules as we worked on making generalizations. These are the rules that were written together as a group over the course of the school year, using a process similar to the one described in the previous excerpt.

- $10 +$ any number from 0-9 equals that number in the teens.
- The plus minus trick or the invisible trick: You take a number away and you add it again and you have the number you started with ($5 - 3 + 3 = 5$).
- This is how to make number sentences that are different but equal the same thing every time. If you know any subtraction number sentence, write it down. If you are trying to equal the same number every time (with other number sentences) both parts of the number sentence get higher by 1 but the number it equals stays the same.

  $7 - 1 = 6$   $7 - 1 = 6$
  $8 - 2 = 6$   $8 - 1 - 1 = 6$
  $9 - 3 = 6$   $9 - 1 - 1 - 1 = 6$

  If the beginning number goes higher, you have to take more (than the 1) away. We put 2 on [the beginning number] and took 2 off and we still had 6. Both sides go higher but the answer stays the same.

- When two numbers come together and one goes away, the one that stays is the answer. (When you add two numbers together.) You've plussed and then you've taken away. [Although this sounds a lot like the minus-plus trick, this was actually an attempt to explain the relationship between $18 + 7 = 25$, $7 + 18 = 25$, $25 - 7 = 18$, and $25 - 18 = 7$.]

Given that I hadn't known where we had been headed, I was pleased about where we ended up. We started out with a generalization that applied to one set of addition facts. This generalization expressed the relationship between numbers from 0 to 9 and numbers from 10 to 19, and it was an early attempt at noticing and articulating a rule. The fact that it applied to a small, finite set of numbers made it easier for them to grasp the idea of something "always" being true. This experience provided a scaffold as they applied this way of thinking to a different set of mathematical ideas. The rest of the generalizations we had worked on apply to an infinite class. For example, the "plus minus trick," which could be represented as $a - b + b = a$, applies to all numbers, though at this point, my students had in mind a much smaller set.

## FIRST AND SECOND GRADERS USE MODELS TO PROVE A GENERALIZATION

As I headed into the second year of the project, I recognized both the children and I were in a very different place than we had been the previous year. I knew I would be working with the same group of children because of the way in which we typically structured the mathematics teaching in the multiage classrooms. I felt very lucky that I could continue my explorations with these children and have a chance to see what kind of foundation we had laid during the previous year.

I began the year with a lot of research questions in mind. Did the work we had done in the previous year have a benefit that I would be able to identify? Would we be able to build on those ideas and take them even further? But my biggest question was: Would focusing on algebraic thinking help my students develop computation strategies that were more efficient?

As my students worked through the mathematics of the first half of the year, I noticed that these children were doing less counting and more numerical reasoning than my other classes had in the past. The idea of using a fact you know to help with one you don't know was present in much of our work. I pointed this idea out when I saw children using it as they shared computation strategies. I also used it as a cue for children who were having trouble getting started, by asking, "What fact do you know that could help you here?"

We also continued having conversations in class about what was happening when students used a fact they knew to figure out a related fact. For example, in January, we were having a discussion about doubles facts (such as 6 + 6) and facts we were calling "doubles + 1" (such as 6 + 7). The children were animated and excited as they figured out 6 + 7. At the time, I wrote, "They begged to share the answer. Whining, pleading to share their knowledge, these children were empowered by this." Various children shared how they used 6 + 6 or 7 + 7 to help with this process of deriving related facts. I was excited by their enthusiasm, but I knew there was a big mathematical idea here that I wanted to get to.

In planning this activity, I had recalled the work of the previous year. Children had been able to use this deriving facts strategy but had not been able to make a generalization about the mathematics that explained why it worked. It seemed like there was a connection missing. They could apply these ideas and even knew how they worked, but did not yet know that they would always work because it was a property of addition. I very much wanted to try to get to that next step with my students.

In our teacher seminar, we had been talking about models and representations, and the role that they play in proving a generalization. What does it mean to show that something is always true, and how is that different from just saying that it is true? I decided to introduce the use of cubes into our classroom discussion to see if the use of this model would help us with our thinking. I prepared one stack of cubes that had 6 dark blue cubes and another stack that had 6 light blue cubes and 1 orange cube. I wanted my students to show me with the cubes the idea that we had been working on—if you add one to one of the addends, it adds one to the total (i.e., if $a + b = c$ then $a + (b + 1) = c + 1$). Here is what happened:

> Teacher:    I'm wondering if there's someone who could use the cubes
> that are in my hand to explain how you use 6 + 6 to help
> you with 6 + 7. What I have is six light blue cubes, six dark
> blue cubes, and then I have an orange one. (Heather
> expressed interest and I called on her.)

Heather explained that 6 + 6 = 12 so 6 + 7 = 13, without even touching the cubes I had handed her. I asked if she could show us with the cubes. She held up the two blue stacks and said that she first did 6 + 6. Then she added the orange, and it was one more. Trevor restated her thinking: 6 + 6 is 12 and then she added one more on. So they had shown with the cubes what was happening, but this still felt like some "aha" or synthesis was missing. I asked why it worked that you can do that—say 6 + 6 is 12 *so* 6 + 7 is 13. (Episode, January 13, 2003)

In response to this question, I had wanted to hear a clearly articulated statement describing what the students had just shown me with the cubes. Though they moved the cubes around in a way that matched my understanding of what was happening, they were not able to get any closer to proving why this was always true.

Soon after, I had another opportunity to explore the use of models with my students. It was March, and we were returning to the question of whether the sum changed when you changed the order of addends in an addition equation. We had talked about breaking numbers apart into chunks and putting them back together in different ways and about whether counting a set of objects by numbers other than one affects the answer. These activities supported my students' developing understanding of numbers. It helped them to be able to move past counting to reasoning numerically when presented with an equation to solve.

We had been using a context of coupons and saving money in our recent work. I offered the following question to the children, "If you wanted to save 50¢, what are two coupons you could have? Let's think about coupons that come in chunks of fives and tens." We talked about one example that a student offered, and the children told me with certainty that the answer would not change if we changed the order in which we added the coupons. As we moved on to talking about proving that you can change the order of the addends and not affect the sum, I told the children that to prove something meant to convince someone. For example, suppose the principal came in and the class had to convince him that what they said about the order of addends was true. I told them they could use any tools they needed to help them explain, and I listed cubes, diagrams, and number lines as possible options. I told them they could use any numbers that they wanted to use to prove this statement, knowing that working with lower numbers often lets a child think more deeply about what is happening mathematically. I also wanted the class to have the experience of trying this out on a variety of numbers, helping them explore the idea of something being true for a larger set of numbers—perhaps all numbers. I suspected that having to convince someone by using a model would change the specificity and level of abstraction of the conversation. This next episode from the classroom discussion describes my students talking about what is essentially the commutative property of addition ($a + b = b + a$).

Teacher:    When you are doing your explaining, I want you to pretend that [the principal] is standing here, and he doesn't believe you. So you've got to be really careful to convince him. Don't assume anything. Say all the things you need to say and really convince him. Like, prove it. (I chose Kathleen to start us off because she is someone who often fits into the category of saying something is true but not being able to say why. But this time she had found a way to express why. She brought a clear diagram with her to our sharing circle.)

Kathleen:   If you take a 10 and a 20 and then you switched them around, it will just equal the same thing. You put the 10 in one place and then you put the twenty, and you put the 20 where the 10 was.

Teacher:    Can you show people your paper, Kathleen? You showed your thinking with a picture, right? So hold the picture up, and show us what you mean by, If you put the 10 where the 20 was. (It seemed to me that pushing for this kind of connection between the representation and what she was saying was key to their level of proof. I really wanted to push for specificity.) Can everyone see Kathleen's paper? So what do you mean, If you put the 10 where the 20 was?

Kathleen:   (She held up her paper and pointed as she talked.) Like right here, the 10 goes here and the 20 goes where the 10 was. (She is pointing to her diagram of 10 cubes in one section and 20 cubes in the other. Then she showed switching them, as if she were moving the cubes.)

Teacher:    And why is it that it doesn't matter, Kathleen?

Kathleen:   Because it's like, any way you switch it, it would just be the same thing. Like, any number you could probably do it with. You could probably do it with any number.

(As I listen to this again I am struck by the word Kathleen chose to use: "switch." Implied in "switch" seems to be a change in position but no change to the quantity or value. I am also struck that the children are so used to thinking about "will it always work" that I didn't have to ask that question this time.)

Teacher:    So are you saying that you think it would work with any number? Like, with any two numbers? You could switch them, and it won't change the answer?

Andrew:    Any, any number.

Teacher:   Andrew, you are agreeing with any, any number you can do that?

Kirsten:   Like 17 and 33.

Child:     And you don't just have to use two numbers.

Teacher:   (I decided to focus on the "any number" part of the discussion before we moved on to more than two numbers.) Like any two numbers, like 17 and 33?

All of a sudden three or four children were talking at once, telling us that it could be any numbers, and that it could be more than two numbers. Andrew even said that you could do a billion numbers. I tried to get all of the ideas heard.

Teacher:   So Kirsten said you're just switching to a different spot. Molly, what did you say?

Molly:     I said you didn't have to use only two numbers.

Teacher:   You didn't have to use only two numbers?

Kirsten:   I know—you could use 10 and 5 and 3.

Teacher:   Wow, you could use three numbers? Like 10 and 5 and 3?

Molly:     You could use eight numbers.

Kirsten:   It doesn't matter.

At this point there were children joining in and talking all at once, saying that you could use more than two numbers and in fact that it didn't matter how many numbers you used. Even a billion numbers! Something about this seems like another level of generalization to me. Not only does it work for any pair of numbers, but also the children have such a clear idea that the order doesn't matter that they know it will not matter regardless of how many numbers are involved. (Episode, March 3, 2003)

As the discussion progressed, the children broadened the conversation to talking about moving the numbers around and breaking the numbers apart into smaller chunks. The students stated that as long as you did not add any on or take any away, when you put them all back together, it would equal the same amount.

This discussion represents two shifts for my class. The first was that they were able to move past just saying that they knew something worked. Perhaps it was because I framed their explanations as needing to convince someone who did not believe them. Or perhaps it was because I had told them that they needed to show us with cubes or a picture. I believe the combination of needing to be specific enough to convince someone and having to create a model that represented what they were thinking is what enabled the students to reach this new level of understanding.

While I was exploring this generalization with my students, my teaching colleagues from the algebra project were also working on these ideas with their students. Our seminar continued to meet every month, sharing our ideas, working on the mathematics and reading cases. As I mentioned earlier in reference to TBI, we began to see ideas developing similarly from classroom to classroom and progressing from grade to grade. Children in each of our classrooms were considering whether the order of addends mattered in single digit addition (3 + 6 = 6 + 3), reconsidering this idea in reference to larger numbers, and then revisiting this idea again in thinking about three addends. Third graders were thinking about these same ideas in the context of a different operation—multiplication. I was excited to see the bigger picture becoming clearer for all of these students.

## ANOTHER LOOK AT ALGEBRAIC THINKING AND COMPUTATIONAL FLUENCY

I was still puzzling over the connection between the development of my students' algebraic thinking and the efficiency of their computation strategies. In fact, this question became a focus for the rest of the work I did in this project.

A colleague who teaches third grade and I spent a lot of time in the spring looking at the children's work and the cases that had been written for the project. We were looking for evidence that the increase in the students' ability to make generalizations about what was happening in an operation had an effect on their computation strategies. We found evidence in several pieces of writing, but I was not fully convinced by what we saw.

I decided that I wanted to structure a discussion that would specifically address this question with my students. During a previous discussion, the children had come up with this series of related number sentences: 99 + 1 = 100, 98 + 2 = 100, 97 +3 = 100, and 96 + 4 = 100. I thought that starting additional discussion in this familiar place would help us to move forward. I asked the children what might come next in the series to make sure that they understood what was happening, and then I asked if they could find the words to explain what was happening in that series of number sentences.

Molly:   Well, you are taking a number.

Teacher:   Which number are you taking, the 100?

Molly:   Yeah. And then you are adding zero. And then you take ninety (she stopped herself here and changed what she was saying before she finished saying 99), one number less than the100 and one number more than the zero.

As I heard what Molly was saying, I knew I had to make a decision about how to represent her thinking. I could write $100 + 0$ and $99 + 1$ since that was the context we had been thinking about and, in fact, the particular numbers that she was referring to. However, last year, I thought sometimes continuing to use the context we had been exploring made us more confused instead of making the ideas clearer. Now, I wondered if the children were ready to move to more of a generalization. Molly seemed to be trying to be more general when she stopped herself from saying 99 and instead said, "One number less than the 100." I decided to try to write what I had heard her say in the most general terms that still reflected her words.

Teacher:   So I am going to call this "any number" (and I wrote those words on the board). We have any number plus zero (I wrote "any number + 0") and then you are saying that we take "any number" and we subtract one from it (I wrote "any number − 1"), and then you add what to it?

Molly:   Well, you have a number, and then you take away one less. Like you have the 100, and you take away one less and it's 99; and then for the zero, you get that one.

Teacher:   So instead of the zero, you add one?

Scott:   Yea, you've got to have one more than the zero.

Molly and Scott were both talking me through this now, and they were carefully watching how I was recording what they said. The chart said "any number + 0" and under that it said "any number − 1." Scott told me that I needed to write a "+ 0 + 1" so that it read "any number − 1 + 0 + 1."

I was blown away by how quickly Scott and Molly moved to this level of abstraction. Had our earlier discussions helped us to get here? I restated what they had said, and Scott added, "We're taking away from that number and adding to the other number." I wanted to hear if the rest of the class understood what was being said, so I asked for someone to restate this idea. I was met with silence. This was really hard work. Scott said again that we were subtracting it from one number and adding it to the other. I thought that if the class saw a model of what was happening it would enable others in the class to verbalize what I thought that they understood.

As the discussion continued, Scott was even able to use a stick of ten to be a model of 100 instead of holding 100 cubes. He took one off of the stack of ten and moved it onto a second stack and continued to do this, showing one stack getting larger and the other getting smaller. As I had hoped, this model helped other children to enter the discussion. Heather was now ready to restate Scott's thinking. She started by saying, "He was saying if you take one off of the 100 and going down to 50, it's always…" and then she trailed off. After Scott's demonstration, several children were able to finish and restate what Heather was saying, and there was agreement that you were taking one from one pile and adding that one to the other pile. Carol clarified that the amount that it equals stays the same, but you keep adding more to the other side.

I was happy with what this discussion was telling me the children understood. They had learned something important about the operation of addition. In fact, when I asked if this would always work, with any numbers, one child said "Yes, because you're not adding any, and you're not taking any away."

I didn't want to leave the discussion at that point because I wanted to know if making this piece of mathematics explicit would enable more children to use computation strategies that are based on these ideas. I wanted to move from the general back to a specific example. With that in mind, I asked if they could use the idea they came up with to make the problem 39 + 14 into an easier problem.

Trevor:   Put the 10 from the 14 on the 39 and that equals 49.

Teacher:  So you're taking a big chunk. You're going to move ten over here and make that into a 49, plus what?

Trevor:   Four. 49 + 4.

Teacher:  Now wait. 49 + 4, that doesn't seem easy enough to me. Can you make it even easier? (Several children were bursting to tell me how to do this.) Trevor, can you make it even easier?

Trevor:   You take one off the 4 and plus the 3 that's left.

Teacher:  Okay, you take one off the 4, and what do you do with it?

Trevor:   Put it over there.

Teacher:  And what does this (pointing to the 49) turn into?

| | |
|---|---|
| Trevor: | 50. |
| Teacher: | So, 50 plus? |
| Trevor: | Three (confidently). |
| Teacher: | So, raise your hand if all of a sudden, 50 + 3 feels a lot easier than 39 + 14. Twinkle if you know 50 + 3. |

Most of the children knew this fact and were excited to let us know. I posed the question, "What did Trevor do to change 39 + 14 into an easier problem?"

| | |
|---|---|
| Corey: | He took a 10 off the 14 and made the 39 a 49. |
| Teacher: | So he took 10 away from here (pointing to the 14) and he added it to here (pointing to the 39). Is that kind of like what Molly said, "You can take one away from here as long as you add it to that side?" |
| Many children: | Yeah. |
| Corey: | Then he said, 49 + 4 = 50. |
| Andrew: | (Who was listening carefully) 49 + 4 does not equal 50. |
| Corey: | I mean… I forget. |
| Andrew: | It's plus one. |
| Carol: | He took one from the 4 and added it to the 49 and got 50. Then he had 3 left on that side and added it to the 50 and it's 53. |
| Teacher: | So here's my question. Is this something you can always do? Start with one problem and change it around to make an easier problem? |
| Many children at once: | Yes! |
| Molly: | Because you're still using the same amount, the same numbers. You're just changing them around. (Episode, March 24, 2003) |

At the end of this discussion, I was both satisfied and excited. My students had demonstrated their understanding of the generalization which they had been exploring [i.e. $a + b = (a - x) + (b + x)$], and they were able to apply it to a computation in order to find an efficient strategy. I was satisfied because their models showed what was happening mathematically in a way that convinced me that they knew it would work for any number. Scott's ability to hold a stack of 10 cubes and have it represent 100 cubes seemed to be akin to saying that those cubes could represent any whole number of cubes, and the class accepted this assumption. This, coupled with their need for me to transcribe their rule precisely so that it represented what they understood could happen with any number, satisfied any questions I had left about missing connections.

I was excited because not only could they prove what they had learned, but they could apply it. At the end of that year and in years since, I have seen that exploring algebraic thinking alone does not increase computational fluency. What has had an affect on the efficiency of my students' computation is asking them specifically how they can use their understanding to make their work easier. What has excited me most has been seeing these ideas come to fruition for not only my competent students, but for several children who previously had no access to these ideas.

## REFLECTING ON WHAT I HAVE LEARNED ABOUT THE MATHEMATICS AND ABOUT BEING A TEACHER-RESEARCHER

I finished that second year of the project having identified what I think was a missing step for my children: the use of models in proving a generalization about an operation. Looking at our work over the two years, I can see where this step fits into the development of children's thinking in this area. Children need to encounter the notion that something can be true for a whole set of numbers or for an operation. They need to understand what is happening in an operation to be able to think about what is true for that operation. And finally, they need to be able to move beyond showing that something is true by using as many examples as they can generate to being able to somehow prove it is always true. I think that this final step of saying "always" means being able to show with a model what is happening mathematically.

Since the completion of the project, I have had the opportunity to see the influence that the work in my classroom has had on the larger mathematics education community. I attended presentations by the researchers who made up the staff of our project (Schifter, 2002; Russell, Schifter, & Bastable, 2003) and listened with interest to the discussions that occurred at those presentations. I read the research article (Monk, in press) that will accompany episodes from the project in professional development materials. I have heard feedback from teachers who have experienced these professional development materials and have seen video of my work with the children (Schifter, Bastable, & Russell, in press).

These experiences have helped me to see how my work as a classroom teacher can both support and be supported by the work of outside researchers. When teachers and researchers work together as a team, we can all learn more about the mathematics and about how children make sense of it. As a teacher, I can then use what we learn to figure out how to better teach my students. Because I am a classroom teacher, my focus remains first and foremost on my students, while my research partners' focus can be to bring this work into the larger research community and perhaps explore it further. Each member of this research partnership has a unique perspective and a unique role, but together we can create a mutually beneficial team that serves both an individual classroom and the larger community of mathematics educators.

## ACKNOWLEDGMENT

The work described in this chapter was supported in part by the National Science Foundation under Grant No. ESI-0095450 awarded to Susan Jo Russell at TERC and Grant No. ESI-0242609 awarded to Deborah Schifter at the Education Development Center. Any opinions, findings, conclusions, or recommendations expressed in this chapter are those of the author and do not necessarily reflect the views of the National Science Foundation.

## REFERENCES

Ball, D. L., & Bass, H. (2003). Making mathematics reasonable in school. In J. Kilpatrick, W. G. Martin, & D. Schifter (Eds.), *A research companion to Principles and Standards for School Mathematics* (pp. 27-44). Reston, VA: National Council of Teachers of Mathematics.

Bastable, V. & Schifter, D. (in press). Classroom stories: Examples of elementary students engaged in early algebra. In J. Kaput, M. Blanton, & D. Carraher (Eds.), *Employing children's natural powers to build algebraic reasoning in the context of elementary mathematics.* Mahwah, NJ: Erlbaum.

Carpenter, T. P., & Levi, L. (1999, April). *Developing conceptions of algebraic reasoning in the primary grades.* Paper presented at the annual meeting of the American Educational Research Association, Montreal, Canada.

Hammer, D., & Schifter, D. (2001). Practices of inquiry in teaching and research. *Cognition and Instruction, 19*(4), 441-478.

Monk, G. S. (in press). The world of arithmetic from different points of view. In D. Schifter, V. Bastable, & S. J. Russell, *Reasoning algebraically about operations: Casebook.* Parsippany, NJ: Dale Seymour.

Russell, S. J. (1999). Mathematical reasoning in the elementary grades. In L. Stiff & F. Curcio (Eds.), *Developing mathematical reasoning in grades K-12* [NCTM Yearbook] (pp. 1-12). Reston, VA: National Council of Teachers of Mathematics.

Russell, S. J., Schifter, D., & Bastable, V. (2003, April). *The role of representation in algebraic reasoning in the elementary grades.* Paper presented at the annual meeting of the National Council of Supervisors of Mathematics, San Antonio, TX.

Schifter, D. (1998). Learning mathematics for teaching: From the teachers' seminar to the classroom. *Journal for Mathematics Teacher Education, 1*(1), 55-87.

Schifter, D. (1999a). Learning geometry: Some insights drawn from teacher writing. *Teaching Children Mathematics, 5*(6), 360-365.

Schifter, D. (1999b). Reasoning about operations: Early algebraic thinking in grades K-6. In L. V. Stiff & F. R. Curcio (Eds.), *Developing mathematical reasoning in grades K-12* [NCTM Yearbook] (pp. 62-81). Reston, VA: National Council of Teachers of Mathematics.

Schifter, D. (2002). *Algebra in the elementary classroom.* Paper presented at the Investigations Users' Conference, Providence, RI and to the CGI Biennial Conference, St. Paul, MN.

Schifter, D. (Ed.) (1996a). *What's happening in math class? Volume 1: Envisioning new practices through teacher narratives.* New York: Teachers College Press.

Schifter, D. (Ed.) (1996b). *What's happening in math class? Volume 2: Reconstructing professional identities.* New York: Teachers College Press.

Schifter, D., Bastable, V., & Russell, S. J. (1999a). *Developing mathematical ideas: Building a system of tens* [Casebooks, Facilitators Guides, and Videotapes]. Parsippany, NJ: Dale Seymour.

Schifter, D., Bastable, V., & Russell, S. J. (1999b). *Developing mathematical ideas: Making meaning for operations* [Casebooks, Facilitators Guides, and Videotapes]. Parsippany, NJ: Dale Seymour.

Schifter, D., Bastable, V., & Russell, S. J. (in press). *Developing mathematical ideas: Reasoning algebraically about operations* [Casebooks, Facilitators Guides, and Videotapes]. Newton, MA: Education Development Center.

Schifter, D., Russell, S. J., & Bastable, V. (1999). Teaching to the big ideas. In M. Z. Solomon (Ed.), *The diagnostic teacher: Constructing new approaches to professional development,* (pp. 22-47). New York: Teachers College Press.

Schifter, D., & Szymaszek, J. (2003). Structuring a rectangle: Teachers write to learn about their students' thinking. In D. Clements & G. Bright (Eds.), *Learning and teaching measurement* [NCTM Yearbook] (pp. 143-156). Reston, VA: National Council of Teachers of Mathematics.

CHAPTER 5

# A LOOK AT A CHILD'S UNDERSTANDING OF MATHEMATICAL IDEAS THROUGH HIS REPRESENTATIONS

**Ana Vaisenstein**
*Boston Public Schools, Boston, MA*

It was Spring. Some students in my second-grade class were not making the progress I expected them to make. My goal was for all of my students to become efficient problem solvers and to be able to operate by decomposing and composing numbers into friendlier parts instead of counting up or down by ones. I wondered why some students were able to use an efficient strategy in some situations but would revert to less efficient ones in other cases. As I began to explore this question I noticed that, for some reason, I had paid more attention to children's talk than to their written work. During the normal course of reviewing student work, I often checked each day's work without connecting it with past work or with my observations of them in class. I had a fragmented understanding of my students' understanding and was missing an important aspect of their sense-making process. I

*Teachers Engaged in Research*
*Inquiry Into Mathematics Classrooms, Grades Pre-K–2*, pages 95–108

decided to improve my ability to analyze how my students communicated their mathematical ideas through written representations and how these representations connected with their work in general. I thought that by having a more comprehensive view of children's work, I would be able to understand why they were not making the progress I was expecting.

As I began to look at student work more closely, I found it was relatively straightforward to develop a better understanding of the work of students who consistently showed clear and efficient procedures and those who made similar mistakes over and over again. For these students, I was able to see how they were or were not making sense of the mathematical ideas. The work that puzzled me the most came from those students who used an efficient strategy for solving a problem one day and showed a less efficient strategy for solving a similar problem the following day. These *discontinuities*, as I will call them, disoriented me. I wondered what these students really understood and where their knowledge might have broken down.

I want all of my students to understand mathematics and to become efficient and flexible problem solvers. However, I am aware that the process of reaching that goal is not a linear one. Sometimes I think I am offering them the experiences they need to reach that goal, but the discontinuities in their work remind me of the complexity of the teaching and learning process. In their book *Making Sense: Teaching and Learning Mathematics with Understanding*, Hiebert et al. stated that "Understanding is built through establishing relationships. Three kinds of relationships are emphasized: relationships between what one already knows and new information, relationships among different ways of representing information, and relationships among different methods of solving similar problems" (1999, pp. 101). I began to wonder about the kinds of relationships my students were making or not making as demonstrated in their written work.

As I looked at my students' work more carefully, I began to realize that analyzing one sheet from each child at the end of the day was not enough to have a clear sense of how that student was making sense of the ideas we were working on over time. I thought that if I looked at a collection of each student's work I would probably be able to identify the discontinuities in their understandings and uncover any missing generalizations of important ideas. This more complete knowledge of my students' thinking would, in turn, inform my teaching.

The words in Hiebert et al. (1999) about relationships resonated with me as I embarked on this investigation. It became clear to me that if I wanted to make sense of my students' understandings, I needed to clarify the types of connections between ideas and representations I wanted my students to make. As their teacher, I needed to establish relationships between my observations of students and what their work revealed, as well as between their various pieces of work and the different ways they were solving problems. I hoped that systematically investigating my students' work would help me establish these relationships. In this chapter I will share what I learned doing this investigation and the implications of this experience for my teaching practice.

## SETTING AND METHODS

I spent a year on sabbatical at the Educational Research Collaborative (ERC) at TERC, a nonprofit organization dedicated to the research, development, and implementation of mathematics and science education. During this sabbatical, I taught at the same two-way bilingual[1] public school in Boston, MA where I had been a teacher for the preceding 5 years. I used the district's $2^{nd}$ grade math curriculum *Investigations in Number, Data, and Space*® with a group of six second-grade students who had been in my class during first grade the previous year and who were below grade level at the end of first grade. I was interested in providing the additional support they needed to meet end-of-second-grade benchmarks while reflecting on my work as a teacher and on my students' mathematical understandings. I met with these six children three times a week during their math block. The other two days these children worked in their class, so I had to keep up with the pace of the whole class for my students to participate successfully.

Eighty percent of the population of the school participated in the free/reduced lunch program, and the students in my small group were representative of this population. Four of the children were boys and 2 were girls. Two of the children in this group were on Individual Educational Plans (IEP) and received services in the resource room. One student was a native English speaker and the other five students were bilingual Spanish/English with various levels of English proficiency. Since I am a native Spanish speaker, the children and I used Spanish in class whenever it was needed to clarify ideas. The six children were below grade level in math at the end of first grade, but all said they loved math and were very enthusiastic about their work. Since we had worked together the year before, they knew they had to think carefully, explain their ideas to each other, prove that their answers made sense, and question each other when things were not clear.

I documented my work very carefully. I kept a journal of every session, which I wrote right after it happened. I audio recorded and transcribed some sessions and videotaped a few others. Judy Storeygard, a researcher at TERC, observed some sessions and took detailed notes of the dialogues, which she then shared with me. I collected all of the children's work and kept copies of all the end-of-unit, midterm, and end-of-year assessments the district developed for second grade. I wanted to have as much detailed information as possible. I knew that the story of my students' understanding and my own was going to unfold as we worked together, and I would need to go back to our work often. My goal during my sabbatical was to examine how the students developed numerical reasoning. It was during the early spring, when I saw that my students' reasoning had not progressed as quickly as I had hoped, that I began to look at their work in a more systematic and longitudinal way.

Because I was interested in gaining greater understanding of my students' work, I decided to approach the analysis of their work with no preconceptions. I would not concentrate on whether or not they used an efficient strategy, but on what their work showed they actually did. I remembered work I had done as a student of Eleanor Duckworth (1987), during which she engaged us in looking at something (a poem, mirrors, a painting, the moon) by saying what we noticed about it. Usually these descriptions led us into considering important ideas. I have also participated in some of the "looking at student work" sessions with Steve Seidel, Director of Harvard Project Zero, in which we teachers spent a good amount of time describing what we saw in students' work—attempting to put all judgments aside. I have found those practices to be useful, so I decided to use them in looking at my students' work.

## MANUEL'S WORK

In this chapter I will focus on the work of Manuel (all students' names are pseudonyms). I selected this student because the discontinuities in his written work pushed me to think more deeply about the mathematical understanding children communicate in writing and to reassess the attention I was giving to students' written work.

Manuel started at the school in first grade. He was always ready to help in the classroom and adapted quickly to the new setting. In mathematics, he made slow but steady progress. At the end of first grade he was able to count to 30, had difficulties remembering the number sequence to 100, and solved addition and subtraction problems using modeling and counting strategies. He often rushed through his work and made mistakes. Consequently, part of my job was to help him slow down, to think problems through, and to double check his answers. Reading and writing were very laborious for Manuel, so he participated in Reading Recovery during the spring. His Reading Recovery teacher and I determined he would need additional support in second grade to continue his progress, and we referred him for a CORE evaluation. At the beginning of second grade, Manuel went to the resource room twice a week to get help with his reading. Although he had made good progress in mathematics, I knew he would greatly benefit from having additional support in this area to meet end-of-second-grade expectations. In the Boston Public School system, we expect second graders to have strong counting strategies and to operate with numbers up to 100 accurately and efficiently. Manuel needed the extra support to become an efficient problem solver. When my sabbatical was approved, I decided to offer that additional support to Manuel and other students who could clearly benefit from more focused work in a small group setting.

In the next two sections I will share three consecutive pieces of Manuel's work as he solved similar problems using two versions of a 100 chart—what I have called the *fast chart* and the *blank chart*. The discontinuities in his answers pushed me to think further about his understanding of the decimal number system and the 100 chart. I will describe and compare his work as I systematically examine and analyze what he understood and what he missed. Then I will elaborate on what I could have done to help him make some additional connections.

## THE FAST CHART

The children were asked to solve the following story problem: *Alicia and Tom were playing Get to 100. They were on number 65. How many more numbers do they need to move to get to 100?* Over the previous weeks, the children had been using the 100 chart and sticks of 10 cubes to solve this type of problem. Manuel decided to work with the sticks of 10. He built 65 using six sticks of 10 cubes and 5 loose cubes. He also collected 40 more cubes, which he built as two towers of 20 cubes each. When he finished I asked:

Ana: So, how many more numbers do Alicia and Tom need to move to Get to 100?

Manuel: 40.

Ana: Manuel, how many cubes do you have altogether if they have 40 and 65?

Manuel: 100… No… [Excited, as he pushed all the cubes together] 105! I messed up! [As he removed 5 cubes]

Ana: So, how many more numbers do Alicia and Tom need to move to Get to 100?

Manuel knew he needed to have 100 cubes at the end of the story; he knew what the whole was. However, I wasn't sure he knew which parts made the whole. I moved on to observe other children and hoped he would continue thinking about the problem. I had asked children to show in writing how they had solved the problem. It was sharing time and Manuel had not worked on his written representation. I called on other children first to allow him to listen to his peers and, in the process, think about a way to represent his work. When it was his turn, he shared his strategy as he simultaneously worked on a representation. The other children listened and contributed.

Ana: So, Manuel, how can you show what you did to solve the problem?

Manuel: I can draw a big one. [He referred to a 100 chart, but he used a vertical-sticks-of-cubes orientation rather than a horizontal-rows-on-the-100s-chart orientation.]

Ana: Ok, but I don't want you to draw every single cube; it will take a long time. Can you think of a way of doing that?

Yanira: He can draw the sticks.

Ana: That's an idea.

Manuel: No, I don't want to do that. I know, I know. I can do it a fast way. [He grabbed a big piece of chart paper and made a big square. He drew 9 vertical lines and 9 horizontal lines very fast. He counted to make sure he had 10 columns and 10 rows.] There! [He certainly surprised me with his speed and clarity of how 100 should look.]

Ana: So how many cubes did you have at the beginning?

Manuel: 65 cubes.

Ana: How can you show that on your chart?

Manuel: Like this. [As he surrounded the area with red marker]

Yanira: That's confusing.

Manuel: [He crossed out 6 groups of 10 and colored in red the other 5 squares to make 65.]

Yanira: It is so messy! I can't understand it.

Denzel: Don't you understand this is 65? [Points to shaded area]

Ana: So, how can you show her that is 65?

Manuel: There! You can see that is 65. [As he wrote 65 on top of the chart above the crossed-out area]

Ricardo: I have an idea; you can use another color to show the other group.

Ana: [I handed Manuel a blue marker, and he circled every square that belonged to the other part. He wrote 5 and 30 above the chart and then wrote 35.]

Manuel:    All reds are 65, the blues are 35, and the reds and
           blues together make 100. [He proceeded to write on the
           paper 100–65=35 and 65+35=100.] (See Figure 5.1.)

Problem:   Alicia and Tom were playing Get to 100. They were on
           number 65. How many more numbers do they need
           to move to get to 100?

Manuel's Answer:    35

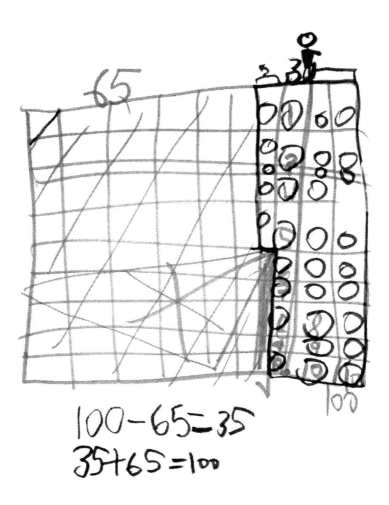

Figure 5.1.    Manuel's fast chart.

I noticed that Manuel's knowledge of how 100 should look with the sticks of 10 helped him find the answer to the problem and identify his mistake. As he worked on his representation, he rejected Yanira's suggestion of drawing the stick and instead picked the 100 chart as the model for his representation. In doing so, he made an important connection: He understood some similarities between the 10 sticks of 10 and the 100 chart he drew. He linked the two representations (sticks of 10 and the 100s chart) that had been available for the students all along, and he knew that both representations communicated 100. This connection indicates he had established "relationships among different ways of representing information" (Hiebert et al., p. 101), which is an important step in the process of understanding an idea.

Manuel seemed to have a better understanding of the problem when he worked from the whole, because he became more aware of the relationship between the parts and the whole. He might have thought: "If Alicia and Tom need to get to 100 and 65 is part of 100, then the rest is what they need in order to get to 100." In his representation, he began with the chart as a whole and then moved on to distinguish its parts, thus appearing to reproduce his actions and understanding. The equation $100 - 65 = 35$ supported that idea. Then to prove it, Manuel wrote $65 + 35 = 100$. He decomposed 100 into two parts by taking 65 away from 100, and he knew that in order to recompose the whole, he had to put together both parts.

During the previous months, we had worked on place value using sticks of ten, and we had played games to collect 100 cubes using those same sticks. In the process we looked at ways to compose and decompose numbers. Manuel seemed to have built on those experiences to solve this particular problem.

I found it fascinating to watch Manuel make the connection between the sticks of 10 and the *fast chart* to represent his understanding of the whole-to-parts relationship in this problem and articulate it clearly orally and in writing (through pictures and numbers). I thought that if he could continue working with this idea, he could become very efficient in solving problems. I decided to have blank 100 charts available in class for the children (particularly Manuel) to use to solve problems. Instead of having to draw the chart himself, he could have it available to use and maybe operate with it directly instead of using the sticks of 10 cubes and then translating those actions into the chart.

## THE BLANK CHART

The following day I showed all children the blank chart and explained they could use it whenever it would be helpful to them. Manuel was not excited about this offer. He wanted to keep drawing the chart himself and whenever possible, to draw it on a big piece of paper. I said that I wanted him to work on a regular piece of paper to get used to the regular format. I added that he could use the charts I brought. He was reluctant to do so, and after going back and forth between drawing it himself on a regular size paper and using the blank chart, he decided to stick to the blank chart to solve the day's problems. Contrary to my speculations, Manuel had not made all the connections I thought he had. When he began to work with the blank chart, he was confused. At first I couldn't understand what happened: What was different about this chart compared to the one he drew the day before? I decided to collect several samples of his work in which he used the chart to analyze what was different and what was the same for each case. For presentation here, I have selected two pieces of his work corresponding to two consecutive days. Manuel worked on Problem A first (see Figure 5.2) and on Problem B second (see Figure 5.3).

**Blank 100 Chart**

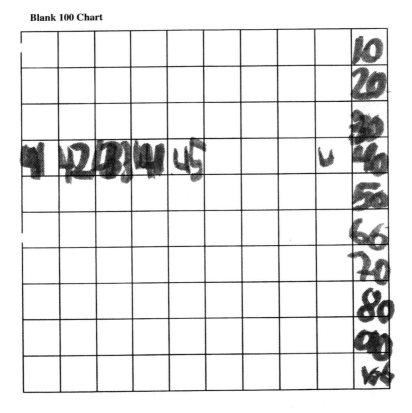

Figure 5.2.    Manuel's Use of the Blank Chart for Problem A.

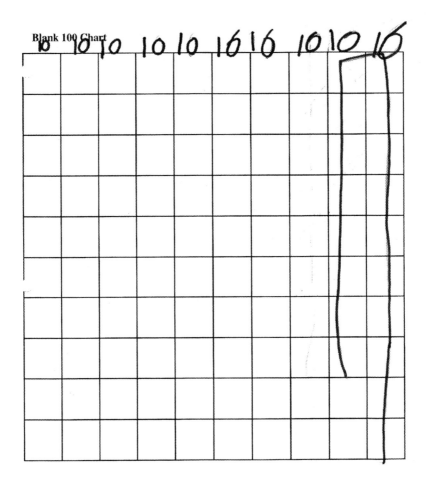

Figure 5.3.    Manuel's Use of the Blank Chart for Problem B.

*Problem A: Kira and Jake were playing Get to 100. They got to number 45.
How far are they from 100?*

Manuel's Answer: 65

*Problem B: There were 100 jellybeans in a bowl. Jeffrey took a handful of jelly-
beans and now there are 82 jellybeans left in the bowl. How many jellybeans
did Jeffrey take?*

Manuel's Answer: 18

When solving Problem A, Manuel had a very hard time figuring out the chart. First he wrote the numbers in the tens column and looked for 45. Instead of moving forward from 40 to the 45, he moved backward without realizing he was on 35 and not on 45. From there he began to count by ones to 100 and counted 65 spaces, but apparently didn't have time to write it down, so his work looks incomplete. During sharing time, his classmates noticed his mistake and tried to help him understand what was wrong. He kept insisting that the number 45 was in the right place, so I decided to bring the sticks of ten to place them on the chart. He had made an important connection between the two representations the day before, so I thought he needed to remind himself of what he had done before. I took 4 sticks of 10 and placed them on the first four rows to support his work and to illustrate what the other children had said to him. Then I took 5 more cubes and asked Manuel to place them on the chart to show the place of the 45. He repeated his mistake and placed them on top of the fourth row. The other children got all excited and engaged in a heated discussion to convince Manuel that he was showing 35, not 45. At first Manuel kept insisting that he was right, but when he observed Ricardo count on by ones from 40, he said he understood his mistake and was very disappointed for not having it right from the beginning. I wanted to make sure what he understood and asked him to rephrase it. He showed us how to count on from 40 to get to 45; not backward as he had done. It was time to go home, and once again he couldn't finish his work.

The following day, Manuel worked on Problem B on the blank 100 chart. This time he made a 100 chart the way he had drawn one previously. Each column represented 10, so he counted by tens to get to 80, counted the two blank squares at the bottom of the 9th column by ones to get to 82, and with a pencil crossed out what was left over and answered 18. He was still moody. I wondered if this resulted from the mistake he had made the day before or because this was not *his* chart, but one I had given him. Either way, he did not put as much care into his work as he had when he created his own chart. There was little evidence on the paper and the equations were missing as well.

So how do these two pieces of work compare to each other? Manuel accepted that he could use the 100 chart to solve both problems. Based on his work from the previous day, he might have thought that if he knew the whole and one part he could determine the other part and find the answer. So what was different in each problem? First, in Problem A he couldn't locate the number 45 successfully on the chart, whereas in Problem B he could locate the number 82 with no difficulties. Second, in Problem A he oriented the chart horizontally and in Problem B he oriented it vertically. Third, to find the answer in Problem A, he counted by ones from 45 to get to 100, and in Problem B, he counted one group of ten and 8 more, which makes 18. One could say that 18 is much less than 55 or 65, as he first thought, and therefore easier to count by tens. However, by taking a look at how he used the charts, I would argue that the quantity didn't necessarily make a difference. It was the way in which he oriented the charts that mattered. In Problem A, Manuel used the blank chart as a conventional 100 chart, in which numbers go one by one in a horizontal sequence. Although he wrote the sequence of 10 in the tens column, he didn't use that information to count by tens to figure out the missing part. The tens sequence seemed to be there, not so much as an understanding of the meaning of ten, but as an observed and memorized sequence. In Problem B, Manuel used the chart to replicate sticks of ten, and since he was accustomed to counting those as 10s, he labeled each column with the number 10 at the top rather than labeling the columns 10, 20, 30, 40, etc. as he had done on the horizontal 100 chart. Did Manuel understand that 10 squares, whether oriented horizontally or vertically, are always 10 and can be counted equally? Had he made any connections between the 10s he wrote on top of each column on Problem B and the 10 sequence he wrote on the right-hand side of the chart when solving Problem A? My conclusion is that he had not connected these two representations. He had not thought about these similarities and differences on his own, so he treated them as two distinct models. This work revealed to me some discontinuities in Manuel's understanding of representations for 10s.

## ANALYZING THE FAST CHART AND THE BLANK CHART

When I analyzed how these two pieces of work compared to the chart he quickly created the first day, I realized that although I thought the blank 100 chart I offered and the chart Manuel drew were the same, Manuel did not seem to think so. I was imposing a representation he had not had the chance to analyze and understand. I should have double-checked my assumptions with him and talked about how his chart and mine were the same or different before asking him to work with it. Although Manuel used the blank chart successfully the following day, I kept thinking about how the difference in orientation affected his capacity to solve the problem. What relationships did he need to notice between these two ways of using the 100 chart?

Whether in its horizontal or vertical orientation, the 100 chart offers the possibility to work in groups of ten. Yet, Manuel had not established that flexible relationship. Although I had thought that he was developing a good grasp of working with tens and had made an important relationship between the sticks of ten and the 100 chart, his work showed that his understanding was bound to a specific use of the model. He needed to make further connections between both ways of using the 100 chart to develop a more flexible understanding of representations of tens. What looked obvious to me was not obvious for Manuel, and as his teacher I should have been more attentive to what might have been causing his difficulties. I could have brought those confusions/hesitations to the forefront and engaged all students in considering them. I could have asked the other children how Manuel's fast chart was the same or different from the one I presented, or I could have asked them whether we could use the chart horizontally or vertically if we wanted to count by tens. This type of discussion may have benefited Manuel and his classmates if they all had engaged in thinking further about these important ideas. After the discussion, children could have used the charts in both orientations to solve each problem and to compare the similarities and differences.

## CONCLUSIONS

Why should I put so much effort into analyzing Manuel's work? Manuel was capable of solving Problem B and others like it relatively efficiently after these experiences. However, I think that analysis of student work at this level of detail can reveal important discontinuities in our students' understandings, and unless we address them, these discontinuities can show up again in other situations. Some students make connections easily by themselves, while other students rely more on their teachers or peers to engage them in thinking about those ideas. As a teacher, I take responsibility for knowing where my students' knowledge breaks down and for bringing those ideas to the forefront of classroom discourse. I need to help my students establish the relationships they are missing if I want all my students to learn with understanding and to develop flexibility in problem solving. Through this investigation, I found that analyzing all of the children's work, both written and oral, is an important part of unveiling children's sense-making process.

Certainly, learning with understanding is more complex than can be shown with one or two pieces of work. However, the complexity of students' thinking can be captured through their words, actions, and representations. I have come to accept that whether their work shows what I expect or not, this evidence tells me something important about what they understand. I have realized that carefully examining an individual student's work longitudinally can add to what I learn from observations during classroom episodes and from examining isolated pieces of work in classroom batches. This more complete view of students' understandings can support better instructional decisions. I regret not having understood Manuel's understandings more clearly as I worked with him. Yet, this deep analysis has allowed me to make better sense of his work and it has affected the way I look at all of my students' work.

At a time when teachers are under much pressure to have all students perform at or above the proficient level, we can easily fall into the trap of thinking that our students understand an idea when they solve one problem correctly. As I have attempted to show in this chapter, understanding encompasses much more than that. A detailed look at students' words, actions, and representations can be time consuming, yet if we are serious about all students achieving proficiency, we may need to more carefully monitor their understanding as it develops.

## NOTE

1.    In a two-way bilingual model, children learn two languages simultaneously; in this case, Spanish and English. Children continue learning content in their home language while they also learn a second language.

## REFERENCES

Duckworth, E. (1987). *"The having of wonderful ideas" and other essays on teaching and learning.* New York and London: Teachers College Press.

Hiebert, J., Carpenter, T. P., Fennema, E., Fuson, K. C., Wearne, D., Murray, H., Olivier, A., & Human, P. (1997). *Making sense: Teaching and learning mathematics with understanding.* Portsmouth, N.H: Heinemann.

Russell, S. J., & Tierney, C. C. (1998). *Investigations in number, data, and space.*® White Plains, NY: Dale Seymour.

Seidel, S. *Project zero.* See project website at http://www.pz.harvard.edu

CHAPTER 6

---

# USING CHILDREN'S UNDERSTANDINGS OF LINEAR MEASUREMENT TO INFORM INSTRUCTION

**Linda Jaslow**
*Northwest Arkansas Education Service Cooperative*

**Tanya Vik**
*Professional Development Collaborative*
*Center for Research in Mathematics and Science Education*

---

Linear measurement is a topic often left to the end of the school year and only addressed in time to prepare for standardized tests, and yet "measurement is one of the most widely used applications of mathematics" (NCTM, 2000). Repeatedly, research cites the complexity of measurement and children's lack of understanding (Stephen and Clements, 2003; Grant and Kline, 2003). In many classrooms, children are taught how to use a measuring tool, but are not given the opportunity to explore the constructs behind the tools they are using (Nitabach & Lehrer, 1996; Lehrer, Jenkins, & Osana, 1998; Lehrer, Jacobson, Kemeny, & Strom, 1999; Grant & Kline, 2003). If we agree that children should "understand the units, systems, and

*Teachers Engaged in Research*
*Inquiry Into Mathematics Classrooms, Grades Pre-K–2*, pages 109–134

processes of measurement" (NCTM, 2000), then we need to rethink our own understanding of measurement and the types of experiences teachers provide children.

What do children understand and not understand about measurement? How do we begin to make sense of children's thinking about linear measurement? When children are taught to read a ruler, we make a great number of assumptions about what they understand. Research shows that children don't have conceptual understanding about the units or partitions marked on a ruler. Often they just read the numbers off a ruler and identify partitions without considering the meaning behind them, resulting in a number of common errors (Nitabach & Lehrer, 1996; Lehrer, Jenkins, & Osana, 1998; Lehrer, Jacobson, Kemeny, & Strom, 1999; Stephen & Clements, 2003; Jaslow, 2005). The development of a measuring tool (ruler) by students can reveal a great deal.

For example, we gave Laurie, a first grader in our study, a non-standard unit and asked her to create a measuring tool that illustrated and labeled both half and whole units. Examine her ruler (see Figure 6.1). What did she do? What does that reveal about what she understands about linear measurement? What does she not understand? What big ideas are embedded in the development of a ruler?

These are important questions to answer if we want to design instruction based on our understanding of children's thinking. In this chapter, we have two goals: (1) to outline the big ideas of linear measurement, and (2) to illustrate how we analyzed what our students learned about linear measurement and used that analysis to inform instruction.

## THEORETICAL BACKGROUND

A number of big ideas are critical to the understanding of linear measurement (Nitabach & Lehrer, 1996; Lehrer, Jenkins, & Osana, 1998; Lehrer,

Using the units the same size as the one below, make a ruler. Label it to show whole units and half units.

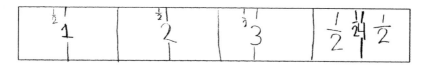

Figure 6.1.   Laurie's Ruler.

Jacobson, Kemeny, & Strom, 1999; Lehrer, 2003; Stephen & Clements 2003). For our classroom investigation, we chose to focus on the features of units, accumulation through iteration, partitioning of units, and zero point, because these ideas lay the foundation for understanding and applying the systems and processes of linear measurement.

*Units.* Understanding units consists of two important ideas: use of identical units and the role of standard units.

- *Identical units.* To communicate the length of an object or a distance measured, the units used must be identical. In the example in Figure 6.2, a car is measured in two ways. In the first measurement, the car is 4 units long. The units used are all identical. In the second measurement, the car is 3 units long, but the units are not identical.
- *Standard units.* Using non-standard units of measure to make sense of measurement is critical, but students also need to understand the limitations of using non-standard units of measure and the need for standard units (e.g., inches, feet, centimeters, etc.).

*Accumulation through iteration.* Length can be accumulated through a process of iterating (reusing) units. For accurate measurement, units must be iterated without leaving gaps. If you have only one or a few units, you can mark the measurement and reuse (iterate) the units across the distance or object being measured without leaving any gaps, as pictured in the first measurement of the car shown in Figure 6.3. The second measurement incorrectly iterates by leaving gaps while measuring.

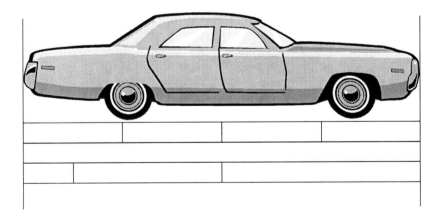

Figure 6.2.    Identical Units?

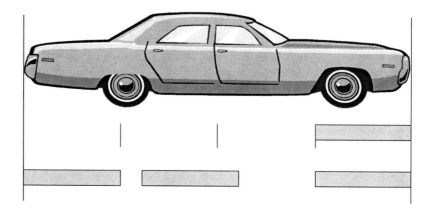

Figure 6.3.   Iteration.

*Partitioning.* Lengths or distances often cannot be measured with whole units alone. Units need to be partitioned (divided) into fractional parts in order to get an accurate measure. For the example, the appropriate measure of the length of the car in Figure 6.4 is 3½ units.

*Zero point.* The measure of length is a distance from a point of origin to an end point. An object is not 1 unit long until you have moved from a

Figure 6.4.   Partitioning Remaining Units.

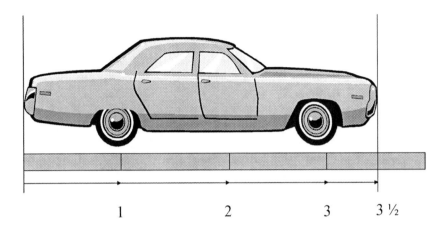

Figure 6.5.   Starting and Ending Points.

zero point (point of origin) to the end of 1 unit. Accumulation of length through iteration proceeds from the starting point to the ending point (see Figure 6.5). While using a length measurement tool with a specified scale (e.g., a ruler), we may begin a measurement at a starting point other than the zero point on the scale.

While these explanations of the big ideas may seem straight forward, we learned that it is extremely complex for teachers to assess students' knowledge of these concepts and to develop instruction to facilitate their understanding of the many layers underlying each concept.

## GETTING STARTED

The second author, Tanya Vik, is a 1st/2nd grade teacher at a high socio-economic status school in Southern California with 82% Caucasian and 18% minority students. She has taught in the primary grades (1–3) for 10 years. The first author, Linda Jaslow, has taught elementary grades (K–6) for 15 years and at the time of this study was adjunct faculty at a nearby university.

For this teaching/research project, we worked on measurement with students two or three days a week over a period of six weeks. Most of the class sessions were about an hour long. We transcribed all of the classroom conversations, documented students' actions, collected all student work, and documented our daily debriefing conversations. To make sense of what students had learned and what they had demonstrated about their understanding of linear measurement, we either debriefed after class or discussed via e-mail what had happened in class. We documented these debriefing conversations and kept a copy of all email discussions. We used these daily analyses of students' progress and challenges to focus on the big ideas of measurement we wanted to develop and to design additional learning experiences.

We had a rough outline of a trajectory for developing students' understanding of linear measurement. As we posed problems, we analyzed and interpreted the students' actions and conversations against that trajectory and tried to make sense of what these meant for our next steps. There were times that students' unanticipated paths forced us to change our line of questioning or to modify the classroom experiences to scaffold or challenge students' thinking.

Our project is based on prior research in linear measurement conducted in elementary classrooms by Dr. Richard Lehrer from Vanderbilt University and what we knew about the big ideas we identified earlier in this chapter. We created the following research question to guide our study: *"How do you get primary children to make sense of identical units, iteration, and partitioning with an eye towards building understanding of a zero point?"*

Our instructional goal was to have children learn to measure and use a ruler with understanding. In order to accomplish this goal, we needed to provide the students with experiences that would result in the guided re-invention of measuring tools for length (a ruler). In designing our learning activities, we built on a series of activities previously tested in other classrooms (Lehrer & Curtis, 2003; Jaslow, in press).

The previously cited research indicates that many of the initial understandings about linear measurement are developed through counting non-standard units. By counting units, children make sense of identical units, accumulation through iteration, and the need for partitioning. Only after they gain these understandings can children learn to view linear measurement as a distance (in units) from a starting point to an ending point. While the process of learning these big ideas of linear measurement is not necessarily sequential, there are some constructs students must understand first. For example, children cannot make sense of the iteration concept if they do not understand the importance of using identical units.

Consequently, we have divided this chapter into two sections to help magnify these subtle differences and how they emerged in our study. The first section focuses on "Counting Units as Measuring." It illustrates the initial classroom experiences and conversations we used in developing understanding of units, the need for partial units, and beginning ideas about zero point (in this case, where to begin and end the process of counting units). In the second section, "Measuring through the Lens of a Zero

Point," we describe experiences that helped our students think about measurement as a distance or movement from the zero point or from a starting point other than zero.

## COUNTING UNITS AS MEASURING

The activities in this section focus on the development of ideas about units, understanding the need for partitions, and beginning conceptions of where to begin the count and where to end it. As you will see, these measurement activities are based in counting processes.

### Playground Pacing

We began with an activity called Playground Pacing. In this activity, we asked our students to measure distances on the playground using their feet. We wanted to see what this activity would reveal about students' understandings of identical units, the reuse of their units (how they iterated), the need for standard units, and how they addressed measuring the entire length (the exact distance or the measurement from a beginning point to an ending point). We watched to see what they did. *Did they leave spaces or overlap their footsteps? Did they recognize that different-sized feet would result in different measures? Did they find such results problematic? Where did they start their count and how did they deal with the left-over space at the end?*

We started the classroom discourse for this activity by having our students share exactly how they paced or measured the length of a painted square on the blacktop. We focused first on what the students' actions revealed about their understanding of identical units and iteration.

Examining the chart in Figure 6.6 shows that Amy and Sophie began by iterating their units, leaving no gaps, and demonstrated some attention to accumulating identical units by walking heel to toe. Both girls suspended this thinking about identical units, or paces, by turning their foot or overlapping it so they did not cross the ending point. They counted all the paces the same. It did not matter if it was a whole pace or a partial pace. Although Shelly and Ron paced the distance differently, neither demonstrated the importance of accurately iterating identical units. Their paces were not equal in length. Shelly took strides and left spaces in between which were not the same length, while Ron sometimes overlapped his feet as he paced.

To push on the students' thinking, we asked them if all of the different ways the students paced were accurate ways to measure the distance. Immediately, the students reacted. Ron stressed that we all have different sized

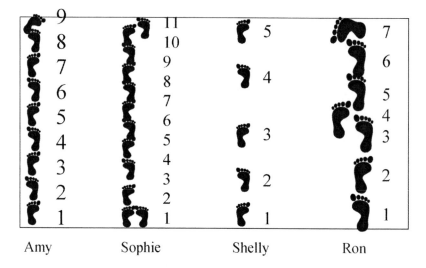

Figure 6.6.   Four Student's Ways of Measuring.

feet: if you have bigger feet, your measure will be smaller, and if you have smaller feet, your measure will be bigger. Maddie challenged Shelly's large steps by saying, "You did not do it heel to toe—you can't leave spaces," revealing her intuitive sense about the need for identical units.

We created the following scenario to help the students think more deeply about the importance of identical units and the need for some type of standard unit. "Let us pretend that Riley goes to Home Depot and tells the clerk he wants a piece of wood that is 11 footsteps long." We modeled the three pacing strategies the students shared and said, "the Home Depot guy might measure out 11 footsteps by walking: heel to toe, normal strides, and baby steps (overlapping)." The class immediately ruled out the use of baby steps and normal strides as an accurate way to measure. They wanted the footsteps to be heel to toe with no spaces left between them. The students were quick to tell us to put our foot on the line to begin the count and put our heel to our toe to keep our units the same size. They also stressed the importance of using some type of standard unit by selecting Riley's feet to be the unit of measure (the length of the square was 11 of Riley's footsteps long). To our surprise, one student pointed out the limitations of even using Riley's feet as our standard unit. "It will always be the same (measure) unless Riley's feet grow and get longer." We felt pretty confident in the students' initial understandings about the importance of identical units and how to iterate the units across a distance.

Next, we wanted to push on an aspect of a zero point—*where did you start your count?* The students began their counts in different places. In Figure

6.7, we show the three places we saw them start. Most of the class thought that the foot needed to be in front of the line and that the first foot should be counted as one. The students explained, "If you start counting in the other places you will get the wrong answer." While they were correct about their conclusions, we were concerned about their use of "wrong answer" instead of "your measurement will be too long/too short" or "you have not measured all the distance or too much distance." For the time being, we accepted their responses, but knew this was an important idea we needed to address.

We continued our conversation and focused on the end point. *How were students making sense of the ending point?* When the students paced the length of the square, most of their measures resulted in a left-over distance, or gap, between their last footstep and the end point. Many of the students rounded the gap up, "it is almost 9 or almost 10" or they tilted their feet and counted a partial footstep the same way they counted complete footsteps. They also didn't discriminate on the length of the remaining distance whether it was just a little bit or if a large gap remained. Making sense of the end point is a critical idea in measuring, so we decided to address this big idea in our next activity.

While the class's conceptions of the big ideas were developing, statements like "you would get the wrong number or answer" concerned us. We wanted to hear them talk about the impact on the distance measured from the different starting points. When we again posed the problem to see if

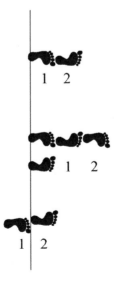

Figure 6.7.   Students' Three Starting Points.

they could explain what it meant to get the right number, they could not explain it. We pondered: *Did the students understand what measurement was or its purposes? Did they understand that they were measuring distance? Did they simply lack sufficient experiences to describe the measure in measurement terms? Did we need to interject language into our conversations that might help the students in describing or understanding measure? If so, what language should we add?*

## Measuring With Books

In our next activity, we had the students use books to measure the distance between two lines. We wanted to focus on their understanding of identical units, iteration, partitioning, and a starting point. We introduced a new unit (books) to see what additional information that change might reveal about the students' understanding. We put out dictionaries (all the same size) and a variety of different-sized smaller books. The different-sized books allowed for conversations about identical units and how to measure a distance that required the use of partial units.

Kathy shared her ideas and our challenges began. "If you used the same-sized books, it will be okay; but if you use different-sized books, you won't get the same number." She placed the same-sized books in a row with the first book butted up against the inside of the first line. When she got to the end, she realized that the book would go over the line. She turned the book on its side to see if she could get it to come up to the line evenly. "It is almost 5 books." We were surprised, after all of our class discussions about identical units, when Kathy turned the book sideways and another student made the suggestion to use another-sized book. The new context and new constraints challenged their fragile conceptions of the importance of identical units.

It was clear that the students were recognizing that they were measuring the distance between two lines and should iterate units the entire distance without leaving gaps. However, they had difficulty describing and measuring the distance between the endpoint and the last whole book. The actual distance was 4½ books long, but they rounded their answer up to 5 (even while recognizing that the distance was not really 5 books long). We continued our conversation and a few students began to contemplate the use of fractions to describe the space or distance that was less than a full unit (see Figure 6.8).

Teacher:   What is the distance between the two lines?

Jill:   [She laid out 5 books all the same size.] It is 5 books long, but you have to cut this last book here. [She pointed to the center of the 5th book.]

Ron:   It is 4½ books.

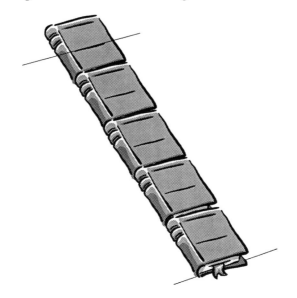

Figure 6.8.    Measuring Length with Books.

Raquel:    No, it is 5 books. See, there is 1, 2, 3, 4 and 5 . [She pointed to the mid-point on the 5$^{th}$ book.] It is book five and half of that.

Thomas:    It is 4½ books. There is 1, 2, 3, 4 and ½ of a book.

Jill:    If you cut the book, it would be 5 books but the last one would be smaller.

Anna:    Just turn the last book sideways and it will be 5 books.

Michael:    They are not all the same size. You cannot do that. All the books need to be the same size.

Initially, the students struggled with whether it was okay to use different-sized units or to round units up. It was also interesting that the students were willing to ignore their initial conceptions about using equal units to make sure all the distance was measured. This indicated to us that measuring the whole distance had more importance to them than using equal units. As the conversation continued, the idea that a unit can be partitioned and described as a fraction was shared. As fractions came into play, new issues arose. Students began to grapple with how to describe units using fractions, but they did not know if the distance was 4½ or 5½ books long. We did not fully comprehend at the time the thinking behind their responses, and, therefore, we were not sure how to help the students see that the distance was 4½ units long, not 5½ units long. We knew our next activity would require the students to continue to think about how to describe the fractional part. We were interested in how that conversation would evolve.

At this point, our minds were full. So many issues had been raised, and we pondered how to address them. We were still concerned about the lack of measurement language being used and what our next steps might be. As we analyzed what our students had done, reflected on the class notes and discussions, and examined the students' work, we came to the conclusion that our students did not have enough experience with measurement to use measurement language. If we wanted them to more accurately describe their thinking in measurement terms, we needed to interject measurement language and further develop various contexts for measuring.

## How Tall is the Turkey?

While the use of dictionaries and other-sized books as units helped to push on the students' conceptions of identical units and the ending point, we wondered if the fact that books could not be cut or folded added to the complexity of the problem. We cut equal sized paper strips to see what impact a foldable unit would have on students' thinking about how to measure a distance that required the use of whole and partial units. We drew a turkey that was 4½ units long (see Figure 6.9). Even with the wavering conversations in the book activity, we were confident the students understood the importance of using identical units, but we needed to strengthen this understanding through discourse.

Teacher:   What do you notice about the strips?

Thomas:   They are all the same length.

Figure 6.9.   How Tall is the Turkey?

Teacher:  Why do you think they are the same length?

Raquel:  If you have different sizes and lengths, it will not measure the turkey correctly. They all need to be the same size.

Sean:  We need to use the same length strips.

Teacher:  Sophie, could you measure the turkey?

Sophie:  [She lined up the 1st unit at the bottom of the turkey's foot. Then she laid the strips heel to toe along the height of the turkey.]

Ron:  [He straightened the strips, and some of them overlapped.]

Class:  [Arguing] You can't overlap the strips.

These students were able to clearly articulate the importance of accurately accumulating equal units. Consequently, we focused our attention on the end point and partitioning.

We then asked the class how tall the turkey was. Various students restated the ideas that had been shared when we measured with the dictionaries. (See figure 9.)

Student 1:  It's 4½ strips. There is 1, 2, 3, 4 and ½ of a strip.

Student 2:  It is 5½ strips. There is 1, 2, 3, 4 and 5½. It's up to the 5th strip and half of that.

There were about four or five students who were able to see that there were 4 whole units and ½ of a unit: $4 + ½ = 4½$ units. The remaining students interpreted the measure the other way. They saw that there were 4 full units and then half of the fifth unit, making the answer 5½ units tall. We struggled to understand this reasoning. *Were the students not recognizing that it is not 5 units until you reach the end of the 5th unit?* Some students' language showed us that they clearly understood there were only 4 complete units and ½ of the 5th unit, but knowing how to correctly describe this was difficult for them.

Through our study of prior research (Lehrer, Jaslow, & Curtis, 2003), we knew this issue was linked to students' understanding of measurement processes, and yet as we carefully listened to the students' language we were not sure if that was the only problem. One minute, we were sure that it was a fraction language issue and the students just didn't know how to mathematically describe the fractions. At other times, we were just as convinced the students were struggling with conceptualizing measurement as a distance from a starting point to an ending point.

## MEASURING THROUGH THE LENS OF A ZERO POINT

After students' thinking about units solidified and they started to use fractions to describe distances less than a unit long, we transitioned into the second half of our project. If we wanted our students to understand whether the turkey was 4½ units or 5½ units tall, they needed to view measuring as movement from a zero point (or a point of origin) to an end point.

Also, we were aware that we still hadn't introduced formal measurement language. The children were talking about strips instead of units, using the language we had given them. If we did not introduce measurement language, then their inability to use it was more about what we did not do instructionally than what they did or did not understand. We made major efforts to consistently use two specific measurement words in our classroom discourse: *units* (instead of strips) and *distance* (instead of space).

### Stuart Little Goes for a Ride

Using the units from the previous day, we had the students remeasure the turkey. We placed a little car just below the turkey and the first unit (see Figure 6.10). We told the students that Stuart Little was planning on driving from the bottom of the turkey to the top of the turkey. We asked them to focus on where Stuart Little (White, 1945) was and how to describe his location. By having Stuart move, we hoped that the class would begin to think about measurement as movement from a zero point.

Figure 6.10.   Starting with the Car at Zero.

Teacher:   Before Stuart Little starts his trip, where would he be?

Amy:   Zero means nothing, so zero would mean he hasn't moved yet. So zero is below the line.

Teacher:   So where would Stuart be if he drove 1 unit? [We moved Stuart's car up the paper a little bit.] Have we driven 1 unit yet?

Amy:   No, you have not driven 1 unit until you reach the end of the 1st unit. [She pointed to the end of unit 1.]

We continued to question the students. "Tell us when Stuart has traveled 2 units. How about 3 units?" The class was able to say that Stuart traveled 2 units at the end of the 2nd unit and 3 at the end of the 3rd unit, etc. We decided to push their thinking further by asking them to identify the half units.

Teacher:   Where am I now? [Stuart was sitting on the ½ mark on the first unit.]

John:   You are at half of the unit.

Teacher:   Where would Stuart be when he has driven 1½ units?

Maddie:   [She pointed to the 1½ mark]

Thomas:   No [He pointed to the 2½ point on the paper units].

Teacher:   Is it 1½ or is it 2½ units? Have we gotten to 2 units yet?

Laurie:   He went 1 and then he went ½ more.

Although this activity helped some of the students recognize that you have not traveled 1 unit until you have traveled the entire length of the 1st whole unit, at least half of the class still identified 1½ units as 2½ units. They were fully aware that they had only traveled 1 whole unit, but they just did not know how to describe the remaining half. We were just as uncertain as before about what this meant. If we didn't understand why students thought this way, how could we help them think differently?

## Stuart Little's Birthday Parties

Since the students were still grappling with the ideas of partitioning units and distance from a zero point, we tried a time context that we thought would be more familiar to them. We asked the students how old they were. It didn't take long for one little boy to say that he was 6½ years old. We asked the students, "Which two years does 6½ years come between? They were all able to say that 6½ came between 6 and 7 years old. We created a number line for Stuart Little's age, marking 0 to 7 years on it. We moved our finger from 0 up the number line and asked when Stuart was ½ year old, 1 year old, 1½ years old, etc. The students seemed to have no problem correctly describing fractions in terms of an age timeline.

We told the class that Stuart had a birthday party every half year and asked where on the number line we could show when Stuart would have his 1ˢᵗ party? Sophie pointed to the ½ mark between 0 and 1. Ron remarked, "He is 0 and ½." We asked the students, "If Stuart is 1½ years old and his friend is 2 years old, who is older?" John, who had previously struggled with naming fractions correctly, pointed to the 1½ mark and said, "This is Stuart." He then pointed to 2 and said, "This is his friend, so Stuart's friend is older." In this number line context, John was able to make sense of fractions and their relative magnitude. The use of a birthday timeline turned out to be quite helpful. The students clearly understood that 5½ years old was between 5 and 6 years. The students, for the most part, understood ½ in the context of age. They did not make the same mistakes they did while measuring distance. We then returned to measuring the turkey and continued the conversation. Many of the students who had previously struggled with correctly partitioning and counting units improved their thinking. We were feeling pretty confident that the students were beginning to think about measurement as a distance from a zero point and appropriately naming distances using fractional remainders.

## Measuring for Meaning

For the next activity, we created a penguin for the students to examine. We asked the students what parts of the penguin could be measured and why they might want to measure them. The students identified different parts of the penguin (flippers, head, feet, etc.) and were able to show the beginning and ending points that would be needed to get an accurate measure. We also talked about why they might want to measure his feet or his head. The students came up with ideas about making him shoes or a hat. Through our conversations, they concluded that if they did not measure correctly, the shoes may be too big or too small. It was important to measure accurately or the clothes that they made him may not fit. At last, the students were using the language we wanted to hear. However, we were not able to determine if this context had helped them to think about the purpose of measure, or if they had just needed additional measurement experiences. It seems that formal language takes time to develop and can't be rushed.

## Mr. Popper's Penguins—Captain Cook

We were still concerned that there were a number of students who still could not accurately describe partitions. We decided to see if a story problem might help the students solidify their thinking and give them a different context for measuring. We posed the following two story problems about Captain Cook, one of Mr. Popper's penguins (Atwater & Atwater, 1938):

> *When Capt. Cook was born, he was ½ unit tall. By his 3$^{rd}$ birthday, he grew 2 more units. How tall was Capt. Cook on his 3$^{rd}$ birthday? Using your units, draw a picture of Capt. Cook when he was born and then draw a picture of how tall Capt. Cook was on his 3$^{rd}$ birthday. Write a number sentence to go with your picture.*

> *Capt. Cook was 2 units tall on his 2$^{nd}$ birthday. He grew ½ unit more by his 3$^{rd}$ birthday. How tall is Capt. Cook now? Using your units, draw a picture of Capt. Cook on his 2$^{nd}$ birthday, and then draw a picture that shows how tall Capt. Cook was on his 3$^{rd}$ birthday. Write a number sentence to go with your picture.*

We selected these story problems because drawing something that is a certain height is a very different skill than measuring an existing object or distance. We also hoped that adding 2 whole units and ½ of a unit (2 + ½ or ½ + 2) would help students see that 2 units plus a ½ unit was 2½ units and not 3½ units.

The students again surpassed our expectations. For the first story problem, they were able to draw Capt. Cook at ½ of a unit, place the 2 units on top of the ½, and draw him again at 2½ units tall as shown on Maddie's paper (see Figure 6.11). They were able to describe him as being 2½ units tall on his 3$^{rd}$ birthday. As a class, they were able to write the number sentence ½ unit + 2 units = 2½ units.

They did equally well on the second story problem. The students drew Capt. Cook two units tall on his 2$^{nd}$ birthday, placed the ½ unit on top of the 2 units, and drew Capt. Cook on his 3$^{rd}$ birthday at 2½ units tall as shown on Anna's paper (see Figure 6.12). As they shared their strategies, they also came up with the following number sentence: 2 units + ½ unit = 2½ units.

We decided to push on the students' thinking even further and asked them if both of these problems were the same, ½ + 2 = 2 + ½. The students

Figure 6.11.   Maddie's Drawing.

concluded that both penguins were 2½ units tall. We were pretty excited. None of the students said that their penguins were 3½ units tall. Maybe the act of having ½ of a unit and adding it to 2 units helped them to see or intrepret a fraction of a unit differently.

## Making Measuring Tools (Rulers)

By this point, the students had demonstrated a pretty solid understanding about the need for identical units, how to accumulate and iterate units, partitioning remainder units, and starting and ending points. We pondered: Could they translate these ideas into the creation of their own measuring tool? They were given a blank ruler and two equal-sized nonstandard units cut out of paper. We asked them to mark and label ½ units and whole units on their rulers. Most of the students were able to iterate the 2 units across the ruler and mark and label the whole units in the correct places. However, when trying to label these units, the challenges in understanding measurement as the distance from a zero point really came to light. Out of the whole class, only two rulers were accurately done by placing 0 at the starting point and numbering 1 through 4 at the end of the corresponding unit. Other students revealed varying degrees of understanding. Many labeled their units in the spaces rather than at the end of the units. We selected a number of problematic student-made rulers and had the class use them as case studies. We asked the students to study the rulers and identify what was correct or incorrect about them. These conversations really challenged their thinking. It revealed that they understood many of the big ideas, but failed to translate them to actions when they created a ruler.

Capt. Cook was 2 units tall on his 2nd birthday. He grew 1/2 units more by his 3rd birthday. How tall is Capt. Cook now? Using your units, draw Capt. Cook 2 units tall and then how tall he is if he grew 1/2 units more. Write a number sentence to go with your picture.

Figure 6.12.   Anna's Drawing.

*Case 1.* Laurie's Ruler (see Figure 6.1 again) - Laurie had marked the units going across the ruler and then labeled them 1 through 4 in the middle of each unit. (She was counting spaces.) She labeled the ½ units right above the numbers that represented the unit. (Her ½ units and whole units were labeled in the same place.)

Teacher:   What do you think about this ruler?

> Shelly:   You can't label it that way. It is not 1 whole unit until it gets there. [She pointed to the end point of the 1st unit.]
>
> Teacher:   What about the 2?
>
> Harry:   [He went up and pointed to the end point of the 2nd unit.] It goes there.

The students began to clarify for themselves that labeling the unit in the middle was not appropriate. It was not one whole unit until you had moved from 0 to the end of the 1st unit. They also found it problematic to label the ½ unit in the same place as the whole unit. Examining Laurie's ruler not only helped the students grapple with how to create a measuring tool, but it helped us understand how some of the students were misinterpreting 2½ units when they measured. Laurie labeled her ruler in the middle of the unit. Also, on the first 3 units, Laurie labeled ½ in the center of the unit, but on the last unit, she labeled ½ on the two sides of the unit. This is similar to labeling a fraction strip that represents parts and wholes rather than labeling a ruler that represents distances from a starting point. With this interpretation, we finally understood a possible explanation for why many of our students initially saw 1½ units as 2½ units. They could have been thinking that the ½ that is embedded in a whole unit should be included along with the name of the next fractional part.

*Case 2.* Maddie's Ruler (see Figure 6.13) – Next, we showed the class Maddie's ruler and had the students look it over. Maddie labeled the ruler correctly at the end points of the units, but at the ½ points, she guessed where halfway marks were and labeled them accordingly. She did not use her paper units to precisely locate ½ of a unit. When the students studied her ruler, they quickly laid a folded unit on top of the units on her ruler and discovered that the ½ units were in the wrong place. This case helped the students to think about the importance of accuracy: ½ is located at the midpoint of the unit. Guessing the midpoint of a unit was not acceptable when creating a measuring tool.

After we had completed the discussions about the rulers, we asked the students to make a new ruler that was more accurate and that could be used to measure. Again, we asked them to label it with ½ and whole units.

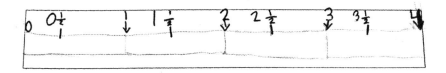

Figure 6.13.   Maddie's Ruler.

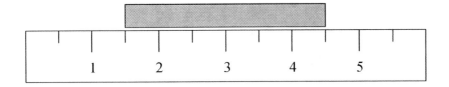

Figure 6.14.    Assessment Task.

Amy clearly illustrated her understanding of a zero point when she was making her final ruler. She laid her paper units on the ruler and marked the whole units. Then she folded her paper unit in half, placed it on the ruler, and marked the mid-point of each unit. When she labeled her ruler, she wrote ½ on the mid-point between the 1st and 2nd unit. We pointed to that spot and asked, "Is that 1½?" She replied no. She placed her hand at 0 and made a sweeping motion stopping at 1½ units and said, "That is 1½ units." Measurement as the distance from a zero point is a complex idea, but she understood it. She was no longer counting units; she was applying concepts of measure.

At this point, we felt like we had accomplished what we set out to do. We helped our students make sense of the big ideas of measurement with an eye towards understanding zero point. With the guided reinvention of a measuring tool (our original goal), our students understood the big ideas of measurement and, most importantly from our perspective, the concept of zero point. All we needed to do next was connect these ideas to reading a standard ruler. "No big deal!" we thought. A few weeks after we had completed our classroom research, we came across an interesting assessment task (see Figure 6.14).

We recognized at once that although we had helped our students think about measurement as a distance from a zero point we had not provided any experiences that began the measurement of length from some other starting point on the ruler. We guessed that our students would not identify the correct measure of the strip in this task. So we began to ponder yet another research question: *How do we build on our previous activities to help children realize that the starting point can be anywhere on a ruler?*

As a new learning activity, we created a large poster of Stuart Little's Street (see Figure 6.15). The street was composed of the blue paper strip units that we had used to measure many items in our classroom. Houses and community locations were placed at the whole-unit and ½-unit marks. We had Stuart Little travel up and down his street in his little car. Initially, Stuart began his travels at 0 (Jarod's house). The students were able to

Figure 6.15.   Poster of Stuart Little's Street.

explain how far Stuart had traveled as he drove up the street. Then we challenged them. If Stuart was at his school (unit 3) and drove to Breanna's house (unit 4), how far did he drive? Immediately, we heard the anticipated response. "He drove 4 units." Jill pointed to the 4 in front of Breanna's house.

Teacher: What if Stuart drove from his house (located at unit 1) to the playground (located at 2½ units), how far would he have driven?

Class: [Students gave two different answers.] 1½ units! 2½ units!

Laurie: He went 1½ units. [She took the car and drove 1 unit.] That is 1 unit. [Then she drove another ½ unit.] There is ½ of a unit. That would be 1½ units.

Anna: It says 2½ units. [She pointed to the label in front of the playground.]

Maddie: It is really 0 because he is at his house and he has not gone anywhere yet, even if he is at 1 unit. He would have driven 2½ units if he drove from Jarod's house [She pointed at the 0 label].

Maddie's observation was profound. She was able to make sense of the idea that the starting point could be anywhere on a measuring tool. If you

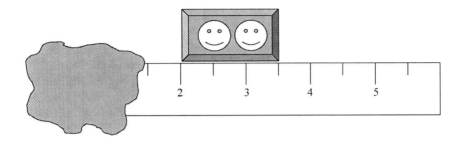

Figure 6.16.    Ink Blotted Ruler.

start at 2 and move 1 unit, then you have only moved 1 unit, not 3. For Maddie to understand that the gas station could represent both 2 units from the zero point on a ruler and the starting point for a different measurement at the same time is an important big idea. Through continued conversations, the students were not only able to determine distances from a point other than 0, but they were able to determine distances going back down the street (i.e., moving from 4 to 3 is also 1 unit of distance).

While most of the students could make sense of the idea of a starting point that changed depending on the question being asked, we still were not sure that this understanding would automatically connect to measuring accurately on a ruler. We gave the students some ink blotted rulers (see Figure 6.16) and asked them how wide the picture was.

Harry commented, "It is just like Stuart Little's Street. It is 1½ units long. From 2 to 3 is 1 unit and from 3 to 3½ is ½ of a unit. 1 + ½ = 1½." Shelly continued the conversation with her justification, "You can start at the 2 and pretend it is 0, the 3 is actually 1 unit and the 3½ is 1½ units. While Harry and Shelly were able to describe the width of the picture, some students had thought the answer was 3½. We continued doing similar problems to help them grapple with this idea. Gradually, the students began to make sense of this situation. We followed up by giving the students an assessment that included items where the measuring started at 0 and items that started at other points on the ruler. All but three students were able to determine the correct measurements.

## CONCLUSIONS

We learned a great deal from this action research project. We felt like we had developed a series of experiences that helped us make better sense about children's learning trajectories for linear measurement and answered our question *"How do you get primary children to make sense of identical units, iteration, and partitioning with an eye towards building understanding of a zero point?"* These experiences illustrated for us that first- and second-grade students, given appropriate experiences and focused conversations, could understand the basic concepts of linear measurement. Our students were able to make sense of the need for identical units, understand that units can be iterated (reused), and recognize that units often need to be partitioned to get an accurate measure. But, most significant for us, these students were able to think about measurement as a distance from any starting point and learned that any point of origin can act as a zero point. The students reflected these understandings in their self-created measurement tools, discussions about Stuart Little's Street, and final measurement assessments. We came to realize that learning about measurement is a journey for both students and teacher/researchers. As teachers, it is our job to assist students in making sense of measurement. To do that, we must first understand the big ideas of measurement for ourselves. It is amazing how much we as teachers had to learn, and that we were able to learn a great deal in the course of reading research, designing instructional activities, and engaging in discourse with students about their thinking. Obviously, if we don't understand what is important about measurement, we can't design instruction to help our students. We cannot teach what we do not understand.

Our conceptual understanding also assists us in interpreting how our students are thinking about measurement concepts and allows us to design learning activities and classroom discourse to deepen their learning. We struggled with our own understanding of a zero point throughout this investigation. It has so many layers—measuring all the distance, interpretation of fractional units, movement from a starting point, and that a starting point can be anywhere on a ruler. While the activities we designed ultimately helped the students make sense of these ideas, we were often very unsure of the best next steps for developing students' understanding. We learned that we could come to understand these concepts, listen to our students, test out the hunches we had about their understandings and misunderstandings, and remain open to surprises both in our students' thinking and in our own.

## ACKNOWLEDGMENT

We thank the Professional Development Collaborative at San Diego State University and the Encinitas Union School District for their support for our action research. We also thank Victoria Jacobs and Jae-meen Baek for their careful reading of this chapter.

## REFERENCES

Atwater, R., & Atwater, F. (1938). *Mr. Popper's penguins*. Boston: Little, Brown.

Grant, T. J., & Kline, K. (2003). Developing the building blocks of measurement with young children. In D. H. Clements (Ed.), *Learning and teaching measurement* [NCTM Yearbook] (pp. 46-56). Reston, VA: National Council of Teachers of Mathematics.

Jaslow, L. (in review). Linear measurement: Designing and redesigning instruction based on formative assessment.

Lehrer, R. (2003). Developing understanding of measurement. In J. Kilpatrick, W. G. Martin, & D. Schifter (Eds.), *A research companion to principles and standards for school mathematics* (pp.179-192). Reston, VA: National Council of Teachers of Mathematics.

Lehrer, R., Jacobson, C., Kemeny, V., & Strom, D. (1999). Building on children's intuitions to develop mathematical understanding of space. In E. Fennema & T. A. Romberg (Eds.), *Mathematics classrooms that promote understanding* (pp. 63-87). Mahwah, NJ: Erlbaum.

Lehrer, R., Jaslow, L. & Curtis, C. (2003). Developing understanding of measurement in the elementary grades. In D. H. Clements (Ed.), *Learning and teaching measurement* [NCTM Yearbook] (pp. 100-121). Reston, VA: National Council of Teachers of Mathematics.

Lehrer, R., Jenkins, M., & Osana, H. (1998). Longitudinal study of children's reasoning about space and geometry. In R. Lehrer & D. Chazan (Eds.), *Designing learning environments for developing understanding of geometry and space* (pp. 137-167). Mahwah, NJ: Erlbaum.

National Council of Teachers of Mathematics. (2000). *Principles and standards for school mathematics*. Reston, VA: Author.

Nitabach, E., & Lehrer, R. (1996). Developing spatial sense through area measurement. *Teaching Children Mathematics* 2, 473-476.

Stephan, M., & Clements, D. H. (2003). Linear and area measurement in pre-kindergarten to grade 2. In D. H. Clements (Ed.), *Learning and teaching measurement* [NCTM Yearbook] (pp. 3-16). Reston, VA: National Council of Teachers of Mathematics.

White, E. B. (1945). Stuart Little. New York: Harper Collins.

CHAPTER 7

# CLASSROOM RESEARCH INFORMS *MEASURE UP*

## A Different Look at Elementary Mathematics

**Claire Okazaki and Fay Zenigami**
*University of Hawaii at Manoa*

**Barbara Dougherty**
*University of Mississippi*

Students are busy pouring water to compare volumes, cutting strips to compare lengths, and using a balance scale to compare masses. They are writing statements on the board and in their notebooks to describe the relationships they find. One student writes:

$A > Q$

$Q < A$

$A \neq Q$

$Q \neq A$

*Teachers Engaged in Research*
*Inquiry Into Mathematics Classrooms, Grades Pre-K–2*, pages 135–152
Copyright © 2006 by Information Age Publishing
All rights of reproduction in any form reserved.

The students in this class are first graders at the Education Laboratory School (ELS), a charter school with curriculum research and development as its primary purpose located at the University of Hawaii's Curriculum Research & Development Group (CRDG).

Elementary students in this school are part of research cohorts involved in Measure Up (MU), an elementary mathematics project undertaken by the Mathematics Section of the CRDG. This chapter describes the work and experiences of three researcher-teachers of the MU project team during the first year of this project. We write about the changes in our understandings about mathematics and its instruction as we experience mathematics through a different lens.

Our involvement in MU began when a Russian team working on a joint project with the University of Hawaii became interested in previous CRDG work in middle and high school mathematics (Rachlin, Matsumoto, Wada, & Dougherty, 2001). As they reviewed the work, they noticed the links between the CRDG mathematics curriculum development and other Russian work (Krutetskii, 1976). Subsequently, they invited us to work collaboratively with them on an elementary project that became known at our institution as Measure Up.

Initially, we were cautious about pursuing the partnership since the original Russian work was conducted in the 1970s and was primarily focused on seven- to eight-year old first graders. Since American first graders are one or two years younger than these Russian counterparts, we wondered if our students would be ready to access the mathematics. After careful review of the research, we realized that this Russian perspective made mathematical sense and was worth pursuing.

In this chapter, we relive the journey of the grade one mathematics during the first year of the project, describe the rationale of the program and the research techniques we used, illustrate the grade one mathematics and discuss the analyses of our work. The project is expected to continue through grade five; however, the focus of this chapter will be on the initial research cohort of grade one students.

## RATIONALE OF THE MATHEMATICAL DEVELOPMENT

Russian mathematicians, mathematics educators, and psychologists (Davydov, 1975a, 1975b; Minskaya, 1975) saw a need for young children to understand mathematical concepts in order to prepare them to deal with more complex mathematics in middle and high school. Rather than taking the path that rearranges the sequence of topics or adds more hands-on activities, the Russian group stepped back from the traditional elementary mathematics curriculum where grade one students begin their mathematical development by learning to count and then move to whole number addition and subtraction. Instead, the Russian team focused on mathematical structures that cross multiple topics and complexity levels so that students looked at the larger picture rather than small fragments that build to bigger ideas. Davydov and his colleagues believed that if students understood structure, then they would be able to apply properties and underlying foundations to any number system. They used that perspective as the basis for the mathematical content development.

A major influence on the Russian research was the work of Vygotsky (1978), specifically his reference to scientific concepts and the idea that instruction can precede development. Based on the Vygotskian perspective, there are two basic means by which students learn. They learn through the development of either spontaneous or empirical concepts, or through the development of scientific concepts. Spontaneous or empirical concepts are developed when children abstract properties from their experiences with specific number ideas or tasks. This idea is most often seen in a traditional progression that children experience when they move from natural numbers to whole, rational, irrational, and finally real numbers, in a very specific sequence. Children learn concepts and skills within each number system, but making connections across the different systems are sometimes difficult for students. Each system seems to be distinct from the other, resulting in student understanding and learning being fragmented and isolated.

Scientific concepts, on the other hand, are developed with the focus on larger, more general contexts that demonstrate, show, or embody properties and ideas relative to, in this case, all number systems. When scientific concepts are the basis of instruction, the teaching focuses on properties of real numbers by using tasks that embody the conceptual side of number and operations, followed later with specific applications in natural, whole, rational, and irrational numbers. Students do not see each number system as a special case but rather see that mathematical structures apply to all types of numbers.

In order to apply scientific concepts to the elementary curriculum, Davydov's group turned to measurement as a context for content development. This makes sense because young children continually compare quantities as they try to determine who has more than, who has less than, and who has the same amount as they do. Mathematically, the measurement contexts allow students to physically model quantitative relationships, build the notion of a 'unit,' and demonstrate the actions of computational concepts.

Utilizing children's natural inclination to compare and describe attributes of continuous quantities such as length, area, volume and mass, sets the tone for the mathematics that follow. Whether the topics are pre-number, number and operation concepts and skills, geometry or algebra, new ideas are introduced through the use of the measurement with continuous quantities. Interestingly, measurement is not formally taught but rather used as the context in which the above-mentioned concepts are the focus of instruction. New topics are introduced through students' previous knowledge so that the learning of new ideas and topics is not done in isolation.

The flow of the mathematics is very different from any curricula we had previously worked with. The movement from one topic to another is naturally fluid. It provides children with the ability to generalize ideas without starting with specific numeric problems. We have been awed by the mathematical discussions that young students generate when sharing their thinking.

Students also begin to understand some algebraic concepts in grade one. The RAND report (2002) recommends an early focus on the development of proficiency in algebra since algebra can incorporate the study of arithmetic but also naturally extends to more advanced, formal concepts and procedures and to connections between elementary and advanced ideas. How early can children learn in an algebraic context? Kaput (1999) indicates that students can learn with understanding in this context if we—

1. Begin early by building on students' informal knowledge,
2. Integrate the learning of algebra with the learning of other subject matter,
3. Include different forms of algebraic thinking,
4. Encourage students to reflect on what they learn in order to articulate what they know,
5. Put a premium on sense-making and understanding. (p. 3)

We feel that MU provides these opportunities for young children.

## OUR RESEARCHER-TEACHER ROLES
## AND RESEARCH METHODOLOGY

During the 2001–2002 school year, we designed and wrote first-grade materials based on translations from the Russian curriculum (Davydov, Gorbov, Mikulina, Savelyeva, & Tabachnikova, 1995, 1999) that stemmed from the Russian research. As part of our research agenda, we decided to use design research methodology (Shavelson, Phillips, Towne, & Feuer, 2003)

Using design research methodology offered us the opportunity to work directly in the first-grade classroom, with all of its complexities and unpredictability. In line with this methodology, each of the project team members took a different role. Fay was responsible for writing the original draft of the materials, including teacher notes, student worksheets and visual masters. As part of the research on student learning, Claire did the classroom instruction for the first cohort group at the ELS, while Barbara observed and recorded information related to the mathematical development. Fay observed and used a classroom observation instrument to document the instructional techniques and students' responses during whole class discussions, individuals working independently, and small groups of students collaborating. After each lesson, the three of us shared observations and made recommendations or suggestions about the lesson and future ones that build on its mathematical content. Discussion each day included addressing questions such as:

- What were critical mathematics learning points?
- Did the mathematics build from previous lessons? Were the problems challenging enough?
- What were the instructional techniques used? Did the techniques provide enough student accountability?
- Did all students have equal access to the discussion and tasks?
- Were the class debriefing techniques appropriate? Did the techniques push students to think?
- What teacher questions moved students to think deeper about the mathematical ideas?
- How do we know students learned?

By studying the intricacies and complexities of the classes, we could consider multiple factors within and across lessons. Individual as well as grade-level analyses of the lessons helped us trace the ways in which the mathematical ideas were connected and how that interconnectivity influenced student learning.

We also utilized the technique of *shadowing*, a technique that allowed us to pilot a lesson with the initial research cohort before it was used at other sites. This process was used in an earlier CRDG algebra project (Rachlin, Matsumoto, & Wada, 1987; Wagner, Rachlin, & Jensen, 1984). The technique required a quick turn-around time to re-craft each lesson with information from our daily lesson analysis at the ELS, to optimize results from the lesson with students. Claire used these recommendations to prepare a revised set of materials. The re-crafted lesson was then used at 1) Connections Public Charter School (CPCS), Hilo, HI, and 2) Univers Laboratory School (ULS), Krasnoyarsk, Russia. Feedback from these sites resulted in further redesigning of the lesson deemed necessary for implementation the following year with a new cohort of students.

The three implementation sites (CPCS, ULS and ELS) were carefully selected to provide a diverse student sample for research purposes. The students are equally representative of larger student populations in regard to 1) student performance levels, 2) socioeconomic status, and 3) ethnicity. For example, at the ELS and CPCS in Hawaii, student achievement levels range from the 5th to 99th percentile in approximately a normal distribution, with students from low to high socioeconomic status and ethnicities including, but not limited to, Native Hawaiian, Pacific Islanders, African-American, Asian, Hispanic, and Caucasian. Both sites are charter schools where no segregation or tracking of students is done and all special education students are part of an inclusion program. At the ELS, the student population is determined by a random selection process. Equal numbers of boys and girls are assigned to each class so the effects of changes in curriculum can be monitored and studied across genders. At CPCS, students are accepted on a first-come-first-served basis. There are no achievement criteria for selection at either charter school, so students within each mathematics class represent a range in abilities and achievement. All three sites have stable student populations that allow the project staff to do longitudinal study into student learning.

## GRADE ONE MATHEMATICS

The development of the mathematics in the grade one MU class began with what children do naturally when they come to school. It is not uncommon to observe young children making informal comparisons and saying, "I have more juice than you." or "Who is taller?" In the MU class students examined, categorized, and sorted objects using different attributes such as shape, color and size of objects. They were then guided to focus on comparing continuous quantities, specifically, length, area, volume (capacity) and mass. They aligned two objects to compare their lengths, overlaid the bases of two objects to compare those surface areas, examined two containers of colored water to compare their volumes, and learned how to use the balance scale to compare two masses.

A typical lesson involved using everyday items that children were already familiar with, such as soft drink bottles, water, and Play-Doh™ modeling compound. Quantities were created with these materials for students to compare. Discussion in class centered on what students noticed when comparing the different quantities. In their own words, they verbalized how one quantity related to another. For example they may have said, "This volume is the same as that volume," or "This length is smaller." The discussion was then guided so comparison vocabulary was introduced—*equal to, not equal to, greater than,* and *less than.* Students also realized that quantities being compared must be the same. In other words, it is not feasible to compare an object's length with its mass.

As students became comfortable describing comparisons through direct measurement, they used paper strip lengths to symbolically represent comparisons. For example, two equal volumes were represented with two equal lengths of paper strips; two unequal volumes were represented with two unequal lengths of paper strips (see Figure 7.1).

Regardless of the quantity (length, area, volume or mass) being compared, the paper strip lengths were used to represent the comparisons.

To further enhance the symbolic representation, students drew line segments. Two congruent line segments represented equality and two noncongruent line segments represented inequality (see Figure 7.2).

Again, whichever quantity (length, area, volume or mass) was compared, the line segments were used to represent the comparisons.

Figure 7.1.   Paper strips for comparing volume.

Figure 7.2.   Line segments showing equality and inequality.

Students were then introduced to the relational symbols (=, ≠, >, and <) which they used with arbitrary letter names (or literal variables) to identify the quantities being compared. For example, when examining two masses on the balance scale, one mass was labeled *D* and the other *L*. Students wrote the statement *D* = *L* but read it as *Mass D is equal to mass L*. They represented the comparison with paper strip lengths as well as drawing line segments. They also labeled the paper strip lengths and the line segments as *D* and *L*. By reversing the order of the masses on the balance scale, students realized that the relationship between the two quantities was the same and were able to record *L* = *D*. When comparisons were unequal, students generalized that the relationship of the quantities (whether the quantity be length, area, volume, or mass) could be recorded in one of four ways: *Q* ≠ *M*, *M* ≠ *Q*, *Q* > *M*, or *M* < *Q* (see Figure 7.3).

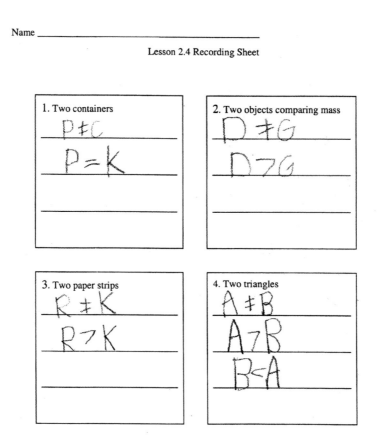

Figure 7.3.   Sample of student work using symbols to represent relationships.

The use of multiple representations (paper strip lengths, line segments, equality and inequality symbolic statements) concurrently with the physical action of comparing quantities allowed students to begin to think abstractly. When shown a pair of equal paper strip lengths or line segments, students showed or described two quantities that were equal either by length, area, volume or mass. When shown a pair of unequal paper strip lengths or line segments, students showed or described two unequal quantities. Their ability to show or describe quantities did not change when they were given only the symbolic statements. In fact, they could not only model the physical comparison, they could also represent the statement with line segments or paper strip lengths.

The use of an intermediate measure was introduced so students could make indirect comparisons of quantities. Students were asked to compare the length of a bookcase with the length of another bookcase that was across the room.

Teacher (T): The principal wants to know if the length of this bookcase is equal or unequal to the length of that bookcase across the room. How could we find out?

Student (S): We could move that bookcase over and measure them.

T: That would be difficult because they are so heavy and we really don't have the time to do that. Let's brainstorm some ideas that would help.

S: We could use paper strips.

T: We do have paper strips.

S: A ruler

T: We don't have a ruler available.

S: String

T: We do have string. What would we do with the paper strips or the string? (Observation notes, ELS, November 2001)

The discussion continued until a plan was formed whereby two students measured the length of one of the bookcases with the string and cut off the length. To keep track of the lengths, students labeled the length of the bookcase $P$ and the length of the string used to measure the length of the bookcase as $C$. A volunteer recorded $P = C$. Another pair of students physically measured the length of the other bookcase ($T$) with length $C$ (the string) and found that they were equal. Another volunteer recorded $T = C$. By then students knew that the lengths of both bookcases were equal and described it as, "Because if length $P$ is equal to length $C$, and length $C$ is equal to length $T$, then length $P$ must be equal to length $T$." The statements were recorded as:

$$P = C$$
$$\underline{C = T}$$
$$T = P$$

This symbolization indicated that students directly compared length $P$ with length $C$ and length $C$ with length $T$. Underlining the second statement helped students to understand that although lengths $T$ and $P$ were not directly compared, one could deduce that the lengths were equal. Length $C$ was also identified as the intermediate measure that helped with comparing two lengths that could not be directly compared. In addition to working with lengths that were all equal to each other, students experienced indirect comparisons of quantities that were not equal to each other.

The development of the concept of addition and subtraction followed. For example, students were shown two identical containers with unequal amounts of colored water. The larger volume was labeled $B$ and the other $A$.

T: Here are two volumes. What can you tell me about how the volumes compare?

S: They're unequal.

T: How do you know?

S: Because one has more and one is lesser.

T: What statement can we write for our volumes?

S: [Wrote: $B > A$] Volume $B$ is greater than volume $A$. [Other students volunteered to write and read other statements: $A < B$, $B \neq A$, $A \neq B$.]

T: What if I wanted to make the volumes equal? How could I do that?

S: Pour some out into the lesser one.

T: Pour some from where?

S: From the greater one and pour into the lesser one.

T: Hmmm… I really want to keep one volume as the "standard." In other words, I only want to change one volume to make it equal to the other. (Observation notes, ELS, November 2001)

The discussion led students to suggest adding enough water to the lesser volume or pouring out enough water from the greater volume. Both actions were done. Students modeled the actions with paper strip lengths. If the action was addition, students added a length to the shorter paper strip length. If the action was subtraction, students cut off a length from the longer paper strip length. *Addition* and *subtraction* were introduced as operations when doing the action. Students also represented addition and subtraction by drawing line segments.

The volume that was added to the lesser volume was identified as the *difference*. The volume that was subtracted from the greater volume was also identified as the *difference*. Students were able to understand that whatever amount you added was the same amount that you subtracted in order to make the two quantities equal.

To record the action in a statement, the difference needed to be labeled ($H$). The + and – symbols were introduced so if students added to the lesser quantity they recorded:

$$B = A + H$$

If students subtracted from the greater quantity, they recorded:

$$B - H = A$$

Students realized that if volume $H$ was added to volume $A$, volume $A$ was no longer the same quantity so another label for the changed quantity was needed. Therefore, if $A + H$ was renamed as $Q$, then the following was true:

$$
\begin{aligned}
B &> A \\
B &= A + H \\
&\quad\downarrow \\
&\quad Q \\
B &= Q
\end{aligned}
$$

Since volume $B$ remained the same, the label for volume $B$ did not change (see Figure 7.4). Students also experienced using addition or subtraction to make two equal quantities unequal as well as adding or subtracting to maintain an inequality.

As students experienced various measurement situations, they realized that it was useful to know more accurately how much of some quantity they had and to describe more clearly how much they needed to add or subtract to a quantity. Only then (midway through the first year) was number introduced. Its introduction was based on the idea of unit—an amount that

Figure 7.4.   Student work samples using addition and subtraction to create or maintain equalities.

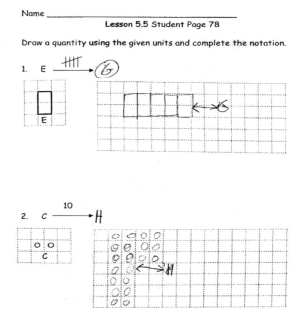

Figure 7.5.   An example of composition.

became the referent for measuring a quantity. After identifying a unit (length-unit, area-unit, volume-unit, or mass-unit), students iterated the unit as many times as needed to create a quantity (composition) (see Figure 7.5). Given a quantity, they also found how many units made up the quantity (decomposition).

Students then made calibrations by iterating a given unit. An example of a calibration based on a mass-unit is shown in Figure 7.6. Each time a mass-unit was added to the spring scale, the unit was marked and numbered. Students realized that in order to replicate quantities by combining or removing amounts, the same unit of measure should be used.

The emphasis on unit was used to construct number rays (or lines or segments). For example, using volume as the context, a volume-unit was identified and a large container was calibrated each time a volume-unit was added. Students marked a drawing of a container with each volume-unit and drew connected, iterated line segments to represent the volume-units. Students realized that since the volume-units were constant, their line segments must also be constant. This resulted in a number ray (see Figure 7.7).

The measurements of quantities with units were recorded on the number rays. This allowed a refocus on understanding addition and subtraction, now with whole numbers. Work continued with emphasis on the

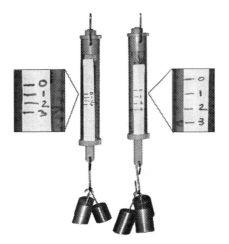

Figure 7.6. Calibration based on a mass-unit.

### Vitamin Recording Sheet

Mark and color the bottle for each volume-unit added. Draw a number line to represent the volume-units.

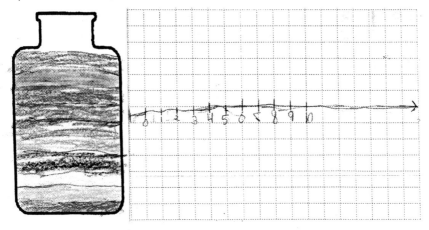

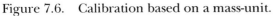

Figure 7.7. An example number ray.

relationship between the whole and its parts. When given two parts and asked to find the whole, students added. When given the whole and one part and asked to find the other part, students subtracted or added-on.

## OUR ANALYSES OF THE CLASSROOM DATA

As we watched the mathematics unfold, we were continually amazed to see that these very young children could deal with very sophisticated ideas. They readily used vocabulary that is typically reserved for older children. In fact, these first graders often asked for a word that would mean what they were working with. For example, when they had to create a way to measure the bookcase, they wanted to know what you would call the length they created. At that point, intermediate measure was introduced. In a similar fashion, they asked for and used relational words, properties such as commutative property of addition, and operational words such as sum, addend, and difference.

In regard to the symbolism used in the comparison statements, we were surprised to find that this actually enhanced students' ability to describe their thinking. It served as an organizer for their thoughts and helped them to structure how they explained and described their thinking. Since young children do not have the complex language skills as older students, the symbolic statements, physical models, and diagrams allowed them show their thinking in multiple ways.

The use of continuous measurement as the mathematical context was powerful. Students could physically model mathematical ideas and those experiences left mental images or mental residues that children could draw upon for later lessons. The connections across lessons and topics enhanced their understanding and affected retention. This meant that after vacation periods, we did not need to spend any time on re-teaching or reviewing ideas that had been introduced prior to the vacation time.

While measurement was not explicitly taught, the concepts about measurement that these first graders developed were impressive. They could easily describe the relationships between the unit and the quantity. As Macy expressed it, "The bigger the unit, the lesser times you need to use it. The smaller the unit the more times you have to use it." (Interview, Macy, March 2002)

She also noted that you have to use the same unit to measure a quantity or otherwise, your measurement is meaningless. Her comments reflect the understandings of a broader student group.

While the use of literal symbols was notable, the students' flexibility with number was remarkable. They were very comfortable decomposing a number into multiple parts, including the use of negative numbers. For example, given the task of showing the parts of 10, Reed explained:

Having negative one and 11 as the parts of 10 is okay because on the number line, negative one goes this direction (points to the left) one unit and 11 goes this direction (points to the right) 11 units. So if you put the one unit on the 11 units, you end up with 10 units. (Interview, Reed, May 2002)

This flexibility continued to impact students' learning when they began numerical addition and subtraction. The idea that a number can be decomposed allowed them to recognize the usefulness of the round number strategy. This strategy involves breaking one addend into parts so that one part combines with the other addend to make a round number (a number that ends in one or more zeroes). As this research cohort entered upper grades, they continued to rely on the round number strategy for multi-digit computation, estimation, and number sense ideas.

Our research team was learning as much as the students. We realized that we had to rethink much of our own understandings of mathematics. Because each of us had learned mathematics from a more traditional approach which framed all of our references in creating lessons, we spent hours un-learning and relearning the mathematics so that we could craft lessons based on the measurement perspective.

This curriculum challenged our perceptions of what children can do when given the opportunity. When we read the research and saw curriculum materials from Russia created on their research premises, our first instinct was to disregard this work because we didn't believe first graders were capable of handling the symbolism. Had we followed that instinct, we would not have seen and heard the incredible insights that these young children created.

Our involvement in MU has also taught us much about the complexities of the elementary classroom. Getting students who are focused on themselves to work together, to share ideas, and to build a mathematical learning community requires much planning and forethought on how to organize and structure the classroom environment. We had mistakenly thought that we could use techniques that had been successful in middle and high school mathematics classes with these first graders. We quickly realized that this age level required a different approach.

## SUMMARY

MU has opened our eyes to a new world of elementary mathematics. The research perspective that we used to design the mathematical tasks and instructional techniques set a course for our work that has changed our perspectives of what could constitute an elementary mathematics program. It has given us hope that young children can emerge from elementary grades with a strong foundation in mathematical understandings that will serve them well as they move to more complex and sophisticated mathematics.

On the other hand, we feel challenged to continue the development to see where these children might go. We are currently developing upper elementary tasks and find that our learnings about the mathematics continue to grow and change our perspectives about mathematical topics. We see mathematics in a different way that often makes us painfully aware of how shallow some of our understandings have been.

Our challenge will continue as we attempt to bring MU to a broader audience. We will be faced with questions from practitioners and parents about the accessibility issues, the benefits and trade-offs for developing mathematical understandings in this way, and pre-requisites needed by teachers if they would like to use this program. We look forward to this challenge because we have seen what can happen when we step out of the box of traditional ideas and open new doorways of exploration. We are hopeful that our work will stimulate the realization that students can thrive and *measure up* with this innovative and exciting approach.

## ACKNOWLEDGMENT

The work described herein was conducted with financial support from Best Practices in Education, Open Society, Quady Foundation, David and Cecilia Lee Foundation, and Curriculum Research & Development Group (University of Hawaii). Any opinions, findings, conclusions, or recommendations expressed in this chapter are those of the authors and do not necessarily reflect the views of the funding organizations.

## REFERENCES

Davydov, V. V. (1975a). Logical and psychological problems of elementary mathematics as an academic subject. In L. P. Steffe (Ed.), *Children's capacity for learning mathematics.* (Soviet studies in the psychology of learning and teaching mathematics, Vol. VII, pp. 55-107). Chicago: University of Chicago.

Davydov, V. V. (1975b). The psychological characteristics of the "prenumerical" period of mathematics instruction. In L. P. Steffe (Ed.), *Children's capacity for learning mathematics.* (Soviet studies in the psychology of learning and teaching mathematics, Vol. VII, pp. 109-205). Chicago: University of Chicago.

Davydov, V. V., Gorbov, S. F., Mikulina, G. G., Savelyeva, O. V., & Tabachnikova, N. L. (1999). *Mathematics teaching grade 1.* Moscow: Miros.

Davydov, V. V., Gorbov, S. F., Mikulina, G. G., Savelyeva, O. V., & Tabachnikova, N. L., (1995). *Mathematics teaching grade 1.* Moscow: Miros.

Kaput, J. (1999). Teaching and learning a new algebra with understanding. In E. Fennema, & T. Romberg (Eds.), *Mathematics classrooms that promote understanding* (p. 3-19). Mahwah, NJ: Erlbaum.

Krutetskii, V. A. (1976). *The psychology of mathematical abilities in school children.* Chicago: University of Chicago.

Minskaya, G. I. (1975). Developing the concept of number by means of the relationship of quantities. In L. P. Steffe (Ed.), *Children's capacity for learning mathematics.* (Soviet studies in the psychology of learning and teaching mathematics, Vol. VII, pp. 7-261). Chicago: University of Chicago.

Rachlin, S., Matsumoto, A. N., & Wada, L. (1987). The teaching experiment: A model for the marriage of teachers and researchers. *Focus on Learning Problems in Mathematics, 9*(3), 21-29.

Rachlin, S. L, Matsumoto, A. N., Wada, L. T., & Dougherty, B. J. (2001). *Algebra I: A process approach* (2nd ed.). Honolulu, HI: University of Hawaii, Curriculum Research & Development Group.

RAND Mathematics Study Panel. (2002). *Mathematical proficiency for all students: Toward a strategic research and development program in mathematics education.* (DRU-2773-OERI). Arlington, VA: RAND Education & Science and Technology Policy Institute.

Shavelson, R. J., Phillips, D. C., Towne, L., & Feuer, M. J. (2003). On the science of education design studies. *Educational Researcher, 32,* 25-28.

Vygotsky, L. S. (1978). *Mind in society.* Cambridge, MA: Harvard University Press.

Wagner, S., Rachlin, S. L., & Jensen, R. J. (1984). *Algebra learning project: Final report.* Athens, GA: University of Georgia, Department of Mathematics Education.

CHAPTER 8

# YOU CHANGED MY MIND
# ABOUT TRIANGLES!

**Lori Renfro**
*Dysart Unified School District, El Mirage, AZ*

Engaging in systematic inquiry in the classroom is a powerful experience that can lead to life-changing results for both teachers and students. Designing tasks to bring out mathematical thinking, observing children engaged in mathematical thinking, collecting data on that thinking, and making instructional decisions based on the data is a powerful sequence of events that leads to a true conceptualization of *teaching for understanding*, a phrase that is otherwise in danger of becoming cliché.

As a first- and then fifth-grade teacher, I had struggled for years trying to figure out what was missing in my mathematics instruction. The children just didn't seem to "get it." And truthfully, I didn't really "get it" either. I was the product of traditional mathematics instruction that emphasized the memorization of procedures and rules. I was never asked to think about the patterns or connections involved with mathematics. Therefore, my content knowledge in mathematics was limited. As I struggled with how to help students become mathematically powerful, an opportunity arose for me to take a "hands-on" mathematics "academy" as part of my school district's systemic initiative. My enrollment in this academy absolutely

*Teachers Engaged in Research*
*Inquiry Into Mathematics Classrooms, Grades Pre-K–2*, pages 153–170
Copyright © 2006 by Information Age Publishing

changed the direction of my life as a teacher and as a learner. I began a journey at that point to learn everything I could about mathematics instruction that builds understanding.

My school district in Phoenix, Arizona—an urban, inner-city district of 20,000 students with a primarily Hispanic population and a free and reduced lunch rate over 80%—was part of a National Science Foundation funded urban systemic initiative called the Phoenix USI. Under this initiative, several of Phoenix's urban districts joined together to provide math and science professional development for classroom teachers. Additionally, funding was provided for a new type of full-time release teacher leader position called a collaborative peer teacher or CPT. The concept behind the CPT model was that classroom teachers would receive intensive professional development in standards-based mathematics and/or science instruction. Teachers that attended the USI academies would then receive support from a CPT as they worked in a risk-free environment to implement standards-based practices in their classrooms. I worked extensively with my CPT while enrolled in USI academies. She supported my growth as a teacher, guiding me as I worked to change my teaching practices and modeling for me when I needed that support in my classroom. I flourished in this environment, and after two years of working with my CPT, I left my fifth-grade classroom to become a CPT myself. I was assigned to two schools in my district, and I began to offer teachers the same type of support I had been offered by my CPT.

## SETTING THE STAGE FOR SYSTEMATIC INQUIRY

My experiences as a CPT were some of the most challenging and rewarding experiences of my educational career. One of these experiences came as part of my involvement in a teacher-as-researcher project that had been organized initially as part of the USI grant, with continuing funding from a Cognitively Guided Instruction (CGI) grant. This two-year project focused on geometry and measurement, a traditionally underserved strand in the elementary curriculum. As part of this project, teachers from USI districts and their CPTs formed a research group called the Phoenix Collaborative. The goal of the project was to engage teachers in systematic inquiry in their classrooms in an effort to improve children's mathematical experiences, especially in the areas of geometry and measurement.

For this research project, I teamed up with two teachers at one of my assigned schools as a CPT. I worked with Jeanette Collins, a kindergarten teacher, and Judy Boch, a second-grade teacher. When the three of us entered into the teacher-as-researcher project, we were highly motivated and ready to engage in systematic inquiry. We hoped to be able to impact the mathematics curriculum in our district, particularly in the area of geometry. We also hoped to provide all of the children with the opportunity to grapple with mathematically powerful ideas while designing a curricular sequence that would emphasize children's understanding of geometric concepts. Our efforts would focus on mathematical content and processes described in NCTM's *Principles and Standards for School Mathematics* (2000). We focused on the content standard for geometry, along with the process standards of problem solving, reasoning and proof, communication, connections, and representation.

Dr. Richard Lehrer, then at the University of Wisconsin–Madison and now at Vanderbilt University, and other nationally recognized mathematics educators and researchers facilitated the work of our group. During the first year, our group focused on developing and expanding our content knowledge in relation to geometry and measurement. We read from *Designing Learning Environments for Developing Understanding of Geometry and Space* (Lehrer & Chazan,1998) and *Mathematics Classrooms that Promote Understanding* (Fennema & Romberg, 1999) to prompt our thinking about how to design appropriate classroom experiences.

We typically met one weekend a month over the two-year period. During these weekends, we engaged in various mathematical activities designed to increase our mathematical content knowledge. We also engaged in discussion about what this would mean for our students. For example, on one of our weekends we created measuring tapes (construction paper strips) using "personal units" and used them to measure various objects. We then talked about concepts of measurement like iteration and zero point. We would then go back to our districts and try out some of these activities so that when we met again we could discuss the successes and challenges that came up as we worked with the students.

During the second year of the project, our group became more focused. We decided to move forward in our learning by engaging in classroom inquiry in a more systematic manner, researching how children thought about geometry and measurement and collecting this information to document our process. Our mission was focused on one central theme—that mathematics should be taught with understanding. We had all witnessed the limitations that traditional mathematics instruction can impose on students, and we were highly committed to assisting students develop mathematical knowledge that they understood and could transfer to other situations. This is why engaging in systematic inquiry became so important to us. As teachers, *we* also needed to learn with understanding.

The Phoenix Collaborative was engaged with inquiry on two different levels. One level was with the students, but the other level involved us as researchers. We had to struggle with defining what *inquiry* was all about, and what practices would qualify as inquiry. It was far from a smooth process, and we made many mistakes along the way! We often didn't have clearly defined research questions and procedures. We would just repeat an activity we had done in the Academy and we would find out all of this interesting information, but we did not always have a clear focus and that hindered our work at first. That was part of the journey—a journey that was sometimes messy but extremely rewarding in the end.

We worked as a group to define the processes and procedures that would be used to guide the inquiry process in our classrooms. Dr. Richard Lehrer facilitated our discussions and gave guidance in relation to designing appropriate tasks for our students. We decided as a group that we would collect information and record growth over time, documenting student thinking using a case study approach. Each team selected 3-5 individual students to focus on when collecting information. We also agreed to collect samples of student work from the students we identified for case studies as well as representative samples from the class. We would also record interviews on audiotapes with the students selected for case studies, and we would use field notes and observational data to further document student learning.

One of the resources that we used to define our work was *Entering the Child's Mind* (1997) by Herbert P. Ginsburg. Ginsburg's discussion of clinical interviews would drive what we did during our interviews with children. Using this resource under Dr. Lehrer's guidance helped us to see the possibilities that interviewing children would present. We would basically be able to assess what individual children knew using specific techniques to draw out children's understanding of mathematical concepts. It was through this dialogue that we discussed the importance of allowing students to solve problems their own way, asking students for justification of their ideas (e,g., How could you make sure you are really right about that?), rephrasing questions when necessary, changing the task if necessary, and offering counter-suggestions.

We would also design thought-provoking tasks for students that would reveal something about their thinking. Dr. Lehrer provided a structure for us to follow that allowed us to gain crucial information. As we designed tasks, we would consider two important ideas: What would we make *problematic?* and What would we design as *transparent?* Two other ideas would also help us in designing our tasks—tools and support. What tools would we provide for children to use during the tasks and what support would we offer them? The support would often prove to be a problematic thing for us as teachers, as we hoped to be working within each student's *zone of proximal development,* (Ginsburg, 1997) while supporting their thinking. At times, however, this proved to be an ongoing struggle—identifying individual zones of proximal development and providing the support necessary to operate in this zone and assist the children in their thinking about mathematical concepts. Based on Ginsburg's work, the Phoenix Collaborative decided that we would offer children support during the interviewing process. As Ginsburg (1997) states, "If the child acting alone cannot solve a problem, perhaps she will overcome the difficulty when provided with some form of social support" (p. 155).

Many of us struggled with this concept of providing support as we worked to collect our data. We continually had to decide how much support to offer and in what format. We had to decide when to give hints and to what degree. We struggled with our questioning, sometimes crippled by limited content knowledge in relation to geometric thinking. We had to think about when to alter a task or when to ask children for justification of their ideas. We had to decide how the available tools were also providing support.

## LOOKING AT KINDERGARTEN

This section shares two episodes from Jeanette's kindergarten classroom that illuminate our research journey together. The first episode, provided as a vignette, focuses on our early exploration of children's definitions for triangles. The second episode focuses on our later inquiry into children's understanding of two-dimensional representations of cubes. Together, these two episodes illustrate the iterative nature of our research, the evolution of our research questions, and the conclusions we have made about the growth in children's definitions for shapes over time.

The vignette that follows is constructed from observational data, field notes, and student interviews from the work Jeanette and I did in her classroom. Jeanette and I were fascinated and, at times, stunned by the thinking that was generated by her 5- and 6-year-old students. This vignette summarizes what her students were thinking in relation to the concept of shapes.

Kindergarteners traditionally have learned about shapes in a very rote manner, and we wanted to see if they could begin to think about shapes as collections of properties. Our initial research question was basically, "How do kindergarten students think about shapes?" The events described below happened during one class session during the second year of our two-year project.

### Kindergarten Vignette

Casey stood before the class looking at the following figure drawn on the board (see Figure 8.1).

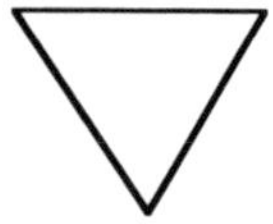

Figure 8.1.   Triangle.

Jeanette had just asked her class if the figure drawn on the board was a triangle. During a prior class session, the class had come to an agreement that a triangle had "three sides" and "three angles." Jeanette and I made eye contact across the room as Casey explained (while "drawing" in the air with her finger) that the figure was not a triangle because it had to be "down, down, and across the bottom." We were both surprised by Casey's observation. As I worked to capture this information in my notes, Jeanette continued the class discussion. Again, Casey reiterated, "triangles have to have a bottom." The other children responded to Casey's observation in a variety of ways. Many agreed with Casey's observation. Others disagreed and said that triangles could be turned in different ways. Jeanette spontaneously began picking up various objects in the classroom and rotating them in different directions. As she rotated each item she asked the students if it was still the same item (e.g., "Is this still a crayon if I turn it this way?"). The students quickly responded "yes" to each of Jeanette's queries.

To enhance the discussion and continue to find out what the children were thinking, Jeanette decided to play the *What is it?* game. This is a game we had used many times in the classroom to help the children refine their ideas. Jeanette drew a shape on the board and had the students use their current "triangle" definition to prove or disprove that the shape drawn on the board was a triangle. Jeanette, using a concept we had learned in our teacher-as-researcher group called "giving counterexamples," drew a three-sided figure on the board to gain additional insight into what the children were thinking. The figure contained three sides, which fit the children's current definition (see Figure 8.2).

As the class discussed whether or not this figure was a triangle, Sage tested the "shape" by pointing to the lines and angles as he counted them. He then explained that it didn't work because "it has 3 sides, but it doesn't

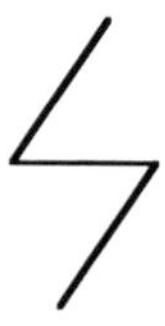

Figure 8.2.   Figure meeting the definition.

△

Figure 8.3.   Isosceles triangle in standard position.

have 3 angles." The class agreed that they could make it into a triangle by moving the bottom line to a different position.

As a point of reference, it is important to note here that the kindergarten students were using vocabulary that they had been exposed to in class. For example, Sage used the word "angles" without hesitation. In a prior lesson, as the students were discussing shapes, Jeanette informed the students that the mathematical term for the property they were observing was "angle." The kindergarten students picked up these terms and used them with ease during discussion. Jeanette reinforced their use of this vocabulary.

Jeanette then went back to the traditional orientation of an isosceles triangle and asked if this shape was a triangle (see Figure 8.3).

Three children tested the shape against the class definition. One child came up and counted the sides and stated, "It has 3 sides." Another child pointed to each angle and said, "It has 3 angles." The class agreed that the shape was indeed a triangle. Another child excitedly came up and pointed at the "vertices" and exclaimed, "I thought of something else! It has 3 points." Vincent added that he thought those were called "corners." It was decided by the class that this was an important attribute, so they agreed to add "3 corners" to the triangle definition. The new class definition, which demonstrated the progression in thinking about the attributes of the triangle as mathematically important, now stood as 3 edges (sides), 3 angles, and 3 corners.

With this definition in mind, Jeanette then redrew on the board the "upside down" triangle (see Figure 8.4) that had proven problematic for some students earlier in the discussion.

One of the children agreed to come up and test this figure to see if it fit the definition of a triangle. As Jeanette led him through the three statements in the class definition, he agreed that it had 3 sides, 3 corners, and 3

Figure 8.4.   "Upside down" triangle.

Figure 8.5.  Shape not closed.

angles and he demonstrated this by pointing to each of those features on the drawing. At this point, Jeanette asked the children if they believed this was a triangle. All of the students agreed that it was a triangle, including Vincent and Casey who had argued against it earlier.

To help the children continue exploring and refining their definition of a triangle, Jeanette then drew the following figure on the board (See Figure 8.5).

Megan tested the shape and counted 3 sides. As Megan was doing this, the rest of the children became very excited and started shouting out that the shape did not have 3 corners. They quickly began to explain that the "sides" had to touch. Jeanette added this information to the class definition. The definition now read: 3 edges (sides) that touch each other, 3 angles, and 3 corners.

With this new information added to the definition, Jeanette revisited the first three drawings and had the children decide whether or not the drawings still fit the definition. The class agreed that the first three shapes were still triangles. Vincent also decided to inform us that the third shape was a triangle, but "it is upside down." Jeanette and I again made eye contact across the room. We were very excited about the class discussion and where it was going. Because the children continued to be interested and engaged in the discussion, we decided to continue. Due to the fact that Vincent still felt compelled to address the triangle as upside down, Jeanette decided to draw the following figure on the board (see Figure 8.6).

Many of the students said it was a triangle, while others remained fixated on the orientation and felt it needed to be rotated. Destiny explained, "It is an upside-over triangle. When it's upside down or upside over it doesn't look like a triangle." Another student who had previously endorsed Casey's idea that triangles had to have a bottom came to the conclusion, "Triangles can go over any way, but they are still triangles."

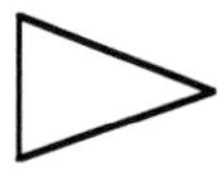

Figure 8.6.  Triangle not in standard positions.

That was a pivotal moment for Jeanette and me as we realized that the children had evolved in their thinking about triangles. We were extremely excited about what seemed like a very productive class discussion, with children beginning to look at a triangle as being composed of certain characteristics, or properties. A child confirmed our belief in this progress when he excitedly explained, as he was leaving school that day, "Mrs. Collins, I learned something new today. You changed my mind about triangles!"

This vignette effectively captures what Jeanette and I were trying to learn about children's definitions for shapes, although we figured out that our research question had really been too broad. Instead of the question, "How do students think about shapes?" perhaps our question should have been, "Through classroom instruction, how can we influence kindergarteners' perceptions of what a shape is in ways that result in conceptual changes?" This process of revisiting and refining our research question was an ongoing piece of our learning.

## EXPLORING TWO-DIMENSIONAL REPRESENTATIONS FOR CUBES

As teacher-researchers, we struggled with two important issues: (1) What was an appropriate question? and (2) What would we need to do to collect information related to the question while continually trying to incorporate practices into instruction that would fit with our mission of teaching for understanding? These issues can be illustrated with the work Jeanette and I did while investigating student thinking in relation to three-dimensional forms. We found out through this process about the importance of student interviews as a research tool; we sometimes struggled with our own limitations with respect to geometric content knowledge; and we continued to refine our identification of research questions.

To work with three-dimensional shapes, Jeanette and I introduced a new tool called Polydrons.$^{TM}$ These are specially designed plastic shapes that can be snapped together to form two-dimensional polygons and three-dimensional polyhedra. This tool allowed us to gain insight into what students were thinking about as they composed and decomposed two- and three-dimensional forms. One of the tasks we designed for students involved using the Polydrons to find all of the nets (two dimensional representations of three-dimensional figures) for a cube. This is also one of the tasks that Dr. Lehrer had us do as participants in the Phoenix Collaborative. We understood that by working with nets students could develop understandings about how solids are constructed, which is an important geometric concept. Jeanette's kindergarten students had already spent time constructing solids, so we moved ahead to see if they could identify different nets for a

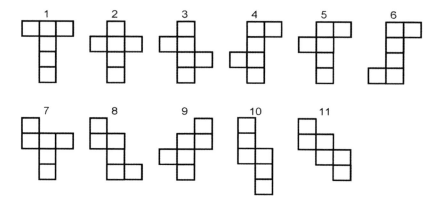

Figure 8.7.   Nets for a cube.

cube. For reference purposes, the chart below shows all of the possible nets for a cube (see Figure 8.7).

Our first task involved having the students make a cube with Polydron squares. Then Jeanette showed the class how to take apart a cube, leaving the squares attached to each other, to make a flat configuration. Jeanette then took apart another cube, which resulted in a different formation. The students were very impressed by this, and we challenged the class to see if they could come up with any more of these flat formations that we referred to as "nets." As Jeanette and I moved through this activity with the students, we recorded our observations in field notes. We were able to document who was having trouble with the activity and who was finding success, but we noticed our field notes were not giving us enough information. We decided at this point that we would conduct student interviews (using the case study students) in order to more thoroughly explore their thinking. At this point, Jeanette and I were struggling with what our research question was. This was partially due to the fact that we were trying to understand what the mathematical purpose of the activity was. It was easy to say, "Let's see if we can find all of the nets for a cube." But, so what? Why was this important in developing geometric thinking? This was a perfect example of how we struggled with content knowledge issues as we conducted our research. We demonstrated the saying "If you don't understand where you are going, then it is difficult to get there."

Jeanette and I decided that we would concentrate on trying to determine how 5- and 6-year olds think about nets for a cube by asking the case

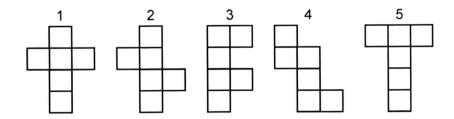

Figure 8.8.   Testing nets.

study students whether a given configuration would fold up into a net or not. The following configurations were shown to the students, with #3 being the only configuration that would not fold up into a cube (see Figure 8.8).

To document student responses, I made audiotapes. Although it was very time consuming to transcribe the audiotapes, it was very helpful in documenting what the students actually had said. These interviews turned out to be very interesting experiences for Jeanette and me, as we learned things from the student interviews that we would not have learned otherwise. We also learned about the importance of asking appropriate follow-up questions to probe further into what students were thinking. For example, as I was conducting the interviews, I decided that when I got to the third configuration I would ask the student (if they predicted correctly), "Is there something you could change on here so that it would fold into a cube?" This wasn't something I had planned on asking, but in thinking about Ginsburg's emphasis on asking children for justification of their ideas, I felt this question would give me better information. By asking this question, I was able to find out that some of our case study students had definite ideas about what configurations would fold up into cubes. For example, Bailey explained (referring to configuration #3), "You don't have anything on the one side," indicating a need to move a square to the other side. Destiny gave an almost identical response. I also decided to go more in depth with Vincent, following Ginsburg's advice about providing support to students during the interview process. I ended up making an additional configuration for Vincent because I felt I still did not know enough about what he was thinking about nets, and he was having a difficult time verbalizing his thoughts for me. I showed Vincent the configuration shown below and asked him if it would fold up into a cube (see Figure 8.9).

He indicated that it would. In order to further understand his thinking, I asked him if he could show me where the bottom would be when it was

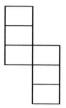

Figure 8.9.   A net to test Vincent's thinking.

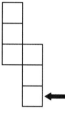

Figure 8.10.   Vincent's idea of where the bottom of the cube would be.

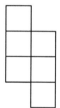

Figure 8.11: Previous net with 3 cubes moved up one position.

folded up. He pointed at the bottom-most square as indicated below (see Figure 8.10).

Still unsure of what he was thinking, I asked Vincent, "What if I took these bottom three off and moved them up? Would that fold into a cube?" (See Figure 8.11.)

I was surprised at what Vincent said. He responded by stating that the figure would not fold into a cube, because "four in the middle won't work." This led Jeanette and I to believe that Vincent did really have some ideas about nets that he had not been able to articulate. From this experience, Jeanette and I learned that conducting interviews was a critical piece of our research efforts if we truly wanted to understand what students understood. Although very time consuming, conducting interviews allowed us to gain information we would not have been able to gain when working with students during regular classroom instruction. We were also able to refine our questioning skills—learning what questions to ask and how far to go to help the students show and explain what they knew.

## RESULTS OF ENGAGING IN SYSTEMATIC INQUIRY

Jeanette and I gained valuable information as we worked with the kindergarten students on shape and dimension. We had begun our work with shape identification by collaborating with the children to create definitions for common shapes—recording student definitions on chart paper, and then modifying the definitions based on class conversation. At the beginning of the school year, as we examined children's thinking about shapes and held active discussions with the class, it was evident that they did not really have a complete understanding of shapes and their properties. Later, as the class worked to create and define definitions, they developed a shared language that would lead their definitions to become more mathematical as the year progressed, depending less on what a shape resembled and more on its mathematical features. For example, in August, a child might have defined a rectangle as "the same as a door." In January, that same child might have said, "A rectangle has 4 sides or edges that touch each other." Jeanette and I are able to make this statement because, as we collected information over time, we noticed patterns emerging— both with our case study students and with the class as a whole.

In order to communicate this information back to the Phoenix Collaborative, Jeanette and I began to develop preliminary frameworks related to the topics we were studying. The chart below (see Table 8.1) shows the progression in thinking that Jeanette and I documented over time and presented to our colleagues in the Phoenix Collaborative.

To construct this chart, Jeanette and I analyzed student responses from our notes that were compiled over several class sessions. These generalizations, although based on our evidence, are preliminary and will need to be revisited with other groups of children to see if the same patterns emerge. We would also like to examine the extent to which these changes are vocabulary based or represent cognitive changes. Based on the data we collected, however, Jeanette and I were able to categorize how the children were reasoning about shapes over a period of several weeks. The goal of our instruction was to have students think about shapes as being made up of properties in order to form the basis for later work with two- and three-dimensional concepts. Although we would have liked to spend more time with this concept, we were able to notice a progression from reasoning about shapes based on resemblance (e.g., "An oval is a circle's cousin... almost the same. A circle would need to be stretched to be an oval.") to

Table 8.1.   Progression of thinking.

| How do Kindergarten Children Define Shapes? | |
| --- | --- |
| *Early Thinking* | *Later Thinking* |
| Triangle | Triangle |
| • a roof, the top of an A, or pointing to triangles in the classroom.<br>• has three sides | • 3 edges (sides) that touch each other<br>• 3 angles<br>• 3 corners |
| Circle | Circle |
| • goes round and round<br>• no sides<br>• looks like a plate, an "o", cookie, etc. | • 1 edge or side that never ends<br>• no angles<br>• no corners |
| Square | Square |
| • looks like a box, the boxes inside a calendar, or a book<br>• 4 sides<br>• 4 the same | • 4 sides or edges that touch each other<br>• 4 angles<br>• 4 corners<br>• all sides need to be the same size |
| Rectangle | Rectangle |
| • 4 sides (2 short, 2 long)<br>• looks like a door, chalkboard, a table, a book, etc. | • 4 edges or sides that touch each other<br>• 2 short sides and 2 long sides<br>• 4 angles<br>• 4 corners<br>• flatter than a square |
| Oval | Oval |
| • no ideas | • 1 side that never ends<br>• no corners<br>• not round, flatter than a circle<br>• like a potato, a lollipop, a tape loop |
| Hexagon | Hexagon |
| • no ideas | • 6 edges or sides that touch each other<br>• 6 angles<br>• 6 corners<br>• sides that are all the same size |

reasoning about shapes based on their characteristics or attributes (e.g., "It has three pointy parts.") to reasoning about shapes as a collection of properties (e.g., "A circle has one side that never stops. It keeps going around and around. It has no angles or corners."). Watching definitions evolve from resemblance-based to attribute-based was an exciting part of what we saw happening in the classroom as the students worked to define triangles, squares, rectangles, and circles.

As students were asked to explain their thinking and allowed to participate in mathematical discussions, their reasoning about shape matured from being guided only by what they could see, to seeing shapes as collections of properties. We also discovered, however, that this predictable pattern was not as stable as we originally predicted. Many children appeared to "come in and out of knowing." For example, one of the children whose thinking we documented through a case study oscillated between thinking of shapes as visual prototypes (what something looks like) and thinking of shapes as composed of attributes or characteristics. For instance, when discussing squares, Bailey focused on the characteristics of the square, pointing to the sides and stating, "It has four sides. Squares have to have sides that are all the same." Later in the same discussion, when a large square was drawn on the board, she looked confused and said, "That's not a square. Squares have to be small." This illustrated for us Bailey's oscillation between what she felt a square should look like (perception) and her knowledge that squares have four sides (conception).

While probing children's thinking in relation to shape identification, Jeanette and I were able to allow students the opportunity to talk about and discover properties of shapes. Our class discussions allowed children the opportunity to clarify their own thinking and make changes in their understanding of shapes. Jeanette, as she facilitated this class discussion, was able to interact with children and help them sift through and organize this information. She asked questions to push children's thinking. Through this type of discussion, the children also learned effective techniques for arguing mathematical points in a constructive manner. If we don't build time in our classrooms for these types of conversations to occur, then we prevent children from expanding their mathematical knowledge in productive ways. Although the kindergarten students' definitions were works in progress, the process of writing definitions provided opportunities to consider shapes as bearers of properties and definitions as ways of thinking about these properties in a manner that could be shared by all.

In addition to experiencing success with the process of defining shapes, we also learned from our mistakes as we worked with three-dimensional shapes. One of the activities we engaged the kindergarten students with when studying nets was to have them draw the nets they discovered. As we collected these drawings, we were surprised at the wide variations in the students' representations. Some students traced their net formations, providing a very literal representation. Others were able to draw the nets without having to trace, using the correct shape and representing the correct number of squares. Some students, however, drew many more squares than needed, and other students used shapes other than squares. Jeanette and I sorted these representations and were intrigued by the selection. As we began to consider the meaning of this information, however, we realized we had left a critical piece out of our data collection. We knew from the NCTM *Principles and Standards* and from our readings in *Mathematics Classrooms that Promote Understanding* (Fennema & Romberg, 1999) that representations can be used to organize, record, and communicate mathematical ideas. We had neglected, however, to interview students or ask any questions of the class as a whole on why they had drawn what they did and what the features of their drawings meant. This was an important lesson in our roles as teacher-researchers. We learned that you have to go one step further than you think you have to if you really want to get at student understanding. Again, our limited geometric content knowledge hindered our ability to come up with a research question that was related to the task of having students draw the nets. If we had been able to do that, we would probably have been able to anticipate needing to question students to determine what the features of their representations meant. For example, we could have crafted a research question like, "What mathematical features will students include in their net representations?" If we had started with that question in mind, then we would have known, for example, to ask the student who drew 16 squares in the shape of a "T" what the individual squares represented. We definitely learned from our mistakes as we moved through the systematic inquiry process.

## CONCLUSION

Engaging in classroom research in the form of inquiry can be a powerful learning tool for educators looking to improve their instructional practice. My involvement in this teacher-as-researcher project expanded my content knowledge in the areas of geometry and measurement and helped me develop questioning skills that enhanced my repertoire of formative assessment strategies. My involvement with systematic inquiry and the experiences I had as a result of struggling through the process with my colleagues in the Phoenix Collaborative helped cement the importance for me of teaching mathematics with understanding. As Romberg and Kaput (1999) state, "The aim of mathematics teaching can be described, in practical terms, as teaching students to use mathematics to build and communicate ideas, to use it as a powerful analytic and problem solving tool, and to be fascinated by the patterns it embodies and exposes" (p. 16). This is what the teachers in the Phoenix Collaborative were really striving for. We are forever changed in the way we view the world of mathematics instruction. The inquiry process can be challenging, but the rewards are great.

## ACKNOWLEDGMENT

I would like to thank Jeanette Collins from Cartwright School District for her amazing ability to provide unwavering support for the learners in her classroom. Jeanette's willingness to expand the traditional kindergarten curriculum allowed us to develop a better understanding of young children's mathematical thinking.

I would also like to thank Dr. Richard Lehrer from Vanderbilt University for his commitment to guiding me and Jeanette as we struggled through the inquiry process. His questions challenged and motivated us both as teachers and learners, and we are forever changed by the experience.

## REFERENCES

Fennema, E., & Romberg, T. A. (1999). *Mathematics classrooms that promote understanding*. Mahwah, NJ: Erlbaum.

Ginsburg, H. P. (1997). *Entering the child's mind*. Cambridge, UK: Cambridge University Press.

Lehrer, R., & Chazan, D. (1998). *Designing learning environments for developing understanding of geometry and space*. Mahwah, NJ: Erlbaum.

National Council of Teachers of Mathematics. (2000). *Principles and standards for school mathematics*. Reston, VA: Author.

Romberg, T. A., & Kaput, J. J. (1999). "Mathematics worth teaching, mathematics worth understanding." In E. Fennema & T. A. Romberg (Eds.), *Mathematics classrooms that promote understanding* (pp. 3-17). Mahwah, NJ: Erlbaum.

CHAPTER 9

# USING CLASSROOM ASSESSMENT TO SUPPORT GROWTH OF NUMBER SENSE IN FIRST GRADE

**Laurie Hands**

As a first grade teacher of mathematics, I worked to focus my teaching to meet the wide variety of students' mathematical abilities in my classroom. It was my goal to move all students to achieve my school district's mathematics standards for first grade. Using the *Investigations in Number, Data, and Space*® (*Investigations*) curriculum materials, I taught mathematical concepts through modeling, student led discussions, games, manipulatives, story problems, and child-centered investigations. Though I believed this curriculum to be effective for guiding students to deep understandings of mathematics, I questioned how I could go beyond the printed units to best assess students' prior knowledge, differentiate instruction to meet various students' needs, and to move students further along the continuum of mathematical understanding. These questions became the focus of my masters' project.

*Teachers Engaged in Research*
*Inquiry Into Mathematics Classrooms, Grades Pre-K–2*, pages 171–210
Copyright © 2006 by Information Age Publishing
All rights of reproduction in any form reserved.

I taught in a small, middle class, neighborhood school in the Northwest United States. The school population was 80% Caucasian, 10% Asian American, and 10% African American and Hispanic. My class of 21 students included 11 boys and 10 girls. The whole school had a close working relationship with a local university. Student teachers were present each year, professors led discussions about research projects at our faculty meetings, and new approaches to teaching were often field tested in our classrooms. The parent community was very involved in all aspects of the students' learning, so parents were often in my classroom during mathematics lessons. The teaching community at my school encouraged collaboration, innovation, and educational research. With the support of an incredible principal, I was able to take risks with my teaching, experiment with improving the effectiveness of curriculum, and collaborate with colleagues to improve my instruction.

My master's project is one example of experimenting with improving the effectiveness of curriculum. I focused my research project on number sense specifically because I believed it provides the foundation for all mathematical learning in first grade. It was also important to me to have a clear picture of each of my students' mathematical understanding, so that I could teach them through connecting to their prior knowledge and move them from concrete understandings to more abstract understandings of number and operations.

Going into my project, I had assessments that were rooted in my district standards and the NCTM Standards (2000), assessments that connected to the curriculum, instructional techniques that differentiated learning, and a strong curriculum to support my teaching. To ensure academic success for all of my students, I felt that I needed to add pre- and post-assessments that connected to my lessons in order to drive my instruction and effectively assess my students' mathematical knowledge. Such assessments were not an integral part of the *Investigations* units.

Another difficulty for me in assessing knowledge and growth arose when I determined that my district's assessments did not align very well with the *Investigations* curriculum. I wanted to get a clearer picture of where my students were starting in their number sense and where they were ending after a series of lessons and activities. I wanted my more advanced students to grow in mathematical understanding as much as my lower achieving students. And although the *Investigations* curriculum addressed learning extensions for students, I felt a need for somewhat richer activities to challenge my most advanced learners. I knew from personal experience that the lessons in the *Investigations* unit on number sense were consistently engaging for my students, but some individual learning activities were not always what I thought every student needed to deepen their number sense knowledge. I came to know these needs and develop these questions based on my seven years of teaching first grade and my four years of experience with the *Investigations* curriculum.

## PROJECT DESIGN

My research project had three main components. The first was pre-assessing, the second was lesson plan analysis and adjustments, and the third was formative and summative assessments that showed student mathematical growth. I created pre-assessments and an interview based on the goals for the number sense unit, district standards, and NCTM standards. At the time, the *Investigations* curriculum did not provide teachers with pre-assessment materials that assisted in targeting students' prior knowledge of the mathematical concepts in the unit. Therefore, I created a pre-assessment that aligned with the district standards and the curriculum, assisted me in targeting instruction, and allowed me to explore what my students already understood about number sense.

### Pre-Assessment Development

The pre-assessment I created was an interview. I chose the interview format because I wanted to be able to observe my students working, analyze their strategies, and listen to their explanations of number and what they understood. An interview allowed me as the teacher to have one on one, uninterrupted time to focus on a student and take notes about their learning processes.

I based the interview on the goals of the unit and the district standards with design assistance from an article by DeAnn Huinker. She explained that the "advantages of using interviews include the opportunity to delve deeply into students' thinking and reasoning, to better determine their level of understanding, to diagnose misconceptions and missing connections, and to assess their verbal ability to communicate mathematical knowledge" (Huinker, 1993, p. 80). She also laid out explicit guidelines to enhance the effectiveness of interviews. She suggested that prior to conducting interviews it is important that teachers ask themselves specific questions in order to narrow their focus and clarify their goals. These questions include: What do I want to learn about my students? How am I going to record the results? Whom do I want to interview? When and where will I conduct the interview? Huinker also provided guidelines to follow during the interview, such as: Students should be asked to think aloud; students should be informed that the teacher will be taking notes; the teacher should observe and listen carefully; probing questions should be asked to further clarify student thinking; and finally, everything relevant to the goals of the interview should be recorded as the interview is happening to ensure key points are not forgotten. I thought Huinker's guidelines were very helpful and I incorporated many of them when creating and conducting my pre-assessment interview.

I also drew from my experience with an interview my first grade team had previously created and administered. The problem with this previous interview was that it was strongly based on district first-grade standards for number sense rather than being closely aligned with the *Investigations* curriculum. We found as teachers that although the information we gleaned from that interview was helpful in analyzing students' number sense, it was not helpful in guiding us to modify lessons or target instruction for specific students. As a first grade team, when we tried to chart and analyze the data from that interview, we realized the goals from the lessons did not match up with the interview goals and questions. We found that we still had many questions about the students' mathematical understanding, and we were unsure about how to modify lessons to effectively differentiate instruction and meet students' needs. It was out of this frustration and confusion that I decided to redesign the pre-assessment interview and better align it with the goals of the *Investigations* number sense unit titled *Building Number Sense* (Kliman & Russell, 1998).

My revised pre-assessment interview was based more closely on the unit's number sense goals, as identified in the *Investigations* program materials, which included:

- Counting to 100 by ones
- Using counting strategies and organization for counting two quantities
- Identifying and reading numbers from 1-100
- Finding the larger of two quantities
- Making 10 using two quantities
- Solving problems in combining and separating situations and showing strategies
- Finding the total of two quantities and explaining strategies
- Writing and sequencing numbers to 100

The pre-assessment interview (see Appendix A) consisted of two pages of questions with space for the interviewer to record comments and observations. I decided not to print these pages two-sided so the interviewer could continue writing on the back of the page if needed. In addition to the interviewer's recording pages, there were three pages for the students to record their work for those questions that involved a written solution. Again, I did not print these two-sided so that the students had the freedom to utilize the back of the page. There was also a blank 100 chart for the students to fill in, and the interviewer utilized a completed 100 chart when asking number identification questions.

I based the format of the pre-assessment on my prior attempt at creating an interview with my first grade team. I found that it was important to have enough room to take notes in order to effectively record the information gleaned from the questions. Also, due to the pace at which the students worked, it was important to have some guiding questions written on the interview document. These questions prompted the interviewer to probe deeper into the students' mathematical knowledge. Along with guiding questions, I also included pre-printed comments that could be circled quickly to indicate student understanding or actions. These were based on prior knowledge of what students often do when asked such questions. These comments were also based on research about developmentally appropriate responses and strategies that children in Grade 1 tend to exhibit. Having comments pre-printed allowed for quicker note taking and guided the interviewer to watch for key elements of understanding that might emerge.

The interview was given in its entirety to individual students, except for the task to fill in a 100 chart, which was given separately because of the length of time most students took to complete that task. Breaks were given during the interview based on student need and school scheduling conflicts such as recess, PE, music, and lunch. The two most effective interview times were at the beginning of the school day from 9:10–10:30 am or the last hour of the day after snack, while the other students were having choice time. These periods provided the most effective one-on-one time without interruptions.

## Differentiating Lessons to Meet Students' Needs

The second component of my project was analyzing and adapting lessons from the first grade unit. I taught some lessons as specified in the curriculum materials. I determined from the student pre-assessment data that a few of the lessons needed extra extensions or remediation. Even though the curriculum materials suggested ways to both remediate and extend lessons for students, these ideas did not always go into sufficient depth, provide concrete examples to use with students, or provide enough extension for the most advanced students. The pre-assessment provided concrete evidence of the wide range of students' number sense which I used to identify the specific areas of the lessons that I needed to modify to provide the most appropriate extension and remediation activities.

The *Investigations* units include a series of investigations with multiple *sessions* (lessons) within each investigation that focus on learning mathematical big ideas. With the students' mathematical understandings in mind, I analyzed the lessons within the number sense unit and differentiated the lesson plans by comparing the goals and objectives from each lesson with the pre-assessment data. I ended up modifying one or two lessons in each of the investigations in the unit. For each session I used a template from Carol Ann Tomlinson's (2001) book on differentiating instruction. The example provided in Appendix B shows how I differentiated one lesson to meet various needs of my students. Differentiating this particular lesson involved an iterative process of trying out the modified lesson with students and revising it to adjust the levels of challenge, particularly for my most capable students.

For this process I also considered the materials I had received during a workshop I had attended given by Dr. Roger Taylor (undated), an educator and advocate for differentiated instruction for advanced learners. One of his models for differentiated instruction calls for the teacher to use the levels of Bloom's taxonomy as a "central hub." He suggested looking at each level of thinking and connecting a process verb to stimulate thought in students. He said to utilize a list of outcome products or projects that match the level of thinking that a student was exhibiting. For example, at the analysis level, one of the process verbs to stimulate student thinking was "compare." Taylor suggested using the idea of comparing in a lesson to exercise that level of thinking about specific content. A comparison diagram or graph is an example of a mathematics end product at that level.

As evidence of the effectiveness of these modifications, and to provide additional data about the range of student growth in number sense, I collected work from six focus students as they completed the unit sessions. I selected these students based on their overall number sense, identifying two students at each of the following levels: above standard, at standard, and below standard in this area. I made these choices by comparing students' pre-assessment results with my school district's standards. During the project, I collected all of the Student Activity Pages from the unit which were completed by these focus students, including those pages that I had modified or had created to support extension and remediation activities.

## Formative and Summative Assessments

The final component of my project was assessing through both formative and summative assessments. Certain lessons within the number sense unit were identified as Teacher Checkpoints and Embedded Assessment Activities, providing opportunities to use formative assessment to check-in with individual students, reflect on how the class is doing overall, and support students' growth. These lessons, which from the students' point of view were no different from other lessons, included (among others): *Twelve Cats and Dogs* (Investigation 2, Session 1), *Three Towers* (Investigation 2, Session 9), and *Solving Story Problems* (Investigation 4, Session 10). For these three lessons, I referenced the *Observing the Students* section in the lesson where clear focus questions were given to utilize while observing students. I recorded my observations on a grid that contained the class list of student's names. I listed key focus questions at the top of the grid to assist in focusing my observations. Examples of these focus questions were, "Do students have a sense of how to begin the problem?" "How do they model the problem?" and "Do they work mentally?"

At the completion of the unit, I administered three post-assessments with the goal that students would show deeper understanding and learning over a period of time. One assessment was a 100 chart fill-in, which was a repeat of the task given during the pre-assessment. Second, I modified and administered a district classroom-based assessment of number sense (see Appendix C). This assessment was modified to better align with both the district standards and the *Investigations* curriculum. Third, I administered one of the assessment tasks designed for this unit from the *Investigations* Assessment Sourcebook for Grade 1 (TERC, undated). I used this assessment task as printed for my below- and at-standard students and created a modified version of this task for my above-standard students (see Appendix D).

The district provided mandatory summative assessments for each of the various math strands to document student achievement. These assessments did not align well with the goals of the *Investigations* curriculum and were not effective measures of my students' understanding and growth. The district's number sense assessment was particularly troublesome, making it a constant frustration for the first-grade teacher team.

I changed a number of things on the district number-sense assessment. First, I changed the format because it did not allow enough room for students to show mathematical strategies. I also changed the format of the computation problems to include both vertical and horizontal arrangements. My students were familiar with both of these formats and needed to be assessed both ways. These computation problems were formatted within boxes that allowed room for students to show a picture of what the problem would look like using a physical representation. This format carried over from the original district assessment, and this format aligned well with the district standards. To better align the remainder of the assessment with the district standards as well as the *Investigations* curriculum, I changed the wording/format of some of the story problems and added two more of them: one combining situation and one separating situation. The new wording asked students to solve the story problems and to show their strategies in pictures, numbers, or words. This part of the assessment was in alignment with the *Investigations* number sense unit. This part of the assessment allowed me to evaluate computation, problem solving strategies, and communication of understanding and thinking.

The final addition to the original assessment was a student self-reflection. I felt it was important for the students to reflect about their thinking, learning, and performance. The students needed to be a part of the assessment process through being aware of teacher expectations, standards, goals, and their role in successfully learning new skills. I used faces for the reflection checklist because I felt it was age appropriate and easy for the students to complete in a timely manner. The students were familiar with self-reflecting using faces in other academic areas such as science.

I drew conclusions about student's number sense development based on analysis of student's work over time and comparing student's pre- and post-assessments. The goal was to show growth for all students in the above-, at-, and below-standard categories. The data I collected assisted me in making further decisions about number sense instruction for my students, both as a whole group and as individuals.

After completing the entire project, I analyzed the changes I had made to the assessments and my differentiated lesson plans. I also reviewed the new ways I discovered that my students approached and solved mathematical problems. Last, I analyzed the entire project as a whole, what I learned, what worked and did not work, and how I might answer my remaining questions.

## ANALYSIS OF THE PRE-ASSESSMENT INTERVIEW

In analyzing the pre-assessment interview, I considered the format of the assessment, its administration, the data I obtained, and how to organize the data for decision making.

### Pre-Assessment Format Analysis

I felt that the changes I made to the pre-assessment format were successful. I had plenty of room to take notes about my students' work and the strategies they utilized. I liked having the freedom to write on the back of the document due to the one-sided format. Although I found it difficult to record everything I desired about the students' thinking, I felt that it was due to a lack of experience recording during interviews and not a formatting issue. The student sheets also provided plenty of room for my students to record answers and strategies. In the future, I would change the format of the student documents to two sided to save paper and assist in organization. The students did not need to utilize the extra space on the backs of the sheets, so condensing the format wouldn't hinder their work.

The pre-written comments were also useful, although I found myself writing everything down in a rush, rather than circling what was already written. These prompts did help me look for certain behaviors or approaches to problem solving. However, with more practice in administering interviews, I think I would become more efficient in circling key components rather than trying to record every detail. As I gain more experience analyzing first-grade work, I will most likely adjust the pre-written comments. As with the guiding questions, having comments pre-written assisted uniformity in administering the interview.The guiding questions were very useful during the interview process. When analyzing a student's thinking and strategies, it was easy to get off track or lose train of thought. The guiding questions such as, "How do you know?" and "Is there another way?" assisted in keeping me focused on leading the students to go deeper with their thinking. These questions also helped with uniformity in administering the interview when others helped interview students.

My choice of manipulatives for students to use during the interview raised additional issues. For the question that asked students to count objects in jars, I provided colored, dry noodles and wooden blocks. Without much forethought, I randomly chose them from a collection of manipulatives I commonly used for estimating activities. I made sure to pre-count the objects so I had an exact total for each jar. What I had not anticipated was that the students might drop or break noodles during the counting process, thus changing the total of the jar. It became difficult for the students to distinguish a broken piece from a whole noodle and to decide whether or not to count a broken piece. In the future, I would make sure that both jars had sturdy objects that would not break with use. The positive aspect to this activity was that the noodle jar and the noodles were smaller in size than the block jar and the blocks. Yet, the total count for the noodles was a higher number than the total count for the wooden blocks. It was interesting to hear the students' comments about the size difference and their responses and reasoning about the relationship of size to total quantity. This was an aspect of the interview question I had not anticipated. For my next version of the pre-assessment, I would make changes in the questions to ensure this area could be revisited purposefully rather than accidentally.

## Pre-Assessment Administration Analysis

Administering the interview was a lengthy process. Each student interview took approximately 25 minutes to complete, not including the 100 chart fill in. I was able to assess 3-5 students per day, thus the pre-assessing process lasted for two weeks. The interview was easily broken into two parts when the school schedule caused an interruption or student fatigue became an issue. Under these circumstances, I gave the student the first five questions, and then administer the last five after the break.

The 100 chart fill in was completed as a whole group within an hour on one day. I carefully observed the students during the 100 chart fill in process and made note of students who struggled and those who finished with ease. I also recorded additional comments about issues that arose during the activity and strategies the students utilized.

To minimize the total time required to administer the individual interviews, I trained an instructional assistant to interview some of the students. This was a successful strategy for me, because I had an assistant who was an amazing educator, and who was willing to take the extra time out of her schedule to meet with me about the pre-assessment process. We were able to establish the same interviewing techniques and be on the same page about how to record data. I could see how this approach, using multiple teachers to assess, could easily be unsuccessful if two teachers did not align closely in their administering and data recording techniques.

One-on-one time with students was achieved by having a structured routine in place for the students who were not being interviewed. I conducted a class discussion so the students were aware of the process and why the interviews were taking place. I asked the students to think about why it would be important for me to have one-on-one time to work with them on math activities. Some of the responses were, "You do that with our reading too," "You need to know what we think," and "You like to watch us do math." Because the students had an understanding about what I was doing, they were easier to manage, thus making the administration of the assessment more successful.

Similarly, when I sat down to interview the students, I told them I would be taking notes about their thinking and their strategies. I told them I was very interested in how they solved the problems and how they got their answers. I asked them to say their thinking out-loud as they worked. These instructions before the interview helped reduce student anxiety and aided note taking during the pre-assessment. Most students shared their thoughts and strategies aloud as they worked; only a few needed to be reminded to do so.

Another management strategy I utilized was to wear a stop sign around my neck during the interviews. The students were familiar with the stop sign from language arts, when I would lead guided reading groups during literacy centers. They knew the sign meant I was working with students and could not be interrupted. The visual cue helped redirect the students to be independent. Thankfully, this management strategy successfully transferred from literacy to math and reduced the interruptions considerably.

## Analysis of Data Examples

The story problem section of the interview led to interesting responses from the students. Across the class, all students understood that they needed to find an answer to the story problem and record it on the student sheet. Conversely, I had a variety of written responses when I asked the students to record their strategy on the paper. The students often would think aloud or orally describe a strategy, and then when asked to write it down, they would record a picture representation of what the problem was asking. For example: Alex (pseudonyms are used for all student names) explained his strategy for solving the combining story: *I have 5 pencils and 4 markers. How many school supplies do I have altogether?* He said "9" right away. When I asked him how he knew, he said, "I hear 5 + 4 = 9 a lot, so I memorized it." Then he added, "5 + 5 = 10, so 5 + 4 = 9." When I asked him to write down his strategy on the paper, he drew a picture of 5 pencils and 4 markers.

Other students like Hally actually recorded the strategy they had used to solve the problem. For the same pencil and marker combining story, Hally had used crayons as manipulatives to assist with her strategy. She had put 4 crayons in one pile and 5 in another pile. She then physically slid the piles together and counted them up by ones. When I asked her to record her strategy, she wrote sentences that described exactly what she had done.

Another point of interest in examining student work was the fact that the majority of the students counted by 1s when counting the objects in the two jars. I told the students I wanted to know the total amount of the objects in the jar, and that they could use any counting strategy to assist them in finding the total. I know that many of the students were capable of counting by 2s, 5s, or 10s, yet only a few students used any grouping strategies in finding the total. I wondered if the question needed to be worded differently to lead them to count in groups if they were capable. Or, I wondered, was it part of the number sense development that they would see a need to use their skills of counting by 2s, 5s, and 10s when finding totals? One student, when told that he could use any counting strategy he wanted, counted by tens and hundreds, even though the number of blocks was between 30 and 50. When counting the noodles, Alex said, "100, 200, 300, 400," then started over and counted "110, 120, 130...." He came up with

137 as a total. When I asked him if 137 was his total, he said, "No, it's 37." He explained that he felt like counting by one hundreds (which was really tens), and that he knew the answer wasn't really 137, but 37. For the second jar he counted by saying, "one-one hundred, two-one hundred, three-one hundred...." He ended up getting to 30-one hundred and stated his answer as 30. Again, when questioned about his strategy, he said that he "felt like counting by hundreds." It seemed that Alex used this strategy for fun or to be creative, though it was not very efficient. This reminds me of students who demonstrate advanced mathematical reasoning, who when asked to record their strategy, draw pictures that are concrete representations of the problem. I think my students still need a lot of exposure to strategy recording and also need to establish their own understanding of what showing strategies means.

## Pre-Assessment Data Organization

Once the assessments were given, I organized the data on a graph that aided in grouping students and targeting instruction. This data led my adjustments to the lessons in the unit. In thinking about charting the pre-assessment results, I wanted something that would be a quick reference for making decisions about instructional groupings and differentiating instruction. My previous experiences working with my teammates in the first grade to chart student data had shown just how difficult this can be. It had been challenging to record meaningful data without including too much detail in a way that provided succinct information. I decided to create a chart with the student names down the left side and the 10 main goals/objectives of the interview across the top. Since the pre-assessment goals were tightly linked to the curriculum goals, instruction was easily modified based on groups of students' needs. I decided to simplify the recording with a plus, check, or minus for each goal as a quick point of reference. I also created a scoring rubric to describe what each rating meant for each of the 10 goals (see Appendix E). It was my thought that if I needed more details about the students' work or thinking, I could always go back and reference the interview notes. I based the scoring rubric on common student responses and kindergarten and first-grade developmental benchmarks.

## ANALYSIS OF INSTRUCTIONAL MODIFICATIONS

I differentiated instruction for my whole class based on the pre-assessment findings. However, for this project, I focused on meeting the needs of six students in particular—two students who needed extra assistance (Alison and Jake), two students who were at grade level (Kelly and Andy), and two students who were advanced learners (Matt and Rachel). The student work examples and reflections about the differentiated instruction were focused around these students' work. I analyzed and modified five lessons from the number sense unit, administered them to the six students, and recorded findings. My analysis of the Counting Pattern Blocks activity within the Number Shapes sessions (Investigation 1, Sessions 5 and 6) provides an example of the process I completed with these lessons.

The guidelines for observing the students during this activity focus on:

- Counting up to about 20 objects in an arrangement while keeping track
- Using numerals to record how many, including none (0)
- Developing strategies for counting and combining collections of objects that vary by color/shape and arrangement
- Becoming familiar with combinations of numbers up to 10 by combining numbers on a recording sheet rather than re-counting all of the objects
- Using names for the object shapes and recognizing relationships among them

The major changes that occurred in instruction for this lesson came at the advanced-learner level. I found, over the years, that this lesson was too easy for the advanced students and easily turned from a counting/combining activity into a pattern block design contest. I made this lesson more challenging in a variety of ways. One option was to raise the number of pattern blocks the advanced students needed to use in the activity. Another made the "worth" of each block vary from each block being counted as one to each block being counted as 2, 3, 5, 7, or 10. The last option had the students combine various combinations of pattern blocks before finding the entire total. Another part of this option was for the students to explain their counting and combining strategies in writing.

I noticed a big difference in the engagement level of the *above-standard* students. They were having to concentrate more and were definitely challenged at this level. Working at their instructional level, they were forced to use strategies they were very comfortable with and try out strategies they were still developing. It was interesting to see the change in approach to problems as the problems took on a more challenging level. Students abandoned more efficient counting strategies for simpler counting strategies or more dependable concrete strategies, which was surprising to me. For example, I was able to discover holes in Matt's number sense as he used strategies to find totals. As he was finding the total of his blocks, with each block worth 2 instead of one, Matt reverted back to counting up by

ones on his fingers. This was a student who had shown abstract mathematical reasoning during his pre-assessments and other lesson activities.
Matt had been able to break apart numbers to make combining easier,
find patterns in equations, and use familiar equations to solve unfamiliar
ones. For these reasons, I was surprised when he began counting up on his
fingers by ones to solve 22 + 14, or 18 + 10. I fully expected him to be able
to go up 10 from 18 without counting. After the activity, I asked him if he
could count by 10s. He said, "Yes," and counted from 10 to 100 by tens with
ease. Then I asked him if he could count by tens from 18. He thought for a
moment and then did so without error. I then asked him why he had
counted on his fingers to solve 18 + 10 on his paper. He said, "So I would
know the answer." I realized that Matt needed more work in counting by
tens from numbers other than 10 and to solve problems that deal with 10s
in ways other than the typical 10, 20, 30... format. I would not have seen
Matt's need for further instruction if I had not challenged him in this lesson. The activity without differentiation may not have forced Matt to use
less efficient but more dependable strategies when problem solving was
more difficult. This allowed me to see the depth of his understanding and
where to target future instruction.

For the *at-standard* students this activity was very appropriate, and it provided me with the opportunity to focus instruction and glean information
about the students' counting and combining strategies. For example, Andy
was able to count up each of his different pattern blocks and then use a
typical strategy for combining those numbers to find the total number of
blocks. He did go straight to the numbers rather than back to the design
for counting up. He started at the bottom of the list of numbers and added
up each time. For example, he added 4 + 7 and wrote 13 out to the side.
Although this initial sum was incorrect, he was able to add on by 10s when
he added 13 + 10 and got 23 and then added 23 + 10 and got 33. He
worked up from there until he reached the top of the page with his answer
of 55. It was interesting to see that Andy fluctuated between mental math
and more abstract reasoning such as "just knowing" 13 + 10 = 23, because
"I know my tens Mrs. Hands," to counting up on his fingers when he com-
puted 33 + 7. It was exciting to see Andy beginning to reason about numbers and find combining strategies that went beyond counting up by ones.
He did need to rely on visual cues around the room when writing his numbers, which also clearly showed me an area of focus for him. It was at this
appropriate instructional level that Andy was able to be challenged just
enough for him to try out new strategies and begin to move into higher
levels of mathematical thinking without being overwhelmed.

For the *below-standard* students who still struggled with counting and
combining, I taught this lesson as the curriculum suggested. I lowered the
total number of pattern blocks to 10 or less, I provided a 100 chart for

visual assistance with recording numbers, and I placed the students with partners for extra assistance. These modifications allowed students like Alison and Jake to complete the activity, challenge their mathematical skills, and begin to stretch their developing number sense.

## ANALYSIS OF THE FORMATIVE ASSESSMENTS

The last session in the unit, which was called Solving Story Problems (Investigation 4, Session 10), followed introductory sessions about combining and separating situations in story problems. The students had been given opportunities to solve both types of story problems with various levels of difficulty. After three days of problem solving and sharing of strategies, the students were engaged once again in solving combining and separating problems as a formative assessment that connects to a future unit on addition and subtraction. Using the observation grid that contained guiding questions for assessment focus, I watched the students work and recorded data. Again, the Observing the Students questions were very helpful for observation and analysis of student growth.

The performances by the six focus students again followed the variability anticipated in the unit. Jake and Allison still fluctuated between counting both groups up by one to beginning to start from one group total and count up to the sum. Kelly and Andy both consistently counted up from one number to the sum, and they were beginning to count mentally without visual or concrete assistance. Matt and Rachel definitely reasoned about numbers using patterns and the way numbers related to one another. They also became more comfortable with manipulating numbers and used familiar number combinations to solve other combinations. The embedded assessment activity helped me better understand the progress of my students' number sense, which provided focus for my preparation of differentiated lessons in subsequent units.

## ANALYSIS OF THE SUMMATIVE POST-ASSESSMENTS

Though the process of modifying and analyzing the results from all three summative post-assessments were interesting and engaging, the results from the district assessment provided the most information. The post-assessments from focus students in the *need extra assistance* category (Alison and Jake) indicated growth in both computation and problem solving. Students who had shown emergent abilities in combining and separating story problems on the pre-assessments had shown growth in these areas after completing the unit. Both students were better able to show their thinking strategies when solving a combining problem. Alison drew a thinking bubble above a drawing of herself solving this problem: *There are 8 cats playing with yarn. 3 more cats come to play. How many cats are there all together?* Within the thinking bubble she wrote "8, 9, 10, 11" to show that she counted on from 8 up to 11. This was an improvement from her pre-assessment, where the majority of her responses included only answers or a drawing that represented the problem rather than her solution strategy.

Subtraction computation problems were still difficult for Alison. On the pre-assessment, she was able to solve subtraction problems, but she only showed her answers in her responses. She indicated that she was unclear how to show her thinking. On the post-assessment, her pictures with the subtraction problems showed pictorial representations of the equation rather than the subtraction action. Though she did use a subtraction sign in her drawings, the pictures did not show the action of things being taken away. If an observer were to count the objects in front of the subtraction sign, they would get the correct answer. The district scoring rubric and the most common first-grade student response for this problem was to show crossed out objects or loops around objects showing what had been taken away.

In the area of self-assessment, Alison rated herself as feeling positive about her ability to solve combining situations and to show her strategies. When rating her feelings toward subtraction and showing strategies, she indicated that she "sort of agreed" that she was successful at solving subtraction problems and showing strategies. This was consistent with my conclusions about her mathematical understanding in the area of subtraction. Alison's representation for the separating story problem also interested me. Alison solved the separating story problem (*There were 10 cookies on a plate. My Dad took 6 cookies to work. How many cookies are left?*) by counting up to 10 on her fingers, then taking down 6 fingers until she had 4 left. When she recorded her strategy with pictures, numbers, or words she drew a thinking bubble and wrote a subtraction equation in it. I wondered why she could show her counting strategy for a combining situation but not for a separating situation. She also reverted back to counting up from one for the first number in the problem, which she had not done when solving the combining problem. I felt that her understanding of subtraction was still at a very concrete level.

When analyzing the growth of the students who I had previously identified as being *at grade level* (Andy and Kelly), I found some pleasing successes in Andy's work. Andy improved in the area of showing his thinking strategies in pictures, numbers, or words. His pre-assessment had provided some indication that he could write his thinking strategies in his response to the pencil and marker combining story problem. He had indicated that

"5 + 5 = 10 so I take one away so 5 + 4 = 9." Clearly, Andy was able to show his thinking in numbers and words in this combining situation, but his other combining situation strategy was limited, and he had not been able to show his strategy for the separating problems. On the post-assessment, Andy did a wonderful job of showing his strategies for both combining and separating story problems. He used sentences that detailed his thinking and provided a picture of his brain doing the thinking with equations for the problems. This was a definite improvement and a good example of the intended growth from taking part in discussions and sharing strategies with peers during the unit.

I had the most difficulty analyzing the growth of the students previously identified in the *advanced* category (Matt and Rachel). Their post-assessment was different from the other assessments in that the combining story problem contained the unknown in the middle of the equation (*There are 15 cookies on the plate. Mom just baked some more! Now there are 24 cookies! How many more cookies did mom put on the plate?*) and the subtraction story did not indicate a clear take-away action (*There are 13 dogs in the backyard. A man has 3 dogs in his truck. 4 dogs have been fed their dinner. How many more dogs need to be fed?*). Rachel was my biggest challenge throughout the whole project. I noticed on her pre-assessment that she could already create a T chart to show all the ways to make 10, which was a major goal for the end of the number sense unit. She also solved combining and separating situations so quickly mentally that she struggled with how to record her thinking strategies. I worried that she would regress in her thinking strategies to more concrete approaches when recording, which would not help her progress. On the pre-assessment, she simply did not record her strategies on the two story problems. Her recording on the pre-assessment problem about pencils and markers showed two ways to make 9 (i.e., 10 − 1 and how it relates to 5 + 5).

On the post-assessment, Rachel did show strategies for solving both combining and separating stories. She knew both answers to the problems instantly in her head and recorded strategies to show her thinking. My concerns about Rachel recording concrete representations of problems rather than her actual thought processes were reiterated when she wrote strategies for the cookie story. The drawing was very concrete and showed 5 + 4 = 9 (a breakdown of the actual answer). When I asked Rachel if the picture showed what she thought about when solving the story she said, "No, I just knew it." For the separating story, she did show a clear representation of her thought process. She said that the picture showed her thinking. This was a clear way to show a strategy, but I wondered if the number problems were still too easy. It was my thought that if the problems were at a level where she was challenged, she would go through a clearer thinking process for solving them and thus be able to reflect on her strategies more easily.

## CONCLUSIONS

This project involved an amazing process, both to explore and to endure. I was surprised at the depth of content, research, and questions that unraveled as I engaged in each component of the project. I am ever more convinced that pre-assessing is necessary for targeting instruction and being able to effectively differentiate instruction to meet individual student's needs. The interview was a powerful tool that enabled me to observe my students' thinking processes, strategies, and ways of reasoning. I was initially concerned about the length of time interviewing took, and I still question how I could better streamline the interview to shorten the time required. Yet I would use two weeks to assess again, because I feel the information I gained about the students was key for creating effective instruction, which led to noticeable growth for all of my students.

I also found that I could have tried many different versions of the interview and could have based the entire project on creating a pre-assessment interview and revising it to improve its effectiveness. Since I also wanted to explore differentiated instruction and post-assessments, I had to narrow the amount of revisions I made. I still think I have more work ahead on analysis of my pre-assessment interview, but I am convinced that this interview was successful because it was linked to both my district standards and the curriculum I was using.

In terms of recording interview data, I still struggle with how to do it best yet make it practical. The reality of teaching is that time is always an issue. I would not take the time to compute intricate scores or make detailed charts concerning assessment, nor would I take the time to use such charts! I need quick references for grouping students and creating lessons. The plus, check, and minus chart worked for me because it was a quick reference and it was easy to create when combining class data. I could see myself using this method in future units because it was an effective tool for me as well as for the instructional assistants and tutors. I gave them copies of the chart and asked them to assist students based on mathematical goals and how the students rated on the chart. I was always able to go back to interview notes if I thought I needed more details about a particular student's thinking or strategies.

In reflecting on the differentiated instruction in this project, I also question the practicality and time required. It took a lot of time to break down each lesson based on goals, expected student outcome, and ways to modify instruction for various groups. I did find that the more tiering I did the faster I got at it. In my opinion, the *Investigations* curriculum is an effective curriculum which benefited all of my students. I did find that differentiating the activities for my more advanced students helped move those students further along the continuum than during my previous experiences with this unit. However, I still struggle with deciding how difficult to make these modified activities, and I worry about making too big of a leap in difficulty and thereby creating holes in students' learning.

There is also the ongoing challenge of meeting the advanced students' academic needs while nurturing the developmental and emotional maturity of all first graders. There are almost always students like Rachel whose performances are currently above and beyond those of other students. I think that some of the activity modifications began to challenge her more, but I think I still fell short in terms of moving her along the growth continuum as much as my other students.

As with the pre-assessment, I think that the post-assessments I modified were effective in showing student growth over time. Although this unit lasted just over a month, I did not see as much growth as I would have liked to see because I was only looking across one unit. I wish I could have extended this project through the remainder of the year to show the full year's growth. Combining results from other units and using pre- and post-assessments with differentiated instruction during all of the first grade units would have yielded many more findings and patterns of growth over the longer period of time and more diverse content areas. Yet I do feel that the post-assessments were practical, teacher friendly, and in alignment with both the district standards and the curriculum. These assessments provided effective points of reference for further instruction and for sharing results with colleagues, administrators, and parents.

# APPENDIX A: PRE-ASSESSMENT INTERVIEW

Name:_____     Date:_____

## Building Number Sense
## Pre Assessment

1. How far can you count by one's? _____ Please count by one's as far as you can.

Comments: * to 40 or higher  *skipped numbers  *with ease  *had to restart/lost track

2. I need you to count the objects in this jar. I want to know how many _____ are in the jar. You will write how many on this post it note. Talk about your strategies and what you are doing as you work.

Student total_____ Actual total_____

Comments: *with ease  *hard time getting started  *organized objects  *counted by 1,2,5,10...other _____

3. I want you to count the objects in this jar #2. I want to know how many _____ are in the jar. You will write how many on this post it note. Talk about your strategies and what you are doing as you work.

Student total_____ Actual total_____

Comments: *with ease  *hard time getting started  *organized objects  *counted by 1,2,5,10...other_____

4. Which jar had the most objects?  How do you know?

Comments:  *did the student change his/her organization?

5. I want $10$ pieces of fruit altogether.  How many apples and oranges can I have to make $10$ pieces of fruit?  You can use this paper, pencil, crayons, cubes.
*What are you doing?  *How do you know?  *Is there any other way to have $10$ pieces of fruit?  *Show me.

Comments:

6. I have 5 pencils and 4 markers. How many school supplies do I have altogether? You can use pencil, paper, cubes to help you.
*What are you doing? *How do you know? *What were you thinking?

Comments:

7. How would you solve these 2 problems? You can use any strategy you would like to solve.

Comments:

8. I have a story for you. I want you to listen to the story and then solve the story for me. I want you to show your thinking on the paper so I know how you figured out the answer. Also, show what the answer is. You can use pictures numbers and words to do this.
*Read story, have student retell back. *Have them solve story problem.

Comments for combining story problem:

Comments for seperating story problem:

9. I want you to fill in this 100's chart as far as you can.

Comments:

10: I am going to show you some numbers on my 100's chart. I want you to say the number.

13        35        9        52        21        77        12        4        40

## *Assessments Story Problems*

5.  I want 10 pieces of fruit altogether.  How many apples and oranges can I have to make 10 pieces of fruit?

6.  I have 5 pencils and 4 markers.  How many school supplies do I have altogether?

8. I went to the store to buy vegetables. I bought 3 carrots, 5 cucumbers and 4 onions. How many vegetables did I buy total?

8b. There were 9 dogs at the park. 3 dogs ran away and 1 went to his dog house. How many dogs were left at the park?

6+5=_____

4+_____=10

## APPENDIX B: EXAMPLE DIFFERENTIATED LESSON

### Counting Pattern Blocks

*1.  What range of learning needs are you likely to address?*

- Learners who are having emerging development of counting with one to one correspondence.

- Learners who can count objects from 1-20 with ease and one to one correspondence.

- Learners who cannot consistently record numerals from 1-20.

- Learners who can consistently record numerals from 1-20.

- Learners who can count objects from 1-20 and higher with strategies other than counting by ones.  They are beginning to group or count by two's, five's, ten's or other combinations.

- Students who are beginning to develop strategies for combining collections of objects that vary by color and arrangement.

- Students who are efficient and consistent with strategies for combining collections of objects that vary by color and arrangement.

*2.  What should students know, understand, and be able to do as a result of the lesson?*

Know:
- How to count up to 20 objects with one to one correspondence.
- Notation stands for number and has meaning.
- There are different strategies for counting and combining collections of objects.

Understand:
- Oral counting connects with counting quantities.
- Written and oral numbers represent quantities.

- When you combine numbers, the total is larger than the addends.

Be able to:
- Count up to 20 objects in an arrangement while keeping track.
- Use numerals to record how many, including 0.
- Total or combine a collection of objects using more than one strategy.
- Name shapes while creating different collection arrangements.

*3. What is the starting point of the lesson?*
- Investigation's Building Number Sense Sessions 5&6 pgs. 19-23
- Referencing counting activity results from the pre assessment interview.

*4. What are some versions for extension?*
- Build an arrangement and complete the totaling task with 20-40 pattern blocks.
- Combine certain block combinations that are less than the entire total. Ex: rhombus + trapezoids + triangles = _____
- Write and explain your counting strategy.
- Write and explain your combining strategy.
- Show three different ways to find the total using pictures, numbers and words.
- If each block was worth 10, or 100, or 25, what would be the total? (Change value of pattern blocks)

*5. What are some versions for extra assistance?*
- Lower the amount of pattern blocks to 10.
- Provide practice in counting objects orally while touching one to one, not in an arrangement.
- Provide hundreds chart or other visual assistance for writing numbers.
- Extra modeling with teacher, or with a partner.

Name_____

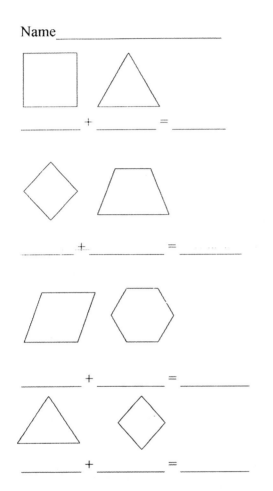

1ˢᵗ try @ extending... still too easy!

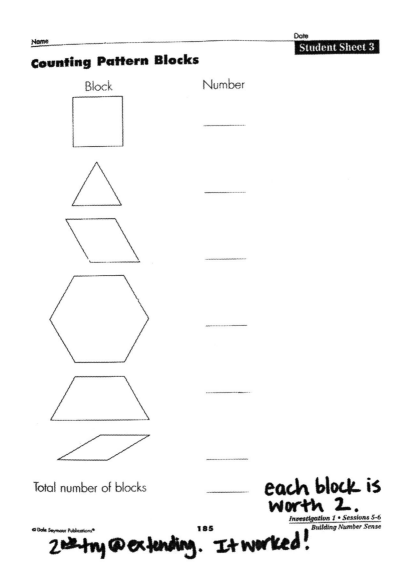

Name _____    Date _____

## Counting Pattern Blocks

Block                          Number

Total number of blocks    _____    *each block is worth 2.*

*Investigation 1 • Sessions 5-6*
*Building Number Sense*

© Dale Seymour Publications®          **185**

*2nd try @ extending.  It worked!*

Kliman, M. & Russell, S. J. (1998). Building number sense: The number system, Grade 1. *Investigations in Number, Data, and Space®* (Student Sheet 3, p. 185). Copyright Dale Seymour Publications. Reprinted by permission of Pearson Education, Inc.

Name:_____ Date:_____

### Counting Pattern Blocks

□ + △ = _____

◇ + ⬡ = _____

▱ + △ = _____

◇ + □ + ⬡ = _____

What is the total of all your pattern blocks? _____

What is your strategy for solving? _____

_____
_____
_____
_____
_____
_____

3rd extension.

## APPENDIX C: ADAPTED DISTRICT POST-ASSESSMENT

Name:_____    Date_____

Add the two given numbers together.
Draw a picture that represents the addition sentence.

| | |
|---|---|
| 2+4=____ | 6+4=____ |
| 3<br>+ 8<br>----<br>☐ | 7<br>+ 2<br>----<br>☐ |

Solve the story problem.  Show your strategy with pictures, numbers, and words in the box below.

*There are 8 cats playing with yarn.  3 more cats come to play.  How many cats are there all together?*

Name:_____ Date_____

Solve the subtraction problems below.
Draw a picture that represents the subtraction sentence.

| | |
|---|---|
| 10-3=_____ | 9-1=_____ |
| 10<br>- 4<br>----------<br>[ ] | 10<br>- 8<br>--------<br>[ ] |

Solve the story problem.  Show your strategy with pictures, numbers, and words in the box below.

*There were 10 cookies on a plate. My dad took 6 cookies to work.  How many cookies are left?*

Name:_____    Date:_____

Self Reflection

I agree          I sort of agree          I disagree

1.  I like adding numbers together. _____

2.  I like subtracting numbers._____

3.  I am good at drawing pictures of number sentences._____

4.  I like solving story problems._____

5.  I can draw pictures to show my strategies._____

6.  I can use numbers to show my strategies._____

7.  I can use words to show my strategies._____

8.  This is my best work._____

**APPENDIX D: ORIGINAL AND ADAPTED
SOURCEBOOK POST-ASSESSMENT**

Name _____ Date _____

Assessment Master 7

### End-of-Unit Assessment Task

**1.** Write numbers in correct sequence
on these counting strips:

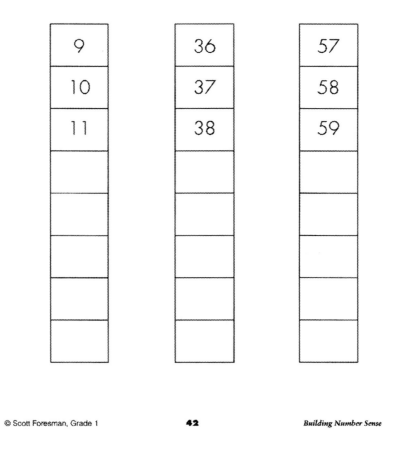

Assessment sourcebook: Grade 1. (undated). *Investigations in Number, Data, and Space*® (Assessment Master 7, p. 42). Copyright Scott Foresman. Reprinted by permission of Pearson Education, Inc.

Name_____   Date:_____

*End-of-Unit Assessment Task*
1.  **Write numbers in correct sequence on these counting strips:**

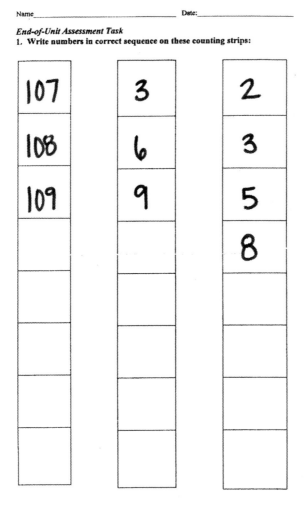

Extended Version

## APPENDIX E: PLUS/CHECK/MINUS RUBRIC
## FOR 10 NUMBER-SENSE GOALS

Plus/Check/Minus Rubric for 10 Number-Sense Goals

| Goal | Plus: Above Standard | Check: At Standard | Minus: Below Standard |
|---|---|---|---|
| 1. Counting to 100 by ones | Counts by ones to 100 with no errors. Counts with a clear, confident, faster pace. Could and is ready to count beyond 100. | Counts by ones with less than three errors. Can count past 50 with no errors. May have some trouble switching decades above 60. | Counts by ones with more than three errors. Can count past 30 with no errors. May repeat numbers, skip numbers, or have trouble with changing decades throughout the entire counting sequence. |
| 2. Counting strategies and organization for two quantities | Automatically groups objects by 2s, 5s, or 10s when counting sets of objects. Counting results in the correct answer. | Is beginning to count objects by grouping or arranging objects. Can group and count by groups if asked to. Generally has correct counting total, or total is close to correct. | Still establishing one-to-one corre- spondence. Counts objects randomly with no particular order. Counting total is incorrect. |
| 3. Reading numbers out of order from 1 to 100 | Reads numbers with ease and no errors. Is begin- ning to read num- bers correctly up to 1000. | Reads numbers to 100 with two errors or less. The error may be minimal, like saying 12 for 21. | Reads numbers to 30 or less with accuracy. Cannot correctly identify numbers above 30 with accuracy. More than two errors during counting. |

Plus/Check/Minus Rubric for 10 Number-Sense Goals

| Goal | Plus: Above Standard | Check: At Standard | Minus: Below Standard |
|---|---|---|---|
| 4. Comparing numbers | Can correctly explain why one number is higher than the other. Uses language about the placement of numbers and may talk about 10s or how many more one is than the other. | Can correctly identify which number is higher than the other. Can begin to explain why. | Cannot correctly identify which number is higher than the other; has no explanation about why; does not attempt an explanation. |
| 5. Making 10 using two quantities | Can show all the ways to make 10 using two numbers. Uses chart or another way of organizing. Can explain the patterns in the numbers when adding. | Shows four or more ways to make 10 with two quantities. Might begin to use patterns in adding, like 5 + 5 = 10, so 4 + 6 = 10. Does not completely organize approach. | Can show two or fewer ways to make 10 using two quantities. Heavy reliance on manipulatives. Uses a random approach to solving. Does not know how many ways there are or how to find more. |
| 6. Solving combining situations | Can easily use and explain strategies for solving combining situations. Compares strategies and uses abstract reasoning when solving. | Can begin to explain strategy when solving a combining situation. Can use physical model to explain, but is pulling away from concrete thinking to more abstract. | Heavy reliance on manipulatives to solve combining problems. Has trouble explaining strategy. |

Plus/Check/Minus Rubric for 10 Number-Sense Goals

| Goal | Plus: Above Standard | Check: At Standard | Minus: Below Standard |
|---|---|---|---|
| 7. Solving separating situations | Can easily use and explain strategies for solving separating situations. Compares strategies and uses abstract reasoning when solving. | Can begin to explain strategy when solving a separating situation. Can use physical model to explain, but is pulling away from concrete thinking to more abstract. | Heavy reliance on manipulatives to solve separating problems. Has trouble explaining strategy. |
| 8. Computing the total of two quantities | Describes and compares strategies when solving computation problems above 18. Can solve a problem with unknown in the middle. | Creates and uses strategies for solving computation problems to 18. Can count on, use doubles, or memorized facts. | Uses concrete manipulatives and counting from 1 when solving computation problems. Strategies are limited. |
| 9. Writing and sequencing numbers to 100 | Writes numbers to 100 with accuracy and very limited reversals. No errors in sequencing. Is on way to writing 1000. | Writes numbers to 100 or at least above 30. Some reversals. Three errors or less in sequencing. | Writes numbers to 30 or less; problems sequencing; many reversals; needs visual clues for help. Recounts orally from 1 to remember what comes next. |
| 10. Oral and written expression of strategies | Describes and compares strategies, both oral and written. Can justify reasonableness and prove thinking with number sense vocabulary. | Creates and begins to describe strategies both oral and written. Needs some extra questioning to pull out thinking. Better at orally describing than writing. Uses number sense vocabulary. | Beginning to demonstrate strategies with manipulatives. Needs prompting and questioning to pull out oral expression of process and thinking. Written recording of strategies is very weak. |

## REFERENCES

Huinker, D. M. (1993). Interviews: A window to students' conceptual knowledge of the operations. In N. L. Webb, & A. F. Coxford (Eds.), *Assessment in the mathematics classroom* [NCTM Yearbook] (pp. 80-86). Reston, VA: National Council of Teachers of Mathematics.

Kliman, M. & Russell, S. J. (1998). Building number sense (Grade 1: The number system). *Investigations in number, data, and space.* White Plains, NY: Dale Seymour.

National Council of Teachers of Mathematics. (2000). *Principles and standards for school mathematics.* Reston, VA: Author.

TERC. (Undated). *Investigations in number, data, and space: Assessment sourcebook (Grade 1).* Glenview, IL: Scott Foresman.

Tomlinson, C. A. (2001). *How to differentiate instruction in mixed-ability classrooms* (2nd ed.). Alexandria, VA: Association for Supervision and Curriculum Development.

Taylor, R. (undated). Workshop handout. For information, see http://www.rogertaylor.com.

CHAPTER 10

# UNCOVERING CHILDREN'S THINKING ABOUT PATTERNS

## Teacher-Researchers Improving Classroom Practices

**Regina Wicks**
*Goulds Elementary School, St. Johns, NL, Canada*

**Rita Janes**
*Rita Janes Educational Solutions*

Children in a Kindergarten class are sorting items by number. They focus on the numbers 2, 3, and 4 based on the book their teacher has read: *What Comes in 2's, 3's & 4's* (Aker, 1990). The teacher asks, "What else comes in groups of 2?" Children readily offer the items they recall from the book. The teacher then asks, "Can you think of any other things that would belong in a group of 2?" The students suggest mittens, boots, earmuffs, earrings, and even thumbs! The teacher moves on to a group of 3. After exhausting the ideas represented in the book, the teacher again asks students to think of other items that would belong in a group of 3. This set

*Teachers Engaged in Research*
*Inquiry Into Mathematics Classrooms, Grades Pre-K–2*, pages 211–236
Copyright © 2006 by Information Age Publishing
All rights of reproduction in any form reserved.

seems a little harder. The students think silently for a few seconds. Finally a little girl raises her hand and offers, "The letter Y." The teacher is puzzled yet intrigued by her response. She asks, "Why do you think the letter Y would belong in a group of 3?" The student answers, "Well, it has 3 sticks." Satisfied with the student's thinking, the teacher adds the letter Y to the group of 3.

## CHILDREN'S THINKING

Children's observations and thinking often differ from those of adults. Yet, by really listening to what children are trying to say and probing into the reasoning behind their thoughts and actions, we can gain insight into the way children see and make sense of the world around them. Teachers must seek to understand what students are trying to communicate and use that information to advance individual students' learning and that of the class as a whole (NCTM 2000). It can be so easy to overlook or disregard young children's comments, especially when they are unexpected or do not fit into our agenda. The teacher above could have easily said, "We are looking for things that come in sets of 3. Does the letter Y come in a set of 3?" Questions or comments, such as "Are you sure...?" or "I don't think...," can actually devalue and discourage children's thinking and even worse, send the message that what they think or have to say is not important.

## TEACHER'S ROLE

According to NCTM (1991), teachers should regularly follow students' statements with "Why?" or other invitations to explain. Doing this consistently, independent from questioning the correctness of students' statements, is an important part of establishing a discourse centered on mathematical reasoning. Opportunities for rich discussion and thoughtful learning are often sparked by children's unique insights and rationalizations. Although young children are working from a small knowledge base, their logical reasoning begins before school and is continually modified by their experiences. Teachers should maintain an environment that respects, nurtures, and encourages students so that they do not give up their belief that the world, including mathematics, is supposed to make sense (NCTM, 2000). The teacher, therefore, plays a pivotal role in involving and encouraging children to think about and make sense of mathematics and to communicate their thinking and understanding.

## BACKGROUND OF THE TEACHER
## AS RESEARCHER PROJECT

### Origination of the Idea

Over the past few years, our school district has been implementing a new math program. This major initiative included new materials and resources as well as new instructional approaches and expectations. This program involved more representation and communication by students as the learning activities encouraged them to make observations or search for patterns in their work, to learn various strategies to solve problems, and to represent their thinking in multiple ways. Students were also expected to solve problems in ways that made sense to them, share solutions in small and large groups, as well as listen to other children's strategies. Although the new math program offered research-based ideas on how children best learn and understand mathematics, it differed significantly from previous programs, especially those experienced by the teachers and parents when they learned mathematics in primary or elementary school. Teachers needed to become familiar with new roles for the teacher and learner in the mathematics classroom. As a result, teachers in Kindergarten and grade one (the grades in which this program was first initiated) started to express concerns as they discussed and questioned the differences between their experienced teaching practice and the instructional approaches expected and encouraged by the new mathematics program. As with any new program, teachers needed time and support to fully understand and integrate the new philosophy of teacher instruction and student learning. The need for more professional development in this area, therefore, focused on teacher practice—identifying and implementing effective instructional techniques as well as exploring how these new approaches can affect optimal student learning of mathematical concepts. The process of designing this professional development led to exploring a collaborative teacher-as-researcher project.

### The Collaborative Team

The professional development team at our school identified mathematics as the focus for improving teaching and learning over a two-year period. To support these efforts, the principal arranged for two professional development facilitators, one in math (the second author) and the other in language, because the new math program integrated many areas of our language program, especially listening, speaking, and writing. Our research team consisted of the Kindergarten teachers, grade one teachers (including the first author), learning resource teachers, the principal, and the two professional development facilitators referred to above (an independent math consultant and an early childhood education professor). This elementary school has 3 or 4 classes at each grade level, totaling approximately 500 students in grades K-4. The school is located in a semi-rural community on the outskirts of the capital city of Newfoundland. The school and the community have both been very supportive of our efforts to improve the environment and interaction in mathematics classes.

Although this research effort was the direct responsibility of the teachers involved, the team agreed that the facilitators would provide support and feedback at each stage of the process—developing the research question; planning methods of inquiry; collecting and analyzing data; reflecting on classroom experiences; and analyzing the processes and products of these research efforts. Having teachers at both the Kindergarten and grade one levels would allow and encourage much discussion and feedback at research team meetings.

According to Johnson (1993), a research study team provides support and a forum for sharing questions, concerns, and results. Teachers advise each other and comment on the progress of individual efforts. By researching the effectiveness of our own teaching methods, we would be both personally and directly involved in the process and product of our own research. Most importantly, this type of research was relevant to us, as teachers, in attempting to improve our classroom environment and teaching practices in order to promote more meaningful and lasting learning in our students. As Johnson (1993) also indicates, teachers engaging in action research attend more carefully to their methods, their perceptions and understandings, and their whole approach to the teaching process.

## PLANNING THE PROJECT

### First Meeting

We met in the Fall of 2000 to plan the implementation of the teacher as researcher project. At that time, we decided to use a unit on patterns as the content focus. We would attempt to provide a variety of stimulating opportunities for children to explore the mathematics of patterns and to discuss their experiences, predictions, and knowledge when observing, creating, and extending patterns in the classroom. According to NCTM (2000), creating and describing patterns offer important opportunities for students to make conjectures and give reasons for their validity. They also provide ideal opportunities for making connections in other strands of the mathematics curriculum, as well as predictions and generalizations based on their mathematical experiences. This sounded like a good place to start!

## Formulating a Focus of Inquiry

Based on our discussions, we formulated our major research question: How can we effectively uncover children's thinking and reasoning of mathematical concepts in an effort to improve instruction and learning in the classroom?

Underlying this major research question, however, were many more questions that addressed various aspects of our research. For example, what kinds of questions do we need to ask students? At what point do we ask these questions? When and how do we encourage students to discover the answers for themselves? We needed to practice wording questions so that they were not only interesting and challenging but also open-ended enough to encourage multiple answers, higher-level thinking, and understanding. In planning lessons, we would not only need to give much thought to the generation of these questions but also to involve students in a variety of working environments (e.g., whole group, small group, partners) to maximize the mathematical discourse in the classroom.

Young children not only lack experience and skills in reading and writing about mathematics but also in speaking about it. According to Andrews (1997), some students think about mathematics in intuitive ways but have great difficulty explaining their thinking. When questioned by a teacher, these students often say "I don't know," "I guessed," or even "I just knowed!" These young mathematicians need help in learning to communicate their reasoning. Therefore, we discussed the importance of modeling metacognitive thinking as well as proper use of mathematical terminology and the language of logic. Which terms should we introduce? When and how should we introduce them? Do we give students tasks that interest and challenge their thinking? Do we encourage them to make connections or do we make the connections for them? Do we give them sufficient opportunities to work together and learn from one another? Do they truly understand the concepts we have done so far? Do we provide time for them to talk about their learning?

We also needed to monitor and assess our success in uncovering children's understandings of mathematical concepts. We planned to observe and record revealing student dialogues, comments and questions. All forms of observation, anecdotal records, and work samples would be assessed in a new light—that of the group during daily and weekly discussions. The culminating effort would be to relate our personal reflections and group experiences to our insights about the process of teaching and learning in the mathematics class-room. Our goal was to strive for professional growth by exploring effective methods of instruction and communication that assist children in achieving true understanding, confidence, and independence in mathematics.

## Planning the Details

The content of our project would consist of the unit outlined in our new program guide in combination with relevant curriculum outcomes in mathematics outlined by the Department of Education. We had an oppor-tunity to work at our own grade level in order to select specific outcomes for our unit, to explore suggested activities in our program guide, and to plan a detailed lesson for the introductory class on patterning. The most important part of our planning, however, was the list of questions we decided to use throughout the lesson in an attempt to encourage class-room discourse and uncover children's thinking and reasoning when cre-ating, extending, and describing patterns.

We also agreed on methods for collecting data, such as anecdotal records, work samples, and quoting student comments and conversations during each lesson. We decided to informally discuss and analyze details of our lessons at each grade level at the end of every school day. We discussed our personal experiences, observations, and reflections based on that day's lesson and then individually or collectively e-journaled the facilitators with reference to any questions, insights, thoughts, or concerns as we shared the details of the day's events. In this way, the facilitators could give direct feedback on our experiences with reference to each of the lessons. We also planned to have a collaborative meeting once a week with all members involved in the project. The purpose of this meeting would be to analyze collected samples of students' work and to share insights from our reflec-tive journals as a means to guide our research and inform our instruction. Therefore, our collection and analysis of data would create an ongoing cycle that would reflect the interdependent relationship of our teaching practices and the students' learning and communicating of mathematical discoveries and processes during the project.

## READING AND REFLECTING ABOUT
## TEACHING AND LEARNING

Throughout the teacher as researcher project, we read a variety of articles that assisted us in gaining a better understanding of the roles of the teacher and student in the mathematics classroom. These readings, in combination with our group discussions, assisted us in planning how we could provide various opportunities and assistance for students attempting to share their ideas and thinking processes related to patterning. We have listed these readings in the appendix for the benefit of other teachers.

The facilitators recommended we read and reflect upon the Reasoning and Proof and Communication Standards from *Principles and Standards for School Mathematics* (NCTM, 2000) before initiating our research project. We engaged in a rich discussion about these readings in the Standards. They were easy to comprehend and offered a wealth of practical and thought-provoking information. They clearly linked children's communicating of mathematical ideas with their learning and understanding of concepts as well as their application of mathematical concepts and skills to solving problems.

## The Role of Questioning and Listening in the Mathematics Classroom

Although we normally engaged children in hands-on activities and discussions in mathematics class, we often questioned the effectiveness of our efforts. Do we give students enough time to discover answers? Who does most of the talking? According to Kincheloe (1991), success is possible only if the teacher creates a situation where students feel comfortable to open up and express what they are authentically feeling. To accomplish such openness, teachers must exercise restraint. They must avoid monopolization of classroom conversation in order to encourage student talk—talk which reveals their thinking and understanding.

The most obvious way to try to find out what children are thinking is to ask them. Questions, however, need to be open-ended, motivating, challenging, as well as relate to children's experiences and the real world in order to encourage higher-level thinking, clarification of ideas, and multiple representations. We discussed the importance of not only inquiring about what children are doing or thinking but also how they know. The key to effective mathematical instruction is to provide ample opportunities for children to become directly involved, in both their thoughts and actions, along with the guidance of their teacher and interaction of their peers, to make sense of the concepts they are learning. Our developing competence in asking questions became the key to our research. We learned the importance of providing time, support, and acceptance for students' answers, whether right or wrong. Our openness to their questions and answers gave flexibility and meaning to our mathematical experiences. The more we listened to students, the more we were able to make sense of their reasoning and to modify our instruction based on their needs. Kincheloe (1991) states that one of the quickest ways to apply teacher research to the pursuit of good teaching involves, simply, teachers listening to students.

Thoughtfully listening to and understanding students is a cardinal tenet of good teaching, as the teacher details his or her observations of the students as well as his or her reaction to the learner. These observations must be contextualized by an examination of the social context in which student and teacher consciousness is formed and education takes place.

## Role of Classroom Discourse and Multiple Representations

The facilitators also encouraged us to create an environment that was communication-rich. NCTM (2000) asserts that students should have daily opportunities to talk and write about mathematics. Communicating about mathematical ideas is a way for students to articulate, clarify, organize, and consolidate their thinking. In Kindergarten and grade one, much of this communication involves classroom discourse and a variety of representations. Through communicating and sharing their learning, children are able to make more sense of the concepts as well as the learning process involved. Moreover, as they listen to other children's ways of thinking and making sense of the same material, they are able to make additional connections and insights. Children realize that there is not just one right answer or way to solve a problem; there can be many. Silver and Smith (1990) state that opportunities for students to create and discuss multiple solution methods for interesting mathematical problems constitute invitations to engage in higher-level thinking in mathematics class, and they represent important opportunities for teachers to learn about and enhance their students' mathematical thinking and reasoning. According to Mewborn and Huberty (1999), restating what someone else has said helps students make sense of others' ideas. It also develops their mathematical vocabulary and critical thinking skills as they attend to what others are saying.

## Communicating Ideas and Reasoning Through Mathematical Language

During the course of our research, the facilitators also encouraged us to create an environment that was rich in mathematical language, which would not only support students' language development but also their ability to communicate mathematical ideas more effectively. Just because young children do not yet have the mathematical language to explain their thinking does not mean that they are not ready or able to learn, understand, and internalize new ways to do so. Steele (1999) asserts that in the early learning of mathematics, children's experiences must be closely connected to the language used to describe these experiences, because exploration in concrete settings is a powerful way to develop meanings of new words.

## DATA COLLECTION

In an attempt to learn about the reasoning capabilities of students at all academic levels and with differing learning styles, we decided that a wide variety of data would need to be collected and analyzed in order to guide, enhance, and individualize our instruction. The various forms of data we collected included: transcripts of classroom discourse (teacher-student; student-student); observations of student interaction and communication; responses to various questions and prompts; student work samples; student math journals; and teacher reflective journals.

Since each teacher involved in the teacher as researcher project had reasonably large class numbers, we decided to select a random sample of 4–5 students on which to focus. We separated our classes into three academic groupings: above average, average, and below average. We then randomly chose 1–2 students from each such grouping. This sample group would not only allow for easier, more manageable collection of data but also more focused analysis of student thinking and reasoning in response to various forms of teacher instruction and questioning strategies used during the project.

### Transcripts of Classroom Discourse

When attempting to uncover children's thinking and reasoning, we felt that what children have to say as well as how they attempt to say it were essential for gaining insight into their knowledge and understanding of mathematical concepts. We attempted to record discussions that we felt were relevant for analysis in terms of justifying children's understanding of concepts or exploring ways to extend their thinking. When children revealed unexpected solutions or theories, we attempted to uncover and clarify their knowledge and learning by asking further questions, redirecting questions to peers, or providing alternate ways to demonstrate their ideas (e.g., drawing pictures, using manipulatives, acting out scenarios).

For example, our first lesson consisted of asking students to tell us what they already knew about patterns. We wanted to offer children the opportunity to share their preconceptions of the mathematical concept of patterning based on previous home and school experiences. This would also give us some insight into their current knowledge as well as their instructional needs for the unit. The following is an excerpt from the discourse that occurred on the first day:

T:  What is a pattern?

S:  Like red, blue, red, blue

S:  The days of the week.

T:  How do the days of the week make a pattern?

S:  Because Sunday, Monday, Tuesday, Wednesday, Thursday, Friday, Saturday, Sunday, and it all starts over again [pointing to the Calendar as she reads or says the days of the week in order].

T:  Oh, so the days of the week repeat over and over again.

S:  Yeah.

T:   Any other ideas about what a pattern is?

S:  It grows.

T:  What do you mean?

S:  It gets bigger and bigger.

T:  Can you show me [unsure if he means longer as in a train of blocks or bigger in terms of a growing number pattern]?

S:  [He uses the container of interlocking cubes to make a simple AB pattern with the colors green and blue. As he adds more blocks to extend the pattern, he points and says] Like this.

T:  OK. So you can extend a pattern to make it longer or bigger.

During the project, we also expected students to justify why their answers made sense or fit a particular concept. This demonstrated for others both *what* and *how* the students were thinking.

## Observations of Student Interaction and Communication

Often children have more knowledge than they are able to communicate. Therefore, we needed to document how children responded when they contributed to group discussions and when they worked on individual and group activities. Children were given the opportunity to represent their knowledge in multiple ways (e.g., using words, letters, manipulatives, pictures, or actions). When asked, "What is a pattern?" some children responded with what a pattern does ("repeats over and over again"), gave examples of what it could look like ("red, blue, red, blue"), searched for examples in the classroom, or used manipulatives or a picture to demonstrate how to make a pattern. By noting the types of information students offered and the settings in which they did so, we were able to gain insight into their knowledge of patterns and how they can be represented as well as valuable data on which to plan for more meaningful and challenging interactions and activities throughout the unit.

Another common observation was that some students would often repeat the same information offered by others when participating in class discussions or copy other students' work when independently creating, extending, or describing patterns. Similarly, other students would create only very basic patterns when writing in their journal, using manipulatives, or completing independent activities. By documenting these observations, we were able to easily identify developing patterns of student behavior as well as provide ourselves with the opportunity to analyze and address these behaviors in immediate and appropriate ways. With friendly, helpful, and gradually more challenging activities and interactions, we could attempt to scaffold more successful and independent experiences for these students to express their thinking based on our direct questioning and indirect manipulation of classroom activities.

## Responses to Various Questions and Prompts

Realizing that questioning can be a powerful tool for provoking higher-level thinking and multiple representation, we explored a wide range of questions and prompts to use at various points in each lesson as well as during various working situations (individual as well as small and large group). We did not simply accept or praise student work at face value but asked many questions to encourage them to explain or expand on their understandings of what patterns are and how they work. Some questions we asked included: Can you read your pattern to me? Can you name it in a different way? Can you predict what will come next? Can you extend your pattern? Can you find any other patterns in the classroom that match yours? How are they the same as or different from yours? How many objects (colors, shapes, etc.) make up your pattern? How many repeats are in your pattern? Can you draw or write about your pattern in your mathematics journal? Can you represent your pattern using other materials or actions?

We also observed students' reactions and noted their responses in an attempt to decide which questions further engaged students or caused them to feel insecure in their responses. This allowed us to decide which methods of instruction were more effective in furthering the students' exploration and understanding of patterning by expressing their ideas and reasoning to others.

Beginning in the earliest years, teachers can help students learn to make conjectures by asking questions: What do you think will happen next? What is the pattern? Is this true always? Sometimes? Simple shifts in how tasks are posed can help students learn to conjecture (NCTM, 2000). We wanted children to explore every aspect of patterning that interested them. For example, one day I grouped the students to make patterns for their partners to "read" and extend. One student was confused with the pattern his partner had created. He asked me: "Miss, is this a pattern?" (His partner had used pattern blocks to form the following: Diamond, diamond, diamond, triangle, triangle, triangle.)

Instead of simply answering the student's question, I referred the question to the whole class and we had a class discussion.

T:  Is this a pattern?

S:  No, it's not a pattern.

T:  Why do you think that?

S:  [shrugs his shoulders]

T:  Can anyone else tell us why Roy thinks that this is not a pattern?

S:  It doesn't look like one.

T:  What should a pattern look like?

S:  I know. It should be longer.

T:  How could you make it longer?

S:  [Uses container of pattern blocks to extend the pattern.]

T:  What did Angela do?

S:  She made the pattern longer.

T:  That's right. She extended the pattern by adding other blocks to it. How did she know which blocks to add to it?

S:  She just looked at the blocks that were there.

T:  So, is this a pattern now?

S:  Yes.

T:  Why do you think so?

S:  Because it's repeating and patterns are supposed to repeat.

This discussion was referred to at a later date when growing patterns were explored and their knowledge and understanding of patterning was expanded.

## Student Work Samples

Many times throughout the unit, we had students complete various small-group or individual activities, such as representing or categorizing letter patterns using various forms (colors, shapes, objects, actions); making quilts using squares of colored paper, or using 3-D objects to create concrete patterns in a home or school project. Students would present their work to the whole class before displaying it inside and outside the classroom for their classmates to observe, admire, and appreciate.

We asked questions to monitor the students at work because, from our perspective, their processes of deciding and creating their patterns were as important as their finished products. Our observations were, therefore, essential in providing evidence of the students' thinking and reasoning while creating their products.

Individual work samples also offered a concrete example of what patterns the children knew and could produce independently. We found that much insight could be gained based on the complexity and accuracy of their patterns as well as how they described the process of creating it. For example, some students could create complex patterns (e.g., AABBC), describe them in multiple ways (e.g., colors, shapes, actions), and relate them to other patterns in the classroom (e.g., those on a display chart of different letter patterns). Others would simply read their patterns as they appeared, or they experienced difficulty explaining how they created their pattern, whether simple or complex. Despite the complexity or simplicity of the completed patterns, the students' ability to explain and describe their reasoning and thinking while making and presenting their patterns provided detailed insight into their true understanding of the concept.

## Student Math Journals

We encouraged students to create and describe patterns in their personal mathematics journals throughout the unit. These journals provided valuable samples of student work and allowed us to monitor students' growing knowledge and competence with patterning, appropriate use of terminology, and increased ability to represent patterns in multiple ways. In Kindergarten, journals were utilized mainly as at-home projects, whereby a parent or caregiver could discuss and assist with transcribing young students' observations. Since children were at various levels of proficiency with writing in grade one, journals became a regular aspect of the mathematics lesson. Students were often asked to copy, create, or describe various patterns (e.g., color, shape, letter, pictures) as well as share their written or illustrated observations with peers, small groups, or the whole class. These journals focused on the concepts being covered and gave the students personal ownership of their work. They could utilize things that were important to them as well as explore their own creativity when designing, analyzing, and describing their patterns. Students were encouraged to search for and make connections with the real world as they discovered objects and designs in the classroom, their own home, people's clothing, in nature, etc.

## Teacher Reflective Journals

The facilitators recommended that each teacher keep a personal journal for reflecting on their daily mathematical experiences. We used these journals to write freely about all our thoughts, questions, concerns, and insights related to the day's events. These journals enabled us to analyze, learn about, and gain insight into the teaching and learning process in our mathematics classroom as well as our own personal growth throughout the process of this project. So much of our data collection was directly related to the students and their ability to communicate their thinking processes that we felt we needed to also account for our growth in terms of how we felt our teaching and instructional strategies were changing and developing as well as how they were affecting us (as teachers) and our students (as learners). After all, our research question included both the role of the teacher and student and the interdependent relationship that is created between the two through the interactions in the classroom. These journals were an important release of information at the end of the day as they allowed us to honestly and openly reveal not only the facts of what occurred during the lesson but, more importantly, how we felt, what we noticed, and what we learned about ourselves and our students.

## Data Analysis

During the analysis of our daily interactions and observations, we often sought out peers, facilitators, and the research literature for answers, guidance, and support in identifying and optimizing our teaching strategies and assisting our students in clarifying and expressing their thinking. Since our analysis was an ongoing process based on our daily interactions in the mathematics classroom, we decided upon frequent sessions whereby we would share, analyze, and discuss our experiences, questions, and concerns as well as validate progress or problem solve ways to improve the instructional learning experiences of the teachers and students. Some of the forums we created for the analysis of classroom experiences included: daily grade level discussions; E-journaling (daily exchange of group experiences and responding to facilitator feedback); and weekly group meetings

## Daily Grade-Level Discussions

At the end of each school day, we would informally discuss our personal experiences during that day's mathematics class. We also planned and prepared specific activities and questions to focus on for the following day based on our current knowledge and experience. By focusing on the same or very similar lesson plans and questions each day, our experiences were often very comparable. We validated the success (or lack of success) that we experienced with each lesson as well as reflected on why we thought each lesson was successful or unsuccessful and how we could improve or enhance our instruction and students' learning in these areas the folowing day. These meetings allowed for the immediate release of freshly experienced knowledge and enthusiasm along with the support of our trusted colleagues who related most closely to our current feelings and experiences with the research project.

## E-Journaling: Daily Exchange of Group Experiences and Responding to Facilitator Feedback

We also posted a daily, collaborative message to a closed online discussion that was accessible only to the members of our research project. Because our grade level group met every day to discuss and analyze our experiences, we would simply send a brief synopsis of our day's lesson along with a description of our group discussion. We would outline any questions or concerns for the facilitators' response. The purpose of our online discussion group was to keep everyone informed of our daily experiences as well as to elicit feedback from the facilitators and/or other colleagues that could help us to better address or improve our instruction and students' learning. The facilitators always gave positive and constructive feedback.

## Weekly Meetings

Most importantly, our collaborative group met once a week to share, analyze, and reflect on samples of student work, observations and transcripts of teacher and student conversations, and any personal or professional insights gained from our reflective journals. The facilitators guided and assisted our analysis of specific teaching experiences with reference to the research. They also asked us thought provoking questions to extend and consolidate our knowledge and thinking about teaching and learning. Their questions and comments also helped to focus our discussions at these meetings as well as encourage and focus our thinking when reflecting in our personal journals. Each meeting was full of energy and enthusiasm as teachers were anxious to share their experiences. The learning environment that developed was very comfortable, accepting, and supportive. We were all dedicated to the teacher as researcher project and the sense of connection and trust we felt in the group led to open and honest disclosures. Since both the Kindergarten and Grade 1 teachers focused on the same content, we made many connections and similar observations across grade levels. The flow of conversation was fast-paced and engaging. We were very supportive of and learned from each other's experiences. It was very common to hear comments such as: "I never thought of doing it that way." "I had a child do the same thing; this is what I did." or "The same thing happened when I tried that lesson."

## SPECIFIC EXAMPLES OF DATA COLLECTION AND ANALYSIS

The collection and analysis of data was a nearly simultaneous process that allowed us to continuously monitor the effectiveness of our instruction in relation to eliciting and supporting our students' ability to communicate their thinking and reasoning skills when working with patterns. Specific examples of this process help to answer our previously stated research question: How can we effectively uncover children's thinking and reasoning of mathematical concepts in an effort to improve instruction and learning in the classroom?

### Making Sense of Each Student's Actions and Thinking

One example of a teacher's experience attempting to make sense of a student's actions and thinking occurred in a Kindergarten classroom, yet it had implications for all teachers in our group. As a follow-up activity to sorting samples of children's winter clothing and making patterns with them, the teacher asked the students to represent their patterns on paper. One little boy immediately sought the teacher's approval when he completed his representation. The teacher saw that he had drawn a row of mittens and a row of hats. However, he had colored all the hats the same color. Instead of simply collecting his work and making note of his error, she questioned the work he had done.

T:   Can you read me the pattern on your mittens?

S:   Red, blue, red, blue, red.

T:   Can you read me the pattern on the hats?

S:   [He hesitated.]

T:   [The teacher did not make a statement, such as "Oh you didn't make a pattern here." or "You forgot to do a pattern with the hats." Instead, she asked him a question.] Have you made a pattern here?

S:   No.

T:   Do you think you can make it into a pattern?

S:   I can color tassels on the hats different colors! [When he returned a few minutes later, he successfully read both patterns.]

This episode provides an example of how a teacher's use of good questions and prompts can enable learners to solve problems for themselves in ways that make sense to them (Rowan & Robles, 1998). By allowing the student to revisit his thinking and to discover and correct his own misconceptions or errors, he demonstrated an understanding of patterns that would not have been obvious from his representation alone.

## Supporting Language Development in Mathematics

Since every group of students has a variety of ability levels within the one class, we all, at one point or another, experienced difficulty reaching some of the quieter, less social and academically weak students in our classrooms. Therefore, we discussed various approaches teachers took in such cases and then explored various methods of encouraging and questioning children in order to include them in safe, successful interactions in the mathematics classroom. Although our students were becoming very proficient with creating and extending patterns, even with support, some children needed additional experiences and practice to acquire appropriate mathematical language. In such cases, the teacher tried to pair students experiencing difficulty with those who had demonstrated a strong understanding of the concept of patterning as well as a good use of the appropriate mathematical terms. The teacher encouraged children to explain their thinking in their own words, but then modeled correct terminology when validating their reasoning.

One particular student constructed a pattern using pattern blocks, but had difficulty naming the pattern. When the teacher asked her to read her pattern she said, "Two of them, and one of them." The teacher then asked other members in this student's group if anyone else could name her pattern in a different way. Some examples of their responses were:

hexagon, hexagon, diamond; yellow, yellow, blue; big, big, small; AAB. Then the teacher asked another child in the group to read his/her pattern and offered the same opportunity to others to name it in a different way. This also gave the student who previously had difficulty naming her own pattern the opportunity to name another child's pattern.

## Clarifying Students' Thinking

Clarifying students' thinking and ideas is also important for processing what they are saying as well as restating their thoughts for the benefit of others to understand as well as make connections with. Following is an example of identifying the pattern or relationship that exists between the operations of addition and subtraction.

T:   Who can tell me what subtraction is?

S:   Like some girls and boys stand up and then sit down. [The teacher writes this on the chart.]

T:   Can you show me?

S:   If me and Robert stand up and then Robert sits down. [He and his friend demonstrate the actions.]

T:   Can anyone tell me another way to say this?

S:   2 take away 1 is 1. [The teacher prints this number sentence on the chart.]

T:   Can anyone else think of what subtraction is?

S:   The numbers get less and less.

T:   Can you explain what you mean?

S:   They start high and then they get less and less; like when you add they get more.

T:   Does everyone agree with this statement? What do you think? [Mixed student answers.] How can we check to see if it is true?

S:   Do some takeaways.

The teacher prints samples of subtraction sentences for students to check (e.g., 5  3 = 2; 8  3 = 5; 3  1 = 2; 9  2 = 7).

T:   Can someone come up to show us if the numbers get less? [A student comes to the chart and points to the answer.]

S:   3 is less than 5 and 2 is less than 5.

T:   [Other students come up to point out that this occurs each time.] So what do you notice about the answers when we subtract?

S:   The answers are less.

T:  Does anyone notice anything else? [Students nod and agree ver-
bally. The teacher then prints a variety of addition sentences and
asks students to find out if the answers are more or less. They discover they are more.]

T:  So what can we say about the answers when we add?

S:  The answer is always bigger.

Rowan and Robles (1998) assert that the teacher's role is more that of a
facilitator to encourage children to build on what they already know than
that of a giver of information and procedures to get answers. Although
these students' knowledge and generalizations will need to be modified as
their mathematical experiences expand throughout the grades (in terms
of adding fractions, negative numbers, etc.), they were learning to make
connections between putting sets of numbers or objects together and taking them apart. They understood these actions in terms of *more* and *less.*

## LIMITATIONS OF THE RESEARCH

### Sampling Process

We decided early on in the research process that we would randomly select
a group of 4-5 students on which to focus our observations, to collect work
samples, and to analyze and reflect on their learning at our collaborative
meetings. Although this number of students was very manageable for gathering data, we were still responsible to the group as a whole in terms of carrying out the lessons and assessing student progress in achieving
curriculum outcomes. In addition, interesting comments and disclosures
were often made by other students, yet we felt somewhat limited and obli-
gated to discuss only those from the random group for the purpose of the
research. As a result, there were many pros and cons to using the small
group instead of the large group for reference and study which caused
some conflict for us when collecting and analyzing data.

### Collecting Data

The types of data we collected, especially the quoting of students' and
teachers' words, was very awkward as the need to gather data was very
much intensified during the period of our research. We found it difficult to
record conversations as they occurred in a small group of students and even
more so when they occurred between ourselves and the students in a larger
group setting. The use of an audio tape would have greatly simplified this
process, as conversations could have been transcribed at the end of the day.

Also, a video tape of one or more of our mathematics lessons would have been very informative and revealing for critically analyzing our interaction with the students.

## Reflective Journals

Our reflections were an important form of data since they revealed personal insights and growth with reference to the research. Yet, finding time to effectively and consistently record our thoughts every day was somewhat time-consuming and problematic, depending on our other obligations, especially since we were meeting and e-journaling on a daily basis. All of our regular school commitments were also ongoing, which left little time at the end of the day to complete all our tasks efficiently.

## Creating a Balance

As primary teachers, we are responsible for teaching all subject areas with the exception of music and gym. Thus, mathematics is one of seven subject areas for which we are responsible. Although we were very excited about researching ways to improve and enhance the teaching and learning processes in our mathematics classroom, we were still responsible for planning, preparing, and carrying out lessons in other subject areas during the day. This sometimes caused extra pressure when trying to meet the demands of reflective and electronic journaling, daily grade level meetings to discuss the current lesson, reviewing plans for the following day, and attending to our regular school commitments throughout the year. However, the need to balance all aspects of personal and professional life is an ever present dilemma in our careers. Prioritizing our responsibilities and seeking time during the school day to meet on our collaborative project would have helped lessen the demands on our time at the end of the school day.

## Sharing Findings

We had a closed discussion group set up on our education server for the purpose of posting our daily reflections electronically. However, due to the privacy of this online discussion group, we could only access the server on our school computers. This added to the amount of time required at school each day to fulfill our research commitments. The flexibility to reflect on daily experiences before e-journaling would have been beneficial if we could have gained access to the site through our home computers later in the evening. In comparison to our collaborative group meetings, we all found the electronic reflections very awkward. They were one-sided conversations that felt very formal and constrained due to the need for written communication. During our in-person meetings, thoughts flowed more freely as there was more than one person actively involved in the conversation. Our oral reflections and discussions proved much more valuable in terms of our sharing, listening, making connections and observations, and learning new ways to think about and carry out activities and discourse in the classroom.

## PROFESSIONAL GROWTH

Many of the major outcomes of this teacher as research project are related to the professional growth of the participating teachers. This growth was reflected in our understandings and practices in four important areas of learning: (1) the importance of language, (2) the balance between processes and products, (3) the role of classroom discourse, and (4) the art of questioning.

### Importance of Language to Mathematics Learning

As primary teachers, literacy is always front and center in everything we do. However, the realization that language is as important to learning mathematics as it is to learning to read (NCTM, 2000) encouraged some deep reflection on our part. We have previously considered mathematics to be a rather separate and distinct subject area dealing mainly with numbers rather than words. However, coming to understand the links between mathematics and language encouraged us to connect teaching mathematics to other subject areas—integrating various ways of expressing and representing mathematical ideas through reading, writing, speaking, and drawing. Mathematics has a language of its own, and both teachers and students can learn to recognize, appreciate, and use this language. Students learn and understand this language best when they are given ample opportunities to explore materials and concepts and are encouraged and supported to make personal connections and discoveries through a variety of classroom settings and experiences. By observing, questioning, uncovering, and sharing students' thoughts and ideas about patterns, we better understood students' thinking and planned more personally meaningful learning opportunities in mathematics.

## Process vs. Product

We realized not only the importance but the necessity of allowing and encouraging young children to become actively involved in their own learning. According to Fennell and Rowan (2001), when students are able to represent a problem or mathematical situation in a way that is meaningful to them, the problem or situation becomes more accessible. Using representations—whether drawings, mental images, concrete materials, or equations—helps students organize their thinking and try various approaches that may lead to both a clearer understanding of the problem and a successful solution.

Children have unique insights and varying prior experiences that directly influence the connections they make to mathematical concepts as well as the way they make sense of what they learn in school. Also since children have different styles of learning and may be more comfortable and proficient in various areas, they not only need to be exposed to concepts in a variety of settings and approaches but they also need to be given choices when representing their knowledge and experience. In our teacher as researcher project, we consciously planned activities that allowed for individual growth and choice. For example, children regularly represented patterns using any combination of choices, including words, letters, numbers, pictures, actions, objects, etc.

We also realized that due to large class sizes, lack of time, and pressure to cover curriculum outcomes, we had previously focused more heavily on the product rather than the process of children's learning. Through this teacher as researcher project, we re-evaluated our mathematics lessons and reconsidered how we assess students' knowledge of concepts. We came to understand the necessity for students to interact with materials and each other in order to explore concepts and ideas. We also came to appreciate the role of the teacher in uncovering and monitoring students' thinking and reasoning to support and extend their understanding of important concepts. In this way, we learned to more appropriately and responsively plan for future lessons and to more effectively assess students' learning. We learned that the more students are directly involved, appropriately challenged, and interested in learning new concepts, the more likely they will be to succeed.

## Classroom Discourse

Providing students with daily opportunities to share their discoveries, discuss their findings, and consolidate their understandings is essential to the learning process. Throughout this teacher as researcher project, time spent communicating proved far more valuable than any time spent doing independent or group practice of skills. Although we included hands-on exploration of materials, whole class demonstration and discussion, small group work and independent practice, we have not always placed appropriate value on pursuing children's thinking in our attempts to maximize learning, nor have we encouraged students to share their discoveries at the end of each lesson. Having students share their ideas and strategies, however, has been very beneficial in assisting other students as well as the teacher to see different ways to solve problems and complete tasks. Students also revealed increased knowledge of the language of patterning and mathematics as the project continued. For example, teachers modeled terms such as *extend*, *repeat*, and *represent*, as children worked with manipulatives. We also posted the terms on the wall for reference when writing in mathematics journals. By the end of the unit, all students were using these terms to one extent or another. Thus, students who have opportunities, encouragement, and support for speaking, writing, reading, and listening in mathematics classes reap dual benefits: they communicate to learn mathematics, and they learn to communicate mathematically (NCTM, 2000). This project exposed us to a new way of thinking about and carrying out our teaching in mathematics class. We learned to listen and observe more as the students did most of the talking, interacting, discovering, and leading of lessons. For example, after children shared their pattern quilts made with squares of colored paper, many students realized that they could have cut out shapes or cut other squares in half in order to add variety and complexity to their patterns. Appreciating their interest in this activity, we encouraged their continued exploration by changing their pattern into different and more complex designs by adding triangles or other shapes. This activity led to a rich and enthusiastic discussion of and appreciation for the patterns represented. Students made observations, comments, and connections with other patterns, such as those with the same patterns (e.g. both AA BB patterns), the same shapes, the same colors, etc.

## The Art of Questioning

The most important aspect of our teacher as researcher project was discovering the power of questioning to uncover children's thinking and to improve not only their learning but the learning and instruction of the teacher. Through questioning, we were able to

- discover children's ideas and thought processes
- clarify children's thoughts and ideas
- extend children's thinking and problem solving skills

- encourage multiple representations
- encourage connections to other areas

By observing, questioning, and listening to students as they interacted independently or with peers, we were able to individualize our investigations and instruction to each student's current level of understanding. We also utilized questioning during student presentations and whole group discussions in an effort to model and share differing opinions and strategies for creating, reading, and extending patterns. Whenever students lacked the language or knowledge to explain their ideas, we would redirect their question to others in the class. For example, if a child had difficulty verbalizing why they named a pattern AB, we learned to ask, "Can anyone tell me why they think Rebecca said it was an AB pattern?" These opportunities also offered valuable learning experiences for the students since they would be able to assist another student as well as be accountable for taking part in the class discussion.

Throughout the project, we consciously planned which questions we would use during the lessons. During our discussions and analyses of daily events, we would always look at the effectiveness of the questions in learning what and how children were thinking. We would often discuss alternate questions or other ways we could approach the same situations. The facilitators were very helpful in these areas, as they provided relevant literature, guided discussions and analysis of classroom discourse, and provided valuable feedback about our experiences. With much practice using a variety of questions on a daily basis, we realized that we were becoming more confident in using questions to guide our interactions with students and to assist in our planning of activities. By simply asking "What do you think?" "Is there another way to figure out the answer?" "How do you know?" "Can you show us?" and "What if...?" we were able to learn information about our students' knowledge and understanding of concepts that directly aided our ongoing instruction and assessment.

## CONCLUSIONS

Through this teacher as researcher project, we learned that children have ideas and thoughts that are often not obvious from what they say or do. However, by simply inquiring into the reasons behind their thoughts or actions, we discovered a wealth of valuable information about their knowledge and understanding of the concept of patterning. By encouraging student interaction and exploration of materials as well as multiple representations of ideas, we established a classroom environment that supported students' needs and interests. And, by observing and analyzing our daily experiences, we planned and implemented instructional lessons and activities that addressed, challenged, and enhanced students' learning in meaningful ways.

Although the teacher as researcher project formally ended, we continue to develop our skills in observation, inquiry, and critical reflection. We have also made connections between our research in the mathematics classroom and many other aspects of our teaching. We can see the value for all subject areas thoughtfully inquiring into children's thinking and providing multiple opportunities for them to represent their learning. Thus, this project has resulted in a cycle of change that has deeply affected our teaching. What we have gained is much larger than the research project itself. It has changed the way we see our roles as teachers and the ways we interact with students.

## ACKNOWLEDGMENT

The authors wish to acknowledge those who participated with us in the collaborative teacher as researcher project. Kindergarten Teachers: Judy Kelly, Karen Lane, Trina Martin, Jan Bailey; Grade One Teachers: Tamara Reynolds, Cindy Sharpe, Florence Rolfe, Karen Adams, Debbie Carey, Penny Pinsent; Principal: Theresa Davis; Learning Resource Teachers: Carol Veitch, Dawn Hayward; Professional Development Co-Facilitator: Dr. Elizabeth Strong.

## REFERENCES

Aker, S. (1990). *What comes in 2's, 3's, & 4's.* New York: Simon & Schuster.

Fennell, F., & Rowan, T. (2001). Representation: An important process for teaching and learning mathematics. *Teaching Children Mathematics, 7,* 288-292.

Johnson, B. (March 1993). ERIC Digest. Washington, DC: ERIC Clearinghouse on Teacher Education.

Kincheloe, J. L. (1991). *Teachers as researchers: Qualitative inquiry as a path to empowerment.* London: Falmer Press.

Mewborn, D. S., & Huberty, P. D. (1999). Questioning your way to the standards. *Teaching Children Mathematics, 6,* 226-27 & 243-46.

National Council of Teachers of Mathematics. (2000). *Principles and standards for school mathematics.* Reston, VA: Author.

National Council of Teachers of Mathematics. (1991). *Professional standards for teaching mathematics.* Reston, VA: Author.

Rowan, T. E., & Robles, J. (1998). Using questions to help children build mathematical power. *Teaching Children Mathematics, 4,* 504-509.

Silver, E. A., & Smith, M. S. (1990). Teaching mathematics and thinking. *Arithmetic Teacher, 37,* 34-37.

Steele, D. F. (1999). Learning mathematical language in the "zone of proximal development." *Teaching Children Mathematics, 6,* 38-42.

## APPENDIX

Andrews, A. (1997). What comes naturally: Talking about mathematics. *Teaching Children Mathematics, 3,* 236-239.

Atkins, S. L. (1999). Listening to students: The power of mathematical conversations. *Teaching Children Mathematics, 5,* 289-295.

Campbell, P., & Chambers, D. (1997). Connecting instructional practice to student thinking. *Teaching Children Mathematics, 4,* 106-110.

Clements, D. H. (1997). (Mis?)Constructing Constructivism. *Teaching Children Mathematics, 4,* 198-200.

Corwin, R. B. (1993). Implementing the Professional Standards for Teaching Mathematics: Doing mathematics together: Creating a mathematical culture. *Arithmetic Teacher, 40,* 338-341.

Cramer, K., & Karnowsky, L. (1995). The importance of informal language in representing mathematical ideas. *Teaching Children Mathematics, 1,* 332-335.

English, L. D. (1997). Promoting a problem-posing classroom. *Teaching Children Mathematics, 4,* 172-179.

Fraivillig, J. (2001). Strategies for advancing children's mathematical thinking. *Teaching Children Mathematics, 7,* 454-459.

Richardson, K. (1997). Too easy for Kindergarten and just right for first grade. *Teaching Children Mathematics, 3,* 432-436.

Schifter, D. E., & O'Brien, D. C. (1997). Interpreting the standards: Translating principles into practice. *Teaching Children Mathematics, 4,* 202-205.

Schwartz, S. L. (1996). Hidden messages in teacher talk: Praise and empowerment. *Teaching Children Mathematics, 3,* 396-401.

Tinto, P. P., Shelly, B. A., & Zarach, N. J. (1994). Classroom research and classroom practice: Blurring the boundaries. *Mathematics Teacher, 87,* 644-648.

Breinigsville, PA USA
12 May 2010
237885BV00004B/8/A